ASIA IN EUROPE AND THE MAKING OF THE WEST
*A series in four volumes examining the spread of cultures
from the east into Europe*

Volume 2

TOWARDS ONE WORLD
Ancient Persia and the West
Warwick Ball

For John Quinn
Ancient History, Newcastle High School, 1968-1969

TOWARDS
ONE WORLD

Ancient Persia and the West

Warwick Ball

OLIVE
BRANCH
PRESS

An imprint of Interlink Publishing Group, Inc.
www.interlinkbooks.com

8/8/11
ww
$ 28.15

TOWARDS ONE WORLD
Ancient Persia and the West

First published in 2011 by

OLIVE BRANCH PRESS
An imprint of Interlink Publishing Group, Inc.
46 Crosby Street, Northampton, Massachusetts 01060
www.interlinkbooks.com

Library of Congress Cataloging-in-Publication Data available

ISBN 978-1-56656-822-7

Cover design: Eleanor Ball
Cover photo: stairway at Persepolis

Printed and bound in Malta at the Gutenberg Press Ltd

To request our complete 48-page full-color catalog, please call us toll
free at 1-800-238-LINK, visit our website at www.interlinkbooks.com,
or send us an e-mail: info@interlinkbooks.com

CONTENTS

SERIES INTRODUCTION

Every culture looks at history in relation to itself, and so it is not surprising that since the nineteenth century our view of world history has been Eurocentric. Perhaps this bias has been overplayed because so many of the world's more powerful nations are rooted in European culture and so the concept of the 'west' and being 'western' has become almost stereotypical and a crude packaging of a whole complex set of cultures.

Whether or not such a view is correct, this questions whether the 'west' is truly 'western'. Or, to put it another way, being 'western' also incorporates a huge amount that is 'eastern'. Hence, regardless of whether the Eurocentric view is correct or not (and in its own terms it can be correct), the traditional view of the European worldwide spread must be balanced by two considerations. First, by the spread of peoples from the east into Europe. And second, that so much of the civilisation we consider to be 'European' is equally Asiatic. In describing the ensuing contact and assessing the affect, much of what it means to be 'European' is challenged. Ultimately, 'eastern' and 'western' civilisations are neither exclusive nor confrontational. In short, it poses the question, what is 'Europe'?

To deny that Arabs and Turks—or Phoenicians, Scythians, Persians, Jews, Huns, and Mongols—are a part of European as well as Asiatic civilisation is not only to fly in the face of evidence, it is to deny some of the greatest achievements of our civilisation: they are integral parts to be acknowledged as much as our Greek, Roman, Norman or Slavic parts. Phoenicians, Persians, Arabs, Turks, Mongols, all form a part of European history, a part that is both European and Asiatic, a part that defines and makes Europe what it is. Arab and Turkish invasions were no more 'attacks on Europe' than Roman or Norman invasions were.

In this series I do not wish to match east against west nor to demonstrate that 'everything came out of the east.' I wish simply to explore the affect of those cultures from beyond the conventional boundaries of Europe that, to a greater or lesser extent, expanded westwards—the counterpart of the 'European expansion'. Since the earliest times, the history of Europe has been inextricably bound up with peoples and cultures from the east. It is an extraordinarily rich and complex relationship. Not only was Europe born and defined out of this relationship, but at every stage in its history it was intimately affected by the lands to the east. This is the story of that relationship: it is the story of Europe itself.

PREFACE AND
ACKNOWLEDGEMENTS

The first volume in our series, *Asia in Europe and the Making of the West*, focussed on the impact that peoples from a broad swathe of the Middle East—from the Arabian Sea through to the Mediterranean—had upon Europe in a movement that was largely colonial in nature lasting several thousand years. In contrast, this second volume focuses on just one people who entered only a very small part of Europe and remained for just a few years. Of all the peoples from the east who entered Europe, the Iranian presence appears the least, covering little more than sixty years—Phoenicians, Arabs, Turks, Mongols, all remained longer or still remain. Furthermore, the contact is usually viewed in terms of conflict: the Graeco-Persian wars and the conquests of Alexander. It is this contact above all others that is frequently viewed as the beginning of some global Manichaean struggle between east and west that continues in various forms to this day. But Europe's contact with ancient Persia was neither short-lived nor conflicting: it was the beginnings of a complex interaction between east and west that continues to this day. This book explores that relationship.

The main people in Europe with whom the Persians came into contact were the Greeks, a contact that was not nearly so one-sided—nor as conflicting—as is thought, and both the Graeco-Persian wars and the conquests of Alexander the Great can be viewed in a radically different light. The contact was as fundamental for the Romans too: it was a Neo-Persian kingdom centred on the Black Sea that came close to stemming the emerging power of Rome in the first century BC, and it was the continued existence of Iran as a great power and its relationship with the Roman Empire that brought about a war at the end of antiquity that wrought more change than any other war in history, with a ripple effect from North Africa to China.

Throughout antiquity, Iranian religious ideas came west to profoundly influence the beginnings of Christianity, and continued to flow west to culminate in the greatest religious upheaval in Western Europe before the Reformation. Most of all, the idea that 'East and West' are locked in some perceived eternal struggle is myth. Indeed, this book and this series questions whether there is such a concept of 'East and West' at all—and ancient Persia was the first to negate such a concept.

For more than anything else, what Persia contributed to posterity was an idea. In articulating the concept of a single universal creator, ancient Persian civilisation was the first to grope towards the idea of a single universal world and put in place 'the base of a future world civilisation' in the words of the historian J M Roberts. The idea of one world was to persist. Today, the ancient Persian idea of a single world transcending political and ethnic boundaries is embodied in an inscription over the entrance of the United Nations building in New York—written by a Persian poet.

*   *   *

This book was written during the course of the past ten years, but in a sense it has been in the making more years than I care to remember. The titles in the bibliography reflect just some of the many works that have contributed to its making; many readers (and reviewers) will doubtless light upon the many equally worthwhile works (usually the reviewer's own) that I have omitted. One work that regrettably only came to my attention after this book was in press is *Cultural Responses to the Persian Wars. Antiquity to the Middle Ages*, edited by Emma Bridges, Edith Hall and P J Rhodes (Oxford 2007). This, and many others, represent just a fraction of the lifetime of reading still to be done.

It is a pleasure to thank Wendy Ball, Frantz Grenet and Michael Roaf for comments, corrections and feedback generally on the various drafts and versions that parts of this book have been through. Such feedback has helped me enormously; I trust that they will blame me entirely for all remaining faults and errors. Oliver Ball prepared the maps again, and once more it is a pleasure to thank Alan Ball, Leonard Harrow and Sahar Huneidi of East and West Publications for their support and their patience.

I have been travelling to Iran for forty years now, but even before then Iran—Persia—always figured largely: Persian carpets when growing up, Iranian friends of my parents, numerous books purchased or borrowed. So many people—both in Iran and outside—have helped me along the way that there is simply not space here to name even a fraction of them. But I do recall when learning about the Graeco-Persian Wars in Ancient History at High School asking my history teacher, John Quinn, why we do not learn more about the Persians? His response was 'Okay, you do the Persians.' So this at last is for him: like then, homework overlong and overdue.

Warwick Ball
Scottish Borders, May 2010

MAPS AND PLANS

LIST OF PLATES

25. The relief and inscription of Darius at Bisitun

26. The beginning of the Royal Road in Sardis (the pavement is Roman)

27. The temple of Artemis in Sardis

28. General view of Xanthos, with the 4th century pillar tombs overlooking the Roman theatre.

29. The inscribed pillar at Xanthos

30. The audience scene on the Harpy Tomb at Xanthos (now in the British Museum)

31. Lycian house tomb at Kaş

32. Site of the Mausoleum of Halicarnassus in Bodrum

33. Scale model reconstruction of the Mausoleum of Halicarnassus in Istanbul

34. Statues of Queen Artemisia and King Mausolus from the Mausoleum, now in the British Museum.

35. The Temple of Athena at Priene, designed by the architect Pytheus.

36. The agora at Alinda, founded by Mausolus.

37. The religious complex of Labraunda, embellished and expanded by Mausolus as a Carian cult centre.

38. The city of Miletus, rebuilt in the Achaemenid period as a planned city on a grid system (standing buildings visible are mainly Roman).

39. The Temple of Apollo at Didyma

40. The sole restored remains of the Temple of Artemis at Ephesus

41. A Persepolitan-Ionic composite bull capital at Ephesus

42. The Greek Serpent Column marking the victory of Salamis, now standing in the hippodrome of Constantinople where it was brought from Delphi by Constantine.

43. Bust of Alexander in the Istanbul Archaeological Museum

44. Inscription of Alexander from the Temple of Athena at Priene, now in the British Museum. © Trustees of the British Museum

45. The country palace of ʿIraq al-Amir in Jordan

46. Iranian style dress at Palmyra

47. View of Armazi-tsikhe, the site of capital of ancient eastern Georgia, on the Mtkvari (Kura) river opposite Mtskheta, the modern religious capital.

48. Excavated remains of a fire temple at Nekresi in Kakheti in eastern Georgia

49. The 7th-century church at Zvarnots in Armenia

50. Detail of the 11th-century Samtavisi Cathedral in Georgia showing the Persian *senmurv*

51. A Sasanian-style hunting scene on the 8th-century church of Ateni Sion in Georgia

52. The ramparts of Sinope on the Black Sea, which became the capital of Pontus in 183 BC.

INTRODUCTION
Which Way West?

Some of the old fault lines which have divided peoples over the centuries … are still very much with us. One of these is the division, and the antagonism, between what was originally thought of as Europe and Asia … each successive wave, as it came to rest, reassumed the ancient struggle between an ever-shifting West and an equally amorphous east. A flame had been lit in Troy which would burn steadily down the centuries, as Trojans were succeeded by the Persians, the Persians by the Phoenicians, the Phoenicians by the Parthians, the Parthians by the Sassanids, the Sassanids by the Arabs, and the Arabs by the Ottoman Turks.

Anthony Pagden 2008[1]

It has become commonplace to assume a state of perpetual war—or at least unbridgeable differences—between 'east and west', a state perceived to go back to the Trojan Wars and continuing today. Any conflict involving eastern and western peoples is explained in terms of some eternal Manichean east-west struggle: often, no other explanation is required, it is assumed self-explanatory. Hence, an invasion of Greece by Persia is explained in terms of an east-west struggle, an invasion of Greece by Rome is not; a conflict between Turks and Serbs is viewed as a part of this perpetual war, one between Turks and Kurds is not.

In explaining east-west relations in such terms, loaded language is often brought to bear: struggles are viewed in terms of 'western values' versus 'Oriental despotism'. The term 'western values' itself thence becomes self-explanatory, implying 'liberty and freedom;' any west-east movement (such as Alexander's invasion of Persia) is thus interpreted as a 'triumph of western values' whilst the opposite (such as Xerxes'—or the Turks'—invasion of

Greece) is regarded merely as 'attempts to enslave Europe.' Any war *within* Europe is not regarded in terms of 'western values;' wars outside Europe are. In other words, the perceived perpetual war soon becomes an eternal struggle between good and bad, right and wrong. It is a neat irony that the term to describe such a struggle—'Manichean'—is an Iranian one.

Are such views commonplace? They lie, for example, not far below the surface of numerous media reports of present day conflicts (and, it must be emphasised, on both sides: many Islamic extremists, for example, view their struggle in such terms). They lie even nearer the surface of current controversy surrounding Turkey's application to join the European Union. Such perspectives form the basis of Samuel Huntingdon's now famous, albeit controversial, thesis on the *Clash of Civilizations*. One recent work sets out to subordinate much of history to this thesis.* The Graeco-Persian Wars are described as 'titanic struggles between east and west' and all subsequent history is viewed as a continuation. Roman history (whose empire is extravagantly described as stretching all the way to India!) is interpreted as supposedly continuing this epic struggle: even Rome's Civil Wars formed a part of it, whilst Hannibal's invasion of Italy from North Africa is described as how 'once again, Asia stood poised, as it had at Marathon, to enslave Europe,' and the victory at Actium (Augustus' battle against Antony and Cleopatra) was 'one in which the future of a free and virtuous west had been preserved from extinction at the hands of a tyrannical and corrupt east.'[2]

Another recent work also views this struggle as 'older by far than the Crusades, older than Islam, older than Christianity, its pedigree is so venerable that it reaches back two and a half thousand years ago.'[†] Language used to describe such conflicts quickly becomes prejudicial: the work is littered with expressions such as 'Mercilessness and repression' 'paranoia on an almost global scale' 'brutal hypocrisy' 'the Persian yoke' to describe Persians and the Persian Empire, while the previous book cited dismisses the Parthian Empire as 'a horde, a mob not a nation' of slaves over which 'Roman virtue' must inevitably triumph.[3]

Such works—and the views they represent—have a significant impact. These are accomplished authors with large followings.[‡] However, to

---

* The historian Anthony Pagden's Worlds at War. The 2,500-Year Struggle Between East and West. Even the title recalls H G Wells' science fictional War of the Worlds.
† Tom Holland's equally emotively entitled Persian Fire. The First World Empire and the Battle for the West; the quotation is from p. xv.
‡ Samuel Huntingdon's work has been hugely influential, Tom Holland has collected

perceive this area of history in terms of a Manichean struggle holds two dangers. First, it stifles historical enquiry and invites glib explanations: complex reasons might be sought for a conflict between, say, France and Germany, but none for a conflict involving eastern and western powers; they are assumed to be in conflict by their innate natures. And second, such views feed the flames of conflict, the glib perception of two clearly defined sides, east and west, locked in perpetual opposition to each other was never true in antiquity and is not true now. Of course, it would be a mistake to deny that there have been wars between eastern and western powers. But wars between successive Iranian dynasties—Achaemenid, Parthian, Sasanian—and corresponding powers to its west imply no more an inevitable and perpetual east-west struggle than various wars between France and England were.

The single event that is almost invariably cited as the origin of this perpetual war was the expansion of the Persian Empire into Greece in the sixth and fifth centuries BC. To some extent, the origins of this view lie with Herodotus, who was the first to suggest this explanation. Nevertheless, even Herodotus gives a more balanced explanation than many today credit him. The Trojan Wars were then retrospectively hijacked to fit into this view (and we will return to Troy later) and subsequent conflicts were viewed as a continuation. The fact that the Greeks were seen to have defeated the Persians turns the perceived Manichean struggle into good old fashioned triumphalism: look how right ('western values; us') always triumphs over wrong ('Oriental despotism; them').

This book sets out to demonstrate, first, that the relationship of Persia with the lands to its west was always complex and never one-sided. And second, that far from dividing the world into opposing neat east-west camps, it was Persia that first created the idea of one world. Both the relationship and the idea have moulded much of what is now considered 'western'. Our term 'western' thus contains within it a paradox: the very strength of the 'west' and of 'western values' lies in the fact that ultimately it is not exclusively 'western'.

---

several prestigious awards, and Antony Pagden is an acknowledged academic whose book is published by a major university press.

A First Foothold

The Persian Empire* was the first major Asiatic power to physically extend its borders into Europe. For unlike the Phoenicians before who come into Europe as merchants and settlers, the Persians came in the sixth century BC as a great power when the Achaemenid Empire sought to incorporate parts of Europe as provinces into a centrally ruled and administered empire. What was the effect?

'Modern Europe owes nothing to the Achaemenids. We may admire their imposing if oppressive architecture, and gaze in something like awe—from prostration-level, as it were—at ... Persepolis, with its marvellous bas-reliefs. Yet the civilisation which could produce such things is almost as alien to us as that of the Aztecs.'

This observation was made in 1970 by an eminent Classical historian.[†] Such remarks might not be so easily made today, as we know far more about global interconnections (often to our cost). But it is a view that still lingers. Even when the wealth of Persian legacy is fully acknowledged (even—often especially—by Classicists), it can appear both remote and irrelevant to the European heritage as a whole. But there is good reason for this view: Persia's foothold in Europe was small, distant and brief—and perceived moreover as ignominious. Of all the peoples from Asia who occupied different parts of Europe, the Persian contact appears the least, covering little more than sixty years. When compared to the five hundred or more that the Phoenicians were in Spain, or the nearly eight hundred that the Arabs were there or the permanence of the Turks in south-eastern Europe after more than seven hundred years, the Persian presence appears

---

[*] The terms 'Persian' and 'Iranian' are problematic. 'Iran' carries the modern implications of ethnicity and the nation state which do not necessarily apply to ancient history. However, 'Iran' is as ancient a term as 'Persia', and the Sasanians at least were conscious of an 'Iranian' identity. See *The Idea of Iran* series ed. by Curtis and Stewart 2005, 2007, 2008. Without entering into the arguments, 'Iranian' is used here to incorporate the Median, Persian, Parthian and Sasanian dynasties, and 'Persia' used more specifically for the Persian Empire, but following conventional usage both are used to some extent interchangably.

[†] Peter Green 1996: 5 (first published 1970). And as recently as 2005 Tom Holland depicted the cities of Susa and Persepolis as merely as exercises in repression. In passing it must also be pointed out that even Green's comparison to the perceived irrelevance of the American pre-Columbian civilisations is inappropriate, as anyone who has eaten a potato, a tomato or the various products of maize, tobacco or a huge range of other plant products first domesticated by pre-Columbian American civilisations will acknowledge.

little more than a minor episode, with no long-lasting effect and of little overall importance—even the Mongols lasted longer in Europe than the Persians did. In contrast, Persian conquests hardly extended into the heart of Europe, but only to its very south-eastern fringes: Greece very briefly and Thrace and Macedonia for only a little longer. One can almost concede the statement quoted that 'Modern Europe owes nothing to the Achaemenids.'

The importance of Persia to European history, however, was fundamental. To begin with, south-eastern Europe has always been a pivotal region. In our own times the Balkans have been at the heart of European events: in the beginning of the twentieth century when events there sparked off World War I, and at its end which saw conflicts at the heart of the post Cold War world. More important, it was a major centre of European civilisation from late antiquity to the Middle Ages, when Byzantium became the receptacle of Classical learning after the rest of Europe had been lost in the 'Dark Ages'. After that it became the centre of one of the largest land empires in Europe since the Roman, under the Ottomans. Most of all, the Balkans saw the first major civilisation on European soil with the flowering of Greece. The contact between Greece and Persia was to change Europe.

ANCIENT GREECE: EAST AND WEST

Up until the time of the Persian Empire the centre of the Greek world and Greek civilisation was as much in Asia Minor as in Greece itself: Asia Minor saw the earliest Greek urbanisation, the beginnings of Greek literature and philosophy, and most of the first colonial expansion beyond the Aegean. With the Persian conquest of Asia Minor the centre of the Greek world passed from Asia to Europe and Greece emerged as the centre of independent Greeks. With the repelling of Xerxes' invasion, Greece— and Athens in particular—became the leader of the Hellenes. The Persian contact thus acted as a catalyst for the subsequent golden age of fifth century BC Athens, the first great civilisation to take place on European soil and seen by many as ultimately the main fountainhead for European identity. Thus, Jacques Le Goff in writing of *The Birth of Europe*: 'Ancient Greece has again and again been looked at by Europeans as a mirror in which to discover themselves.'[4] From this contact with Persia, European civilisation was born.

5

What was this civilisation that was thus born? Or, to put it another way, was it 'European?' To a large extent, the definition of 'what Europe is' becomes simply one of perspective. To take just two examples, in a book entitled *The Birth of Europe*, itself a part of a series entitled *The Making of Europe*, the author throughout refers to 'Christendom' solely in terms of Latin Christendom: Byzantine Greek or Russian Orthodoxy is by implication neither a part of 'Europe' nor 'Christendom. A similarly entitled work, *The Making of Europe*, also excludes eastern Europe (as well as Muslim Spain) from the idea of 'Europe'.⁵ Many more such instances could be cited. The only part of eastern Europe considered 'European' is ancient Greece: after its decline (i.e., after 'ancient history' became Roman), eastern Europe was until recently largely forgotten by mainstream history apart from occasional passing references. In their own terms there is nothing necessarily wrong with such perspectives (and both works cited offer excellent insights), but for all that ancient Greece is usually viewed as the beginning of Europe, a study of Europe from a Balkan perspective would be very different to the many around now. Greece is hijacked by western Europe when it seems useful—mainly its flowering in fifth century BC Athens and the occasional quixotic event since, such as Greek independence movements against Turks or Nazis—but 'Europe' still remains firmly fixed at the western end of the continent. A history of 'Europe' and European identity from a Balkan perspective would focus, first of all of course, upon ancient Greece, but also equally upon Constantinople and Byzantine civilisation,* and then upon places and events usually passed over by histories of 'our' Europe: the rise of the Bulgarian kingdom perhaps, as Europe's first nation state rather than Merovingian France; the beginnings of the Hungarian monarchy instead of the Holy Roman; the defeat of the Arabs at the second siege of Constantinople in 717 rather than their defeat at Poitiers by Charles Martel in 732 as the iconic battle that 'saved Europe from Islam;' and most of all the rise and spread of Turkish and Russian ascendancies as the most important historical processes in 'Europe'. Western histories focus more on the Roman legacy, hence especially Italy and France, but the Roman legacy was as great (or greater) in the east, and it was Byzantine, Bulgarian, Russian, Seljuk and Ottoman monarchs who continued the title 'Caesar', as opposed to just two in western Europe.† Western concern with the emergence of

---

* Equally a part of broader 'Greek' civilisation—and of far longer duration than Fifth Century Athens' flowering. Indeed, many Greeks themselves today still regard Constantinople as the city.

† German Kaiser and British Qaysar-i Hind, the official Indian title of British monarchs

the Germanic peoples into European history would be balanced by, say, the emergence of the Slavs or the entry of the Turks. Orthodox is no less 'Christendom' than Catholic.

Probably the one reason more than any other why modern western Europe regards ancient Greece as the birth of Europe is because Greece alone is accredited with the origin of Europe's most precious idea: democracy. Thus, Norman Davies writes in *Europe East and West*:

> One East European country, significantly, was *not* written off [at the end of the Second World War]. It has been well argued that the Western leaders were preconditioned to abandon Eastern Europe to Stalin at Yalta and Potsdam because 200 years of cultural propaganda had desensitised Western opinion to the loss of Warsaw, Budapest or Sofia. But Athens was a different matter. The mythology of Western civilization insisted that Greece was 'ours'. Greece was not seen as eastern, alien, exotic or backward, and she had to be saved at all costs. In the Percentages Agreement of 1944, Churchill made Greece the sole exception. In his Fulton Speech of 1946, where he warned of the Iron Curtain, he also boasted that 'Greece with its immortal glories is free.' Similar sentiments were expressed forty years later to support Greece's entry to the European Community.[6]

Greek origins of European democracy are only true up to a point. Even such an avowed Tory and Hellenophile as Edward Bulwer Lytton in the mid-nineteenth century was at pains to point out that 'the Greek republics were *not* democracies, even in their most democratic shape;—the vast majority of the working classes were the enslaved population … to increase the popular tendencies of the republic was, in fact, only to increase the liberties of the few.'* Democracy in any case has no single origin: in its simple early form (such as in ancient Greece), it was little more than a gathering of tribal elders common to most early societies. Such gatherings are equally a feature of, for example, traditional Arab societies. The myth of western democracy, that 'western values' stand for democratic ideals and freedom and strives alone to promote and spread democracy throughout the world (especially in opposition to 'Oriental despotism'), forgets the

---

from Victoria to George VI.
* Lytton 2004: 153. Modern European democratic institutions originated, on the one hand, with the Viking councils of the Dark Ages (of which the Icelandic and Isle of Man parliaments are the direct descendants) and, on the other hand, with the foundation of the Swiss Confederation in 1291. Cf. Davies 2006: 130-1 and 297.

fact that modern western nations spread throughout the world almost *solely* through blatant imperialism—indeed, in almost all cases democracy was explicitly denied the subject peoples. The idea of Greece and democracy thus become a part of retrospective re-invention to accord with modern self perceptions.

The Persian contact with Greece may only have been brief, but it was only a small part of a much larger story: that of Persia's contact with *Greeks*: and the people are as important as the land. This contact with Greeks began long before the first invasion of Greece and continued long after. The relationship between Greek and Persian was complex and many sided, one of the more important themes of ancient history. The Greeks of Asia Minor—Ionia, Caria and adjacent lands on the west coast of Anatolia—had been absorbed into the Persian Empire in its first outward expansion in the previous century and made a Satrapy. The end of Darius' and Xerxes' brief flirtation with Greece did not mark the end of this contact with Persia. On the contrary, it was the beginning of a very complex relationship that was to last for many centuries and was to end up fundamentally changing both civilisations.

For the Persians did not disappear, either with their defeat by Athens at the Battle of Salamis in 480 BC or their defeat later on by Alexander at the Battle of Gaugamela in 331 BC. Indeed, the Iranian peoples had been a constant factor on the Near Eastern stage ever since the Medes arrived with a bang at the sack of Nineveh in 612 BC, and were to remain a major factor in Middle Eastern and eastern Mediterranean politics for a further 1200 years or more until the last Persian empire of antiquity finally collapsed with the defeat of the Sasanians at the Battle of Nihavand in 642 AD at the hands of the Muslim Arabs. Long after Classical Greek civilisation had declined and the centre of civilisation passed to the Romans, the relationship with Iran remained a constant factor for European history.

A TROJAN PRELUDE AND POSTSCRIPT

Herodotus viewed the beginnings of the conflict between Greeks and Persian as the Trojan Wars, and so many studies of ancient Greece and of its relationship with its neighbours inevitably lead back to both the epic event itself and to its chronicler, Homer. The Trojan Wars is one of the ancient world's most potent and enduring symbols (Pl. 1). For thousands of years it has been taken to symbolise east versus west, Asia versus Europe. In 1999, for example, the Council of Europe launched a major travelling art exhibition at the National Museum of Denmark in Copenhagen, *Gods and Heroes of the Bronze Age*. From Copenhagen the exhibition went on to Bonn for the summer 1999 and Paris for winter 1999-2000. It was essentially an exhibition of European art of the Bronze Age and for once offered a refreshingly holistic view of 'Europe', including objects from Bulgaria, Czech Republic, Greece, Hungary, Poland, Romania, Russia and Slovak Republic as well as the 'usual suspects' in western Europe. But the final part, entitled 'The Birth of Europe', finished with the Trojan Wars: an east-west conflict was seen as a key to Europe's identity.[7]

Writers as diverse as T S Eliot, Edward Said, Francis Fukayama, Norman Davies and J M Roberts, to take some examples at random, describe Homer as a 'European' writer: indeed, as the very beginning of 'European' literature.[8] The statement in other words is a literary truism that requires no qualification or justification. Yet we have no evidence that Homer even visited Europe: the little evidence that we do have suggests that he was probably from Smyrna in Asia Minor (if he existed at all, as some authorities doubt). But because the Homeric epics are written in Greek (a language, one must remind ourselves, that was spoken as much in Asia Minor as in Greece), Homer has become unambiguously 'not only the first European literature but the first world literature'[9]—literature, by implication, is perceived as a European innovation. I recall the first time I took my family to visit Troy, when my (then) six-year old son bought a Turkish comic book (in English) on the Trojan Wars. The book concluded with the words, 'An Anatolian poet, that grand Homer, who lived hundreds of years henceforth, wrote these for us all …' Perhaps it takes a Turkish perspective to place Homer in a more balanced context.[10]

Greek myths were essentially fluid: they were always being developed and reinterpreted to fit changing ideas, tastes and circumstances, to illustrate or form parallels to the ideas of the day. Hence, any view of the Trojan Wars can be taken as valid. But originally, the historicity of Homer's *Iliad* was no more real than Shakespeare's *Hamlet*: it was simply a great story superbly told. However, from the fifth century BC onwards it came within the interests of various people with axes to grind to reinvent the story in their own mould: Athens to justify its leadership of the Greeks against the Persians, Xerxes to launch his war in Greece, Alexander to launch his own war in Asia, Rome to provide it with ancient and eastern roots, Mehmet the Conqueror as a stick to beat the Greeks with. In the nineteenth and twentieth centuries there arose an archaeological obsession to discover Troy and prove Homer's history of the Trojan Wars. This reached its height with Schliemann, but even long after Schliemann's interpretations have been discredited, this obsession shows no sign of abating: the far more professional current German excavations are still concerned with the historicity of the *Iliad*, the German-Russian dispute over the Trojan gold is as much to do with the Trojan legacy as the gold itself (long proven to be far older than, and quite irrelevant to, the Trojan Wars). For Troy has become a symbol above all else of a perceived struggle between east and west—a perception and a construct that has not the slightest foundation in Homer's great epic itself. Homer must be weeping.

Shortly after the Persian Wars, Homer and the Trojan Wars were reinvented by the Greeks to provide a ready-made precedent for the Greco-Persian wars, and Homer's epic was recast as the first episode in an eternal struggle of east versus west, Greek freedom-lover versus Asiatic barbarian, and the Trojans were retrospectively barbarised. There is, of course, no evidence for such a theme in Homer. On the contrary, Homer was probably from the Trojan side of the Aegean as we have observed, and in his Trojan epic the Trojans are never 'barbaric' but as heroic as the Achaeans (note: *not* 'Greeks'; Homer never uses the term)—or indeed moreso, as it is the city of Troy itself that is cast as the tragic hero, and it is Priam for whom one ultimately weeps, not Achilles. Up until the fifth century BC Trojans were depicted—for example, on vase paintings—as identical to Greeks. Homer's *Iliad* was never a war between 'Greek' and 'barbarian' nor even 'Asian'. But by the fifth century the Achaeans were turned into 'Greeks' and the Trojans reinvented as barbarians, precursors to the Persians, and vase paintings henceforward depict them in oriental costume. 'Here it became part of anti-Persian rhetoric, symbolizing the victory of Greek over non-Greek. Athenians could have it invoked in speeches, look at the depictions of the sack of Troy in the Painted Stoa, read the verses on Kimon's Herms in the agora, watch barbarian Trojans on the stage.'[11] Even that far back, history had become 'an unending dialogue between the present and the past' in the words of E H Carr.[12] In an era that has seen governments, backed up by a vast media barrage, demonise Germans, Communists and Muslims, it all sounds tiresomely familiar.

*   *   *

The world-spread and domination of 'western civilisation'—the first world-wide civilisation (although not the first world civilisation—that was the Persian) and the most successful one in history—is not in doubt here. But it is not as simple, and certainly not as one-sided, as it appears. I have not dealt here with those essential borrowings from the east that made the expansion possible—printing, paper, gunpowder, the compass, and so forth, to cite just a few of a very long list. But far more important than these borrowings, so much of the foundation of 'western civilisation'—indeed its very definition—is eastern: the alphabet and Christianity, for example. Most of all, our glib cultural divisions of east and west on analysis do not fit—and never have. By adhering to them it simply creates further divisions and misunderstandings.

One of the great paradoxes of the 'west' is that its very strength and worldwide success lies in the very fact that so much of it is not, after all, 'western'. We divide history into individual units of convenience, as indeed we must: east, west, Asia, Europe, Middle Ages, antiquity, and the hair-splitting refinements in between. Without doing so, history is so cumbersome that it becomes impossible to make meaning of the whole. But when those units of history become the purpose rather than the tool, history becomes oversimplified, and can feed a dangerous message. History *is* complex and it is wrong to oversimplify it. Any explanation must of necessity be complex. It must, therefore, be emphasised that any view given here is just *one* view: just one part—and a small part at that—of this complexity. To come up with any simple explanation is to deny the immense and complex variety that has contributed to making what we are today, not just 'Europe' but all of us, whoever 'we' are. History is nothing if not collective experience; the greater the 'collection', the richer the experience.

I do not intend to glibly claim that 'eastern' civilisations are superior. It is simply not a question of that: it is a nonsense to think of a single, defined 'eastern' civilisation at all. But is it also a nonsense to think of a single 'western' civilisation as it is normally taken to mean. We are not exclusive culturally, and our western and European identity is not as glib as we like to think. 'A living civilization must be able not only to give but to receive and to borrow' in the words of Fernand Braudel.[13] The central theme of history is not the domination of one civilisation over another, the momentary hegemony of one single region or group or even idea, be it European or Roman, Near Eastern or Ottoman, Communist or Islamic. Instead there is a continual, on-going ebb and flow of ideas that pass from one area to another, undergoing modifications by different cultures all the time. To force all cultures, peoples, civilisations into some preconceived 'east-west' mould is not only confrontational, it simply flies in the face of historical fact. Most of all, if we have any regard at all for our own European civilisation, we must strip aside blithe assumptions rooted in prejudice and understand it in its fullest, richest and broadest sense. Not to do this is to belittle it.

Chapter 1

THE LEGACY OF CYRUS
The Iranian Background

Ex[alted Marduk, Enlil-of-the-Go]ds, relented. He changed his mind about all the settlements whose sanctuaries were in ruins, and the population of the land of Sumer and Akkad who had become like corpses, and took pity on them. He inspected and checked all the countries, seeking for the upright king of his choice. He took the hand of Cyrus, king of the city of Anshan, and called him by his name, proclaiming him aloud for the kingship over all of everything.

Cyrus Cylinder (translated by Irving Finkel,
www.britishmuseum.org)

Thus says the Lord to Cyrus his anointed, whom he has taken by the right hand, subduing nations before him and stripping kings of their strength; before whom doors will be opened and no gates barred.

Isaiah 45: 1

There was one Cyrus, the Persian, who reduced to obedience a vast number of men and cities and nations, we were then compelled to … decide that to rule men might be a task neither impossible nor even difficult, if one should only go about it in an intelligent manner.

Xenophon *Cyropaedia* I.i.3

Persia is one of the great, classic civilisations of Asia that has fascinated people to its west ever since the foundation of the Persian Empire by Cyrus the Great. The land of Iran, constrained by the Caspian Sea to the north and the Persian Gulf to the south, has acted an east-west channel throughout history that connected the lands of Central Asia, India and ultimately China with the Near East and ultimately Europe. Hence, it is one of the more pivotal regions in history.

GEOGRAPHICAL BACKGROUND

In travelling eastwards across the vast lowlands of central and upper Mesopotamia, one sees in the distance a great mountain barrier. These are the mountains of Kurdistan, the beginning of the Iranian Plateau, rising abruptly like a wall beyond the Tigris (Pl. 2). Few geographical features demonstrate more graphically just how distinct Iran is, culturally and geographically, from the lands of the Near or Middle East to its west. Behind stretches the level plains of the Tigris-Euphrates basin and the Syrian desert further west, interrupted by the Anti-Lebanon and Lebanon ranges before meeting the Mediterranean. This is the Arab world of today, the world of the great ancient civilisations of the Semitic Near East. But ahead is a very different world, a world of high mountains and upland plateaux, of long winter snows and winds coming out of Inner Asia: Iran is more a part of 'High Asia' than of the conventional 'Middle East' further west. Its people speak languages unrelated to those of the Semitic Near East, and although today they share the same religion (Islam), Iranian Shiʿism is different to the mainstream Sunnism practised by most Arabs. In reaching this mountain barrier one senses the traditional 'Middle East' to be left behind: the Iranian Plateau is where Central Asia begins.

The Iranian plateau is mostly between 100 and 2000 metres high, dominated by the Alburz mountains in the north and the Zagros in the south-west; in Iran one is rarely out of sight of mountains. The two mountain ranges meet in a knot towards the Caucasus mountains in the north-west. This latter region, known as Azerbaijan (the Republic of Azerbaijan further north is an extension) is one of the hilliest and best watered parts of Iran. The country remains hilly and well watered further south-east following the Zagros ranges, through Kurdistan, Luristan and Fars, but in the extreme south-west it opens out into the low, flat plains of Khuzistan (ancient Susiana or Elam), an eastward extension of the lowland of the Tigris-Euphrates river basin of Mesopotamia. The Zagros range becomes more arid further south, plunging abruptly in places into the Persian Gulf, isolating the plateau from the sea and leaving only a very narrow, arid coastal strip. The Alburz ranges to the north isolate the Caspian littoral from the central plateau in a similar fashion. The Caspian coastal plain, however, could not be in more contrast to the Gulf: the combination of its altitude several hundred feet below sea level with the barrier effect of the Alburz ranges has provided an enclosed, humid, greenhouse environment of dense rain forest, rice fields and tea plantations. To the east of the Caspian, where the Alburz gradually peters out, the country opens out into the high, wide pastures of the Turkmen steppe and Khurasan. Between the two ranges of the Alburz and Zagros lies the bulk of the Iranian plateau, a largely level area of plains and semi-desert (although interrupted by low ranges of hills throughout), gradually giving way to the great deserts of sand and salt in the central and south-eastern parts of the country (the Dasht-i Kavir and the Dasht-i Lut). This region contains some of the great cities of Iran, such as Tehran and Isfahan, and a string of caravan cities—Yazd, Kerman, Bam—skirt the southern edges of the desert towards the south-east. The eastern parts of the country are generally far more arid and desert-like—although still very hilly—merging into the desert regions of Seistan and Baluchistan. In the deserts of Seistan, however, have been found traces of some of the earliest civilisations in Iran, civilisations about which very little is still known.

Culturally, the civilisation has spread over a considerably greater area than the modern boundaries of Iran itself, reflecting the fluctuations of different Iranian empires throughout history. Regions as widely separated as parts of the Balkans and the Black Sea in the west to India in the east, and the Aral Sea in the north to southern Arabia in the south have at different times been ruled by various Iranian dynasties. More immediately, adjacent parts of Mesopotamia and Central Asia can be said to come under the cultural orbit—a 'greater Iran'. Hence, important works of Persian architecture can be found in Iraq, Turkey, Afghanistan and Uzbekistan.

At the same time, the present boundaries of Iran incorporate minorities from all surrounding regions—indeed, the ethnic makeup of Iran is one of the most varied in Asia. The largest community in Iran, after the Persians themselves, are the Azerbaijanis to the north-west whose language is close to Turkish; another Turkish dialect is the language of the Turkmen to the north-east as well. The hills and valleys of the Zagros to the west and south shelter a variety of other minorities: Shahsavan to the north-west, a semi-nomadic group who speak a dialect of Turkish; Kurds and Lurs to the west, two distinct, mainly sedentary groups whose languages are related to Persian; and the great nomadic nations of the south, Bakhtiari, Qashqai and Khamsa, who are of

Persian, Turkish and Arab origin respectively (with considerable admixture). Arab communities are also to be found in Khuzistan to the south-west as well as along the Persian Gulf coast; in the far south-east the population is Baluch, who speak a language distantly related to Persian.

Iran has also been home to numerous religious minorities, often for thousands of years. The oldest are the Zoroastrians, examined more in Chapter 7, but there is also an ancient Jewish population dating from the time of the Persian Empire. The largest Christian community are the Armenians, who mainly arrived after the sixteenth century (although Armenians were in Iran in the Sasanian period), but there is also a small community of Assyrian Christians, descendants of the Nestorians expelled from the Byzantine Empire. There are also Muslim minorities: the Arabs, Turkomen and Baluch are mainly Sunni, and there are several Sufi schools. Smaller religious communities are the Ahl-i Haqq in Kurdistan and the Mandaeans in Khuzistan, distinct religions that incorporate elements of Gnosticism and Manichaeism. Another distinct religion that emerged in Iran in the nineteenth century was the Baha'is, although these are not recognised by the present government and have mainly moved abroad. The idea of a world transcending political and ethnic boundaries, therefore, is inherent in the nature of the country itself and its history.

Strictly speaking the country is called 'Iran' rather than 'Persia'; Iranians themselves refer to their country as Iran. This is not a modern name, as is often thought, but is as ancient as Persia. 'Persia' derives from the Hellenised form of *Fars* or *Pars*, the southern province bordering the Persian Gulf. Calling the country 'Persia', therefore, is much like calling the Netherlands 'Holland' or Britain 'England'. In antiquity the Iranians referred to their country as *Eranshahr* or 'country of Iran'—the Sasanian kings added the title *Eran ud Aneran* to their names, kings of 'Iran and non-Iran'. The name derives from *aryan*, the general Indo-European ethno-linguistic group of which the Iranian peoples form a part; the name survives in the place-name Herat (ancient Aria) in Afghanistan. Nonetheless, 'Persia' has been in common usage in the West since ancient Greek times and is now used more in a cultural sense: it is conventional to speak of 'Persian art' or a 'Persian carpet'. The language, moreover, is known as Persian, not Iranian (again, analogous to the 'English' language, which is never called 'British').* The Persians were originally a sub-tribe of the Iranian peoples. Persian

---

* 'Iranian' or 'Iranic' in fact has a specialist linguistic meaning referring to a group of languages all related to Persian.

(known as 'Farsi' in Persian—not to be confused with Parsee, which is a Zoroastrian community of Iranian origins in India)* is an Indo-European language that is Central Asian in origin, not belonging to the Semitic group of languages spoken by most inhabitants of the Middle East (apart from the Turks). The only other countries where Persian is largely spoken are Afghanistan and Tajikistan,† although there are Persian-speaking minorities in Bahrain, Turkmenistan, Uzbekistan and China as well. At different times in the past, in some cases as late as the nineteenth century, Persian was also a *lingua franca* in much of Central Asia, China and India.

PREHISTORY AND THE ARRIVAL OF THE IRANIANS

There were civilisations in Iran long before the arrival of the Medes and Persians. The story begins between about 10,000 and 7000 BC, with the gradual change from nomadic hunter-gathering groups to settled communities and the beginnings of the first agriculture, the so-called 'Neolithic Revolution'. The Zagros hills of western Iran were among the first places in the world where this process took place. Over the ensuing millennia these small settlements in western Iran—distinguished mainly by their brilliantly coloured pottery—gradually grew and expanded, with flourishing sedentary cultures being firmly established throughout Iran and elsewhere in western Asia: with the Caucasus, Mesopotamia, Central Asia and the Indian borderlands. By about 2000 BC civilisation in Iran revolved around two important centres: Seistan in the south-east and Elam in the south and south-west, with Fars in the south acting as a major link between the two regions. That in the south-east has only recently become fully apparent, with major discoveries still being made, so it is not yet fully understood. It covers an area stretching roughly from Kerman eastwards

---

* There is a pedantic tendency nowadays to refer in everyday contexts to the language as 'Farsi' rather than 'Persian'—I have even been corrected on occasion and told quite sternly that 'no, the language is not Persian, it is Farsi.' This is surprising: one never (in an English-speaking context), refers to the language of France as 'Français' or of Germany as 'Deutsch'.

† In Afghanistan and Tajikistan the language is known variously as Dari, Farsi and Tajik, but are essentially dialects of the same language that are mutually understood. In some ways, the name *Dari*, meaning '[language of] the court, is probably a more correct term for the language than *Farsi*, '[language of] Fars' is, for it was in the Samanid court of Bukhara in the ninth and tenth centuries that modern Persian emerged. Technically, therefore, the language should perhaps be 'Khurasani' rather than 'Farsi'.

to where the present Iranian, Afghan and Pakistani borders meet in the deserts of Seistan and southwards to the shores of the Gulf of Oman. This brilliant—and as yet un-named—civilisation produced an extraordinary art with many terracotta, steatite and bronze sculptures discovered, and wrote on clay tablets in a little known pictographic script called proto-Elamite. There are many connections with Central Asia, and this may have been its origin.

The better known civilisation is that of Elam in the south-west, if only because of its strong connections with the early civilisations of Mesopotamia. Indeed, the plains of Elam are geographically an extension of Mesopotamia, and the Elamites share many characteristics with the Mesopotamians: they built ziggurats, they wrote in the cuneiform script. But the Elamites were at the same time distinct from the Sumerians and Babylonians of Mesopotamia: their language, Elamite, is unrelated to the Mesopotamian languages (it may have been related to the Dravidian language group of India). The centre of this civilisation has traditionally been viewed as Susa, in the centre of Elam in the lowlands, but recent discoveries have indicated that other centres existed in the highland area of the Iranian plateau at Anshan near Persepolis and even further east in south-eastern Iran, suggesting less Mesopotamian influence than originally thought.

The Iranian peoples themselves are relative newcomers to the country they gave their name to: Iran. They were originally a Central Asian people, coming into Iran in a series of migrations that might have begun as early as the late third millennium BC and only ended in the first century BC with the arrival of the last Iranian tribe from Central Asia, the Parthians. Both the date and the route of the arrival of the first Iranian tribes—or the Indo-Iranians—has been much disputed, and forms a part of the much wider discussion over Indo-European origins and dispersions.* With the first Iranian tribes known in the historical period—the Medes and Persians—being centred on western and southern Iran, it was previously thought that they arrived in Iran via the Caucasus to the west of the Caspian. The centre of earlier peoples speaking Indo-European languages in Anatolia, such as the Hittites and the Mitanni, seemed to support this view. It is now more generally recognised, however, that the Iranians came via the north-east, direct from Central Asia, particularly through the Gurgan 'corridor' to the south-east of the Caspian, as excavations at sites such as Tureng Tepe, Yarim Tepe and Tepe Hisar tend to suggest. More recent studies

---

* This is discussed more in Volume 4 of this series, *The Gates of Europe*.

have indicated that the Indo-Iranians might have migrated from Central Asia first to south-eastern Iran, before dividing into two major groups, one migrating eastwards to India, the other westwards to southern Iran. But whatever the facts—and there is still a great deal more archaeological investigation to be carried out—the pattern of Indo-Iranian movements was probably a more complex one than first appears. It is unlikely that there was a sudden invasion, such as the Mongols in later history, and their appearance in Iran was more likely to have been the result of a series of slow and largely peaceful migrations and gradual assimilation along a number of different routes.

The archaeological record indicates the period after about 1400 BC to be a particular era of mass movements and migrations, with new peoples arriving on the plateau, mainly in the northern and western parts of the country. These new peoples are associated with a distinctive type of grey pottery which is found on many sites of this period (often with burials), and archaeologists have suggested that this 'grey-ware people' might be evidence of the arrival of Iranian tribes, but there is not enough information to draw ethnic or linguistic conclusions. The best known of these cultures is one that emerged after about 1000 BC in the Zagros mountains, and produced the now famous Luristan bronzes. These exquisite bronzes, nearly all originating from Luristan in the west of Iran, are some of the finest products of the metallurgists' craft to have come to us from early antiquity. They began to flood the world's museums after the 1920s, but since most of them came from clandestine excavations—and many are forgeries—we still know very little about the people who produced them. Many of the bronzes are horse trappings, so it has been suggested that they represent the arrival of the Indo-Europeans onto the Iranian plateau, as it is known that the Indo-Europeans introduced new horse-riding techniques. Once again, there is not enough information to draw ethnic or linguistic conclusions.

But whether or not the grey-ware people or the Luristan bronze people were the first Iranians, we certainly know from Assyrian sources that from the ninth century BC the first great Iranian tribe had established themselves on the plateau. These were the Medes.

THE MEDES AND THE PERSIANS (MAP 1)

The year 612 BC is one of those watershed dates that occasionally occur in history. It was an important one for Western Asia, for in that year the city of Nineveh, capital of the Assyrian Empire, was sacked and destroyed by an allied army of Babylonians and Medes. The Assyrian Empire was the greatest power that the ancient world had hitherto known, and the extinction of such a power is reason enough for that date to be an important one. But more than that, the sack of Nineveh marked the arrival of an entirely new people on the world stage: the Medes. The Medes were the first of the Iranian tribes to form themselves into a coherent group. Initially, their 'empire' was probably little more than a loose confederation of tribes in the hills of western Iran, but their overthrow of the Near East's greatest power up until that time thrust the Medes—as well as their close allies and ethnic cousins, the Persians—firmly into the Near Eastern arena. Up until then, the Near East had been dominated by the lowland Mesopotamian civilisations of antiquity: Akkadians, Babylonians, Assyrians, Aramaeans (mainly peoples belonging to the Semitic group languages). There was a brief resurgence under the Neo-Babylonian kingdom of Nebuchadnezzar and his successors, but soon Babylon was to go the same way as Nineveh when the Medes gave way to a new, mightier, Iranian power: the Persians under their dynamic new leader, Cyrus the Great, who conquered the Median empire.* The Near East was to be dominated by successive Iranian dynasties—Persian, Parthian and Sasanian—for over 1200 years until the rise of the Arabs under Islam.

The Medes established an empire that extended into northern Mesopotamia and eastern Anatolia, with its capital at Ecbatana, modern Hamadan. The heartland was the hills of western Iran and northern Iraq, roughly the same area that is today peopled by Kurds. This has led some authorities to regard the Kurds as the modern descendants of the Medes. The Kurdish demographic centre is now generally further west than the original Median homeland around Hamadan: the mountainous areas of northern Iraq, south-western Turkey and north-eastern Syria, but this is viewed as a 'Celtification' where later incomers—notably the Persians—pushed the earlier Medes into the less desirable mountainous fringes.

---

* A recent study, however, has suggested that Cyrus' coup represented a re-assertion of the Elamites and not a rise of the Persians—see below.

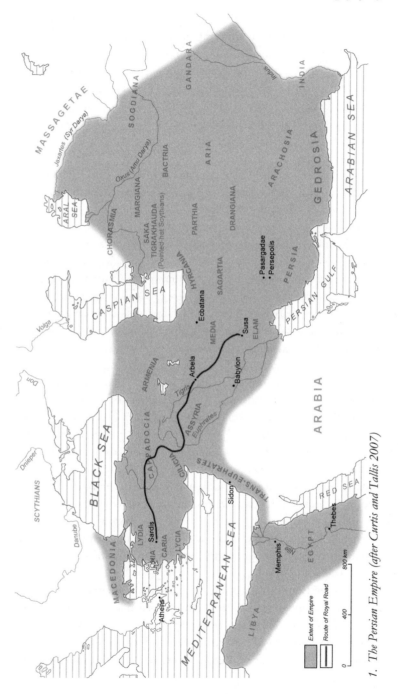

1. The Persian Empire (after Curtis and Tallis 2007)

Closely allied to the Medes in the upper echelons of their army and administration was another confederation of tribes from the same Iranian stock: the Persians. Whereas the migration of Median tribes had settled in the west of the country, the Persian tribes settled in the south in the region that eventually took their name, Fars or Persia proper. The Persian tribes united under the house of Achaemenes, and their leaders eventually married into the Median royal family. It was one of these leaders, Cyrus who, in 550 BC, deposed the last Median king, Astyages, to found the Achaemenid Empire.

Cyrus is traditionally held to be the founder of the Persian Empire. That he founded a great empire has never been in serious doubt, but a recent re-examination of the evidence by archaeologist Daniel Potts has plausibly suggested that Cyrus himself was an Elamite, not a Persian, and that the Persians themselves did not assume power until Darius' coup some thirty years later.[1] The suggestion has certainly aroused considerable controversy amongst Iranians themselves, many of whom revere Cyrus as the greatest Persian. To some extent the ethnic affiliation of Cyrus is irrelevant, for the empire—and the civilisation—that he founded was above all an eclectic one that drew upon both Persian and Elamite elements—as well as many others—to found a new international order that transcended cultural barriers.

Whatever he was, Cyrus rapidly established a great empire. His conquest of King Croesus' kingdom of Lydia in western Anatolia brought the Persian Empire to the frontiers of Europe. Acting on a prophecy that if he crossed the Halys River (forming the eastern boundary of his kingdom) he would destroy a great kingdom, Croesus invaded Cyrus' territories—and destroyed his own! The Persian Empire then absorbed most of Anatolia as far as the Aegean. Cyrus soon added Central Asia as far as the Jaxartes (Syr Darya) River, as well as Babylonia and Syria to the empire. Cambyses, his successor, added Egypt, and Darius, the greatest Achaemenid Emperor after Cyrus (and perhaps the real founder of the *Persian*, as opposed the Achaemenid, Empire), added Sind and Punjab in the east and northern Greece in the west. By about 500 BC, the Persian Empire was the largest the world had seen (Map 1).

The Persian Empire was also the world's first multinational empire. For unlike the few comparable empires before it—such as the Assyrian—the subject peoples were allowed a large degree of autonomy, often under their own governors and kings. Local institutions and religions were respected, even encouraged: the gods of Babylon were restored and protected, the exiled Jews were allowed to return and the Temple of Jerusalem rebuilt with the aid of imperial funds. A massive new system of organisation and administration was instigated: provincial government, roads, taxation, banking—all solid new institutions that survived the eclipse of this empire by many centuries. A universal art form came into being. J M Roberts thus writes in his *History of the World*: 'The monuments fittingly express the continuing diversity and tolerance of Persian culture. It was one always open to influence from abroad and would continue to be. Persia took up not only the language of those she conquered, but also sometimes their ideas. She also contributed … Right across the Old World Persia suddenly pulled peoples into a common experience. Indians, Medes, Babylonians, Lydians, Greeks, Jews, Phoenicians, Egyptians were for the first time all administered by one empire whose eclecticism showed how far civilisation had already come. The era of distinct units of history in the Near East was over … The base of a future world civilisation was in the making.'[2] Moreover, it laid the foundations of a distinctive *Persian* civilisation: a civilisation of gardens as much as fortifications, a civilisation that was at once both mighty and gentle—it is significant, for example, that unlike the Assyrians or Egyptians, the Achaemenids generally did not exalt military conquest in their inscriptions or their art.

The Persian Empire experienced revolts of course—notably by the Egyptians, but also by the Ionians and even its own satraps—and it would be a mistake to regard the empire with rose-tinted spectacles as one huge harmonious family living at peace under the loose but benevolent rule of the Great King. It would also be a mistake to deny what it is most accused of: Oriental despotism. Of course it was despotic—but the empires of Alexander, the Seleucids, the Romans or the Byzantines were equally 'orientally despotic;' Xerxes' despotism was no more 'oriental' than that of Charlemagne or Henry VIII, and despotism does not discriminate between east and west.

But the Achaemenids *were* noted for their tolerance, and their empire was remarkable for the comparative lack of revolts: there is no record of revolts, for example, in Syria or inland Anatolia or in the ancient lands of Bactria or Arachosia. Almost alone of ancient 'despotisms', the Persians had solved the problem of 'how to rule an empire without continuous and repressive force on its inhabitants'.[3] There was none of the large-scale and continuous blood-letting that characterised so many empires of antiquity: Assyria and the Hellenistic successor states, for example, or Rome with its interminable civil wars, or the countless numbers—probably in the millions—who died when Qin Shih Huang-di established the first Chinese empire. Persepolis has been regarded as the very embodiment of despotism, as the remarks by Green and Holland in the Introduction show—but it is remarkable that the reliefs there do not depict a single battle.

AN INTERNATIONAL STYLE

Persepolis and the monuments of this civilisation are a fitting place to pause. The empire had four capitals (or royal cities), Pasargadae, Hamadan, Susa and Babylon, but a fifth outshone them all (if only because it is the only one to have survived): the royal seat and dynastic centre of Persepolis (Pls 3-20). All were deliberately chosen not only to reflect the cultural and ethnic diversity of the Persian Empire but also to provide continuity with the past. Pasargadae, an upland pasture, was probably the original tribal area of the Achaemenids, perhaps the site of Cyrus' first victory against the Medes, hence of immense symbolic value to the Achaemenids (Pls 3-6). Hamadan was the original Median capital, and although the Persians replaced the Medes they were particular to include the Medes in the upper echelons of their administration; to a large extent the Persian Empire was projected as a continuation of the Median Empire as much as its successor (Pl. 7). Susa was the ancient Elamite centre, and Elamite culture—and language—remained a part of the Persian imperial vocabulary; indeed, Cyrus himself might have been an Elamite as we have seen (Pls 8-9). Babylon was, of course, a reaffirmation of the importance of ancient Mesopotamian civilisation which the Persians incorporated (Pl. 10).

Strictly speaking, Persepolis was not a capital city like the others, but was an immense royal residence, largely the work of Darius and Xerxes in the sixth and fifth centuries BC that was both an assertion of the new Persia and a re-assertion of the older Elamite capital of Anshan nearby (Pls 11-20). Its precise function is disputed, but it may have been built to host the New Year festivities on the spring equinox (usually 21st March) each year, the main annual event of the Iranian calendar, when representatives of the subject peoples of this immensely widespread empire would come together to bring tribute and pay homage to the court of the Great King (Pl. 19). Persepolis was, above all, the architectural embodiment of Persian dynasticism, of kingship. It is significant that with the sole exception of

Cyrus at Pasargadae, all Achaemenid kings were buried here or at the adjacent necropolis of Naqsh-i Rustam (Pls 21-24). Persepolis is thus the ultimate inspiration of a whole range of dynastic cults expressed in architecture, from Surkh Kotal and Mathura in the east to Mt Nimrod and the Mausoleum in the west. The sheer scale, splendour and majesty of Persepolis (not to mention the other Persian imperial palaces which have not survived) might conjure up images of grand 'oriental isolation' like no other. But the opposite was true. Migrating between capitals, the Persian kings went out into their empire as few others did, before or after.

The ruins of Persepolis convey another, deeper message. To a greater or lesser extent, all empires, benign or brutal, impose some form of unity over the nations that they rule: the Assyrian no less than the Roman or any other empire of antiquity. But amongst ancient empires, the Persians added another dimension. On the reliefs at Persepolis it is very graphically illustrated how every year delegates from all corners of the empire—Nubians from the south, Cyrenaicans from the west, Scythians from the north, Indians from the east, and just about every other nationality in between—would travel to Persia to pay homage (and taxes) to the great king in his magnificent court (Pl. 19). Many empires were content to receive their taxes and allegiance simply by remissions or through agents sent out from the centre to the peripheries to either receive or seize them. But Persia imposed obligatory annual travel from all corners upon its peoples (or at least their representatives): for the first time in history a Nubian would rub shoulders with an Indian and a Scythian (and a whole host of others)—and not at a once in a lifetime chance meeting, but on a regular basis. This was true internationalism. Even under the Roman Empire such internationalism did not exist: a subject king, such as Herod, might only visit Rome once in a lifetime, and the governors were always sent out *from* Rome. There was no system where the provincials were forced to visit Rome on a regular basis. Such an internationalism, and with it an intermingling of different cultures and ideas, was not to emerge again until the concept of the obligatory annual pilgrimage to Mecca that Islam required of its believers.

When wandering through the ruins of this vast palace complex it is possible to observe styles from Egypt, Greece, Anatolia, Central Asia and Mesopotamia in the architecture (and more influences exist in the art)— many of these styles occasionally even reflected in a single column (Pl. 15). From a purely aesthetic point of view it does not often work: it can appear simply a jumble with too many styles, architecture by an international committee. But that is not the point. This extraordinarily eclectic style reflects the internationalism and deliberate syncretism of the Persian kings—part of a policy to weld together the disparate cultures of its vast multi-national empire: 'an idea not an art'.[4] Thus, with the Mesopotamian, Anatolian, Greek, Egyptian, Central Asian and Indian styles combined with its own native Persian style, we see a deliberate syncretisation: the beginnings of an international architecture.

Two further monuments reflect another important facet of Persian governance: that of oral transmission. The Royal Tombs at Naqsh-i Rustam, not far from Persepolis (Pls 21-24), and the great inscription and rock relief at Bisitun overlooking the ancient Royal Road between Susa and Hamadan (Pl. 25), both with important inscriptions from the reign of Darius. His tomb inscription, often known as the 'Testament of Darius', is engraved on the face of his tomb at Naqsh-i Rustam far above the ground and well beyond legibility. This has been interpreted as, at best, merely 'his view of royal invincibility and infallibility'[5] or at worst irrelevant: it was too far for anyone to read anyway. The same can be said of his inscription at Bisitun. But even if it were posted in public places in towns throughout the empire, it would be just as unintelligible: most people were probably illiterate. Who were these addressed to therefore?

The explanation lies in oral transmission: just as the sacred books of Zoroastrianism were disseminated orally, this and other statements of the Persian kings would be memorised and proclaimed orally at important occasions in public places throughout the empire so that all would know, and not just the literate (or far-sighted) minority. A parallel situation occurs much later in Islam, when a Qur'anic verse is inscribed around the top of a minaret far beyond its legibility: there was no need for it to be read, as believers would know it anyway. After all, we know that Darius' testament was repeated virtually word for word by Xerxes: it had become as fixed, in other words, as a written constitution. Copies—or at least versions—of the Bisitun inscription have been found elsewhere (as indeed Darius instructed it to be in his inscription), such as an Aramaic version written on papyrus at Elephantine in Egypt dating to the time of Darius II, as well as other versions found in Babylonia and Susa. One can assume that Greek versions would have been circulated in Anatolia as well. Darius' laws were admired in both the Bible and by Plato, and its legal terms and forms were borrowed in Armenian and Syriac.[6] And, whilst it is true that it is a case for 'royal invincibility and infallibility', it is more importantly an explicit statement of the principles of good government.

As a final look at this legacy one returns not to the grand halls of Darius and Xerxes but to one of the more modest: the Tomb of Cyrus at Pasargadae (Pl. 6). It is a comparatively plain building: a relatively small single chamber with a pitched roof raised on a stepped podium. The effect is enhanced by the tomb standing in isolation. As a monument it is unique in Iran—as, indeed, is its creator.

Originally perhaps an Elamite, the Persians since have regarded Cyrus as their own, their greatest king. Babylonian documents hail him as the benefactor of their religion and the restorer of the ancient gods of Babylon to their rightful place. The Jews went even further, and the Old Testament proclaims Cyrus as the 'anointed one', a messiah or prophet, for allowing the exiled Jews to return to Jerusalem and rebuild the Temple. In Syria, cuneiform tablets confirm Cyrus' tolerant policy of allowing deportees to return.[7] The Greeks made him the hero of one of their great literary works, the *Cyropaedia* or *Education of Cyrus* by Xenophon. This has been one of the more influential works of literature written and has been 'in print' probably for longer than any other book in history. Xenophon was in the employment of a Persian prince, Cyrus the Younger, who challenged his brother Artaxerxes II for the throne. Although Cyrus lost and was killed, Xenophon was a great admirer of both Cyruses, and wrote his *Cyropaedia* in answer to Plato's *Republic* as a eulogy for good government and a model for princes. Machiavelli, in writing his own 'mirror for princes' some two thousand years later, numbered Cyrus the Great among the four ideal princes of the ancient world (along with Moses, Theseus and Romulus). Although certainly based on a core of fact, the events Xenophon narrates in the *Cyropaedia* are essentially fictional. But Iran had a long tradition of the cult of kings and their dynasties, with monuments from Surkh Kotal and Mathura in the east to Nemrut Dağ in the west all stemming from the cult of kingship expressed at Persepolis.*

---

* Surkh Kotal in Afghanistan and Mathura in India were dynastic cult centres of the Kushan kings of the first century AD, as is Khalchayan in Uzbekistan. Nemrut Dağ in Turkey was a dynastic cult centre of the first century BC Commegenian kings, themselves of Iranian origin. Nemrut Dağ is discussed further in Chapter 5. The continuing symbolism of Surkh Kotal into the Sasanian period was graphically demonstrated by the dramatic discovery of the rock relief of Shapur near there (hunting hippopotami!) a few years ago by Jonathan Lee. See Grenet *et al.* in Cribb & Herrmann (eds) 2007. The great Buddhas of Bamiyan in Afghanistan belong within this tradition as a dynastic cult centre for the Turk *kagans* (Bamiyan is also discussed in Volume 3 in this series).

In this context, it is worth recalling a parallel Indian tradition of the 'mirror of princes' genre, going back to the *Arthasastra* of Kautilya and probably written for Chandragupta Maurya in the fourth century BC. This might be a completely independent tradition, but a common link between Indian and Greek was the Persian Empire. We know too that such traditions would also have been disseminated orally: Zoroastrianism confirms the Iranian oral tradition long before the Achaemenids (see below Chapter 7). Of all princes, therefore, Cyrus was the obvious choice for Xenophon's model in an overt idealisation of monarchy. A Persian king of kings, a Babylonian benefactor, a Jewish prophet, a Greek hero: no ruler in history has been so honoured by his subject peoples. *

---

* Briant (2002: 40-49) downplays both the Babylonian and Judaic traditions of Cyrus, the one as exaggerated by Persian propaganda, the other as realpolitik. For the *Cyropaedia* see Tatum 1989.

Chapter 2

PERSIANS AND GREEKS
The Beginnings of a Complex Relationship

It's time we admitted the truth:
we're Greeks also—what else are we?
but with Asiatic tastes and feelings,
tastes and feelings
sometimes alien to Hellenism.

It isn't correct, Hermippos, for us philosophers
to be like some of our petty kings
(remember how we laughed at them
when they used to come to our lectures?)
who through their shadowy Hellenified exteriors
(Macedonian exteriors, naturally)
let a bit of Arabia peep out now and then,
a bit of Media they can't keep back.
And to what laughable lengths the fools went
trying to cover it up!

No, that's not at all correct for us.
For Greeks like us that kind of pettiness won't do.
We simply can't be ashamed
of the Syrian and Egyptian blood in our veins;
we should really honour it, delight in it.

C P Cavafy[1]

Among the many different subject peoples depicted on the Persepolis reliefs were Greeks (Pl. 19a). It is this relationship between Persian and Greek that formed the basis of much of ancient history and the beginnings of perceived east-west conflicts. It is a relationship, therefore, that it is essential to examine.

It is also a relationship that is almost invariably viewed from the perspective of the Greeks. It seems almost impossible to be objective about Greek civilisation. Of all the ancient civilisations, that of the Greeks seems to be the most filtered through the perceptions of subsequent civilisations. We first view the Greeks through the Roman perception (almost literally, since many 'Greek' works of art are Roman copies, and Greek architecture first becomes familiar via its Roman and Neo-Classical descendants). The Romans admired and emulated their art, but the Greeks themselves were viewed as a slave people (albeit a learned one)—it is notable that for all Rome's Hellenic heritage, there was not a single Greek emperor until the Greeks themselves dominated the empire after its move to Constantinople; Rome had more Arab emperors than Greek. Up until the eighteenth century the Greeks were viewed by western Europe as debased, duplicitous and decadent, hence the negative connotations of the word 'Byzantine'. Indeed, the Latin church openly persecuted the Orthodox Greeks who were regarded as heretics—even the 'terrible Turk' was often viewed as superior. Throughout the Middle Ages the Greeks were regarded almost as much an objective of the Crusading movement as the Muslims were, hence the notorious Fourth Crusade of 1204 against Constantinople.*

Next is the Renaissance, whose rediscovery and interpretation of Greek civilisation largely defined the period. The latest filter—and still, perhaps, the most dominant—is the eighteenth century Enlightenment and the nineteenth century Romantic, through whose eyes Greek civilisation became both the ultimate root and the ultimate ideal. Ancient Greece has now become both the embodiment and fountainhead of European civilisation: '… that one small East European country to be regularly acclaimed as "the mother of Europe", the "Source of the West", a vital ingredient if not the sole fountain-head of Europe.'[2] One is left wondering, like Cavafy, what exactly is 'Greek': what really lies behind so many masks?

In attempting to strip away these filters and glimpse what lies beneath,

---

* It is interesting that an anonymous eleventh century Italo-Norman text, the *Gesta Francorum*, asserts the myth that both Turks and Normans had a common ancestry, both being descended from the Trojans. Hence, both were natural enemies of the Greeks. If the Turks would only convert to Christianity, it was argued, no nation would be their equal. See Cardini 2001: 83 and 142.

Greek civilisation remains as enigmatic as ever. It remains like Greek sculpture, which inspired both Rome and the Renaissance: the secret is preserved. Beauty is undoubted, but it represents the ideal: the faces are anonymous, blank, they are not 'real' people. When comparing Greek sculpture to its poor cousin, Roman (as one must: the definition of 'Classical' is Greek *and* Roman), the Roman faces are immediately recognisable as portraits of real people—even the mosaics combine both realism and naivety: we feel we *know* the Romans.

A particularly important and widely read book on Greek civilisation is John Boardman's now classic *The Greeks Overseas*, a seminal account of the expansion of Greek civilisation throughout the Mediterranean and into Europe, Africa, Asia and the Black Sea. But in a sense the title of this book begs a basic question: so much of Greek civilisation took place outside and beyond Greece—especially in Asia Minor—that the Greeks are as much 'at home' overseas as in Greece itself. This may appear nit-picking (and certainly implies no criticism of Boardman's book). But it serves to highlight two important points.

First, our view of Greek civilisation is heavily biased towards fifth century BC Athens. Remarkable though the Athenian achievement was, it was not the first centre of Greek civilisation nor was it the last, but only one part of a broader (and richer) Hellenic achievement. For example, the first centre of Greek philosophy—often viewed as Greece's greatest contribution to civilisation—was Miletus in Asia Minor in the early sixth century BC, and the last upsurge in Greek learning was in Constantinople in the fifteenth century. It is important to bear in mind, therefore, how un-homogeneous Greek civilisation as a whole was, and that there was no such thing as a single 'Greek mind' or single set of 'Greek values'. E H Carr in his now classic *What is History?* emphasises this when he writes: 'Our picture of Greece in the fifth century B.C. is defective not primarily because so many of the bits have been accidentally lost, but because it is, by and large, the picture formed by a tiny group of people in the city of Athens ... we know a lot about what fifth-century Greece looked like to an Athenian citizen; but hardly anything about what it looked like to a Spartan, a Corinthian, or a Theban—not to mention a Persian, or a slave or other non-citizen resident in Athens. Our picture has been preselected and predetermined for us, not so much by accident as by people who were consciously or unconsciously imbued with a particular view and thought the facts which supported that view worth preserving.'[3]

Our second point is that Greek civilisation is viewed as the roots of our own European civilisation—indeed, as the very origin of our European identity: 'Greek therefore European' becomes a self-evident statement that is not questioned.* But Greek civilisation has flourished so much *outside* Europe: the early civilisation of the Greeks of Asia Minor—mainly Ionia—and then the Greek intellectual centres of the Hellenistic successor kingdoms: Pergamon in Anatolia, Antioch in Syria and—most important— Alexandria in Egypt. One might also point to far less well known later centres of Hellenism: Babylon in Mesopotamia, Gundishapur in Iran, Bactria in Central Asia and Gandhara in India, for example.† The longest lasting Greek state apart from Byzantium was the Bosporan kingdom on the Black Sea with its capital at Panticapaeum: from its foundation in the sixth century BC to its eventual disappearance in the fourth century AD, a continuous history of a thousand years. Miletus, Cnidus, Panticapaeum, Antioch, Seleucia, Alexandria, Bactris, Taxila, Constantinople: all centres of Greek civilisation far away—in some cases many thousands of miles away—from Athens. Even today, the third largest concentration of Greek population in the world is Melbourne, Australia.

Greek civilisation, as it has come down to us through successive Roman, Renaissance, Enlightenment and Romantic filters, is seen as the root of European civilisation, indeed as the origin of European identity. That Greek civilisation is *in* Europe goes without saying. But is it *of* Europe? For more than most, Greek civilisation, right from its beginnings, has been born from and subsequently defined by its relationship with other peoples: the 'barbarians'.⁴ The relationship which underpinned so much of ancient Greek history was that with the Persians. It was a complex relationship, frequently troubled and always reciprocal. But it was a relationship that formed so much of what came to be viewed as 'Europe'.

---

* Archaeologist Loring Danforth (in Roisman (ed) 2003: 355), for example, emphasises that 'The dominating ideology pervading the field of archaeology in Greece has been that of Greek nationalism. Its primary ideological purpose has been to construct a romanticized image of ancient Hellenism as the origin, not only of Greek national culture, but of all Western civilization as well.'

† Few apart from specialists might have heard of such places as Balkh in Afghanistan or Taxila in Pakistan, especially as centres of Hellenism, but through these, elements of Hellenism (mainly art) influenced, India, Central Asia and China, making them as important for the dissemination of Greek civilisation as Athens or Alexandria were.

GREEKS, HELLENES, IONIANS AND PERSIANS

The Greeks refer to themselves as 'Hellenes' and their home country as 'Hellas'. A Hellene is any Greek speaker, east or west, but Hellas applies only to the modern country of that name (modern Greece).* But to the Persians, Greeks both east and west of the Aegean were 'Ionians', *Yauna* or *Yunan* (and still are: the modern Persian for 'Greece' is *Yunanistan*): the Balkan Greeks, in other words, were viewed as a branch of a people based in Asia. When a differentiation had to be made, the Balkan Greeks were referred to as the 'Ionians beyond the sea' or 'the Ionians in Europe' with the Asia Minor Greeks as the 'Ionians by the sea'.† A salutary corrective to most modern works which refer to the Balkan Greeks as 'Mainland Greeks' and the Greeks of Anatolia as 'East Greeks'—or even simply as 'the mainland and Asia'—with the implied differentiation of mainstream and periphery (surely Asia is equally—if not more—a 'main land'?).‡ Indeed, a recent study of the origin of the Greek peoples places their original homeland in eastern Anatolia.[5] This suggestion has many flaws and remains controversial, but it does at least demonstrate that the question of the European or Asiatic identity of the Greeks is by no means settled.

With this dichotomy in mind, it is important to appreciate the difference between 'Greek' and 'Ionian'. The blurring of 'Ionian' with Greek not only misses much of the wealth and diversity of Hellenic civilisation as a whole, but it underlies our perceptions of 'Greek' civilisation as a uniquely European one. Much of what we call 'Greek' civilisation is strictly speaking Ionian, i.e, it took place in Asia rather than Europe. To some extent many scholars recognise this distinction and get around it by labelling the Greek

---

* The terms 'Greece' and 'Greek' are Latin, applied first to Greek immigrants in southern Italy and then to all Greeks. After Christianity the term 'Hellene' fell out of favour among Greeks, being equated with 'pagan;' it was only very late in the Byzantine period when 'Hellene' was revived in order to underline the difference with the Latins. Throughout the Byzantine period the Greeks referred to themselves as 'Romans' and to this day, Greeks in Istanbul still refer to themselves under that name: *Rhomaioi.*

† Although the exact difference between 'Ionians beyond the sea' and 'Ionians by the sea' is unclear in the inscriptions: which sea is meant, for example, the Aegean or the Marmara? The term might well refer to Thessalians, Thracians and Macedonians as well, or mean simply 'westerner' generally. When the Persian term *Yauna* entered southern Indian literature as *Yavana*, it had broadened to include Romans and 'westerners' generally, including—ironically—Persians.

‡ The terms 'Balkan Greeks' and 'Anatolian Greeks' seem to be the least biased terms, and are used here.

civilisation of Anatolia as 'East Greek'. But this simply exacerbates an already confused situation: the term 'East Greek' implies an off-shoot (hence poor cousin?) of the Greek peninsula, hence of Europe. However, Ionia acted as the Greeks' channel of communication with Asia and with Near Eastern Civilisation, out of which Hellenic civilisation as a whole evolved. This in turn has meant that Asia has always perceived the Greeks—and Greek civilisation with it—through Ionian spectacles. Straddling both sides of the Aegean, Greek civilisation forms as much a part of eastern civilisation as western.

The terms 'Greek' and 'Asian', therefore, are loaded with a whole baggage of cultural ramifications to the European mind; whenever they are used one must bear this in mind. From the 'Asian' viewpoint, it is significant that all Asian languages, ancient and modern, refer to Greece and the Greeks as 'Ionia' and 'Ionian': Arabic, *Yunan*, Assyrian *Yawan*, Sanskrit *Yavana*, Chinese *Ye-meï-ni*, Old Persian *Yauna*, modern Persian *Yunan* and *Yunanistan*.*

IONIA: A QUESTION OF IDENTITY (MAPS 2-3)

The west coast of Asia Minor—the Aegean coast—is where the Anatolian plateau plunges abruptly into the sea. Hence, the area is very mountainous, leaving in some places only a narrow coastal strip. This has provided the Ionian coast of Asia Minor with its two most characteristic features that have moulded its cultural development since earliest times: the mountains and the rivers. The run-off from the mountains has provided the coast with a number of important river estuaries—the Maeander is one of the better known—which act as a natural focus for both settlement and, more importantly, for harbours. But the run-off brings more than water: it also brings silt. An important side-effect of these rivers, therefore, has been the constant silting up of the harbours that the rivers created, with consequent expansion of the coast line resulting in many of the important coastal sites of antiquity now lying inland.

The end of the Bronze Age in the eastern Mediterranean in about 1200 BC is marked by an event referred to vaguely as 'the invasion of the Sea Peoples'. The event itself, however, was far from vague: it was cataclysmic. Indeed, the invasions of the Sea Peoples is one of the great watersheds in the

---

* The name 'Ionian Sea' on the west coast of Greece is coincidental, and has no linguistic relation to 'Ionia'.

2. *Ionia and the Near East (after Cook 1962)*

3. *Asia Minor under the Achaemenids (after Burn in Gershevitch 1985)*

history of the eastern Mediterranean and Near East. It was probably sparked off by an initial invasion by nomads from the north, possibly the Dorians, ancestors of the Greeks, but the exact identity or nature of the invaders is not clearly understood. This does not matter so much as its ramifications, which had a knock-on effect of displacements, movements and invasions that lasted a considerable time. Some theories have tried to link it with natural cataclysms, such as tidal waves, earthquakes or the massive volcanic eruption that destroyed Santorini (Thera). The 'Sea Peoples', therefore, refers to a fairly general series of events rather than anything or anybody specific. With it, the old powers of Ugarit, Troy, Crete, Mycenae and even great powers like the Hittites disappeared. Egypt itself was destabilised, and in its wake we see the arrival, movement and eventual emergence of new peoples: Dorians, Etruscans, Aramaeans, Hebrews, Philistines, Greeks, Phrygians, Assyrians.

Soon after this, by about 1000 BC, the Ionians began to emerge as a distinct people on the coast of Asia Minor. According to some traditions they migrated to Ionia from the Peloponnese; according to others, some originated in Crete. Such traditions are probably just indirect references to the movements of the Sea Peoples; in fact there seems to have been mixed migrations, only becoming 'Ionic' in identity on arrival. They were mostly settled by the tenth-ninth centuries, with the main Ionian cities organised into a league in the ninth century. Miletus and Smyrna are the oldest settlements, probably pre-Ionian, and so represent continuity as much as new arrivals. The Carians, immediately to the south of Ionia, were a much older, pre-Greek Anatolian population speaking a distinct non-Greek language, only gradually becoming Hellenised after about 900.

In the early formative stages of this new culture we see the emergence of probably the greatest name in Greek civilisation: Homer. As far as we know, Homer was an Ionian from Smyrna (and there is controversy over whether he even existed), living in about 850 BC, but the events that he wrote about occurred several hundred years previously in about 1250 BC. The *Iliad*, the first great work of literature in Greek was probably inspired—or at least made possible—by the adoption and adaptation of the Phoenician alphabet through Ionian contacts in northern Syria some centuries before. Indeed, the literary roots of the *Iliad*, and to a lesser extent Hesiod's *Theogony*, have been recognised in Hittite and Mesopotamian literature, such as the *Epic of Gilgamesh*.[6] This raises an important issue. Homer is generally regarded as the father of 'European' literature: but is Homer, his background and the world of the *Iliad* European or Asian?*

Much the same question may be asked of Thales, considered the 'father of Greek philosophy', not to mention the Ionian philosophical 'school' of Anaximander, Heraclitus, Hecateus, Anaxagoras and their followers who came afterwards, mainly in Miletus. Also forming a part of the general Ionian philosophical tradition were Pythagoras, a Samian who migrated to southern Italy, the Phocaeans Parmenides and Zeno, and Hippocrates of Cos. The indebtedness of this earlier 'Ionian school' to Babylon and Egypt is widely acknowledged (indeed, Thales is believed to have travelled to Egypt). Western philosophy is frequently regarded as beginning with Thales,† and philosophy is rightly regarded as one of the greatest—perhaps *the* greatest—achievements of Greek civilisation. But again, can the beginnings of a tradition that took place almost wholly in Asia be regarded as a solely European achievement?

Asia Minor was also the origin of much of the Greek expansion elsewhere in the eastern Mediterranean in antiquity (Map 2). In the sixth century BC colonial expansion, mainly from Miletus, resulted in the foundation of large numbers of colonies around the Black Sea and elsewhere in the eastern Mediterranean. Indeed, so extensive was Greek colonisation from Asia Minor into the Black Sea that it became virtually a Milesian lake, with its more important colonies of Sinope, Amisus and Trapezus containing Greek populations until recent times. This was to culminate in the foundation of the Greek Bosporan Kingdom with its capital at Panticapaeum in the east of Crimea (Pls 54-55). In addition, it was a navigator from Asia Minor, Scylax of Caria, who charted the Indus on behalf of the Persians in the fifth century BC. In the west, Phocaeans from Asia Minor founded Marseilles and other settlements in Spain and Gaul. The Ionians also established colonies on the coast of Syria and in the Nile Delta, with the foundation of Naucratis in the sixth century BC in some ways anticipating Alexandria.

---

* Interestingly, in Federico Fellini's cinematic masterpiece, *Fellini Satyricon* (1969), the scene where Homer is being recited (in Greek) at Trimalchio's banquet, a voice-over is translating it into: Turkish! See also Jon Soloman (2001), *The Ancient World in Cinema* (New York and London): 277. However, such a detail might be as irrelevant as the later gladiatorial combat with the Minotaur, fought against an arena backdrop of: the small seated Buddha at Bamiyan in Afghanistan!

† 'Without the hardy errors of Thales, Socrates might have spent his life in spoiling marble, Plato might have been only a tenth-rate poet, and Aristotle an intriguing pedagogue' as Edward Bulwer Lytton's (2004: 176) characteristic wit puts it.

ASIA MINOR AND THE PERSIANS (MAP 3)

Having set the Ionian scene in relation to the Greeks to the west, it remains to examine Ionia in relation to the Persians to the east. The contact between Greek and Persian began in Ionia earlier, lasted longer, and had a deeper effect upon Europe than any other area. The Achaemenid conquest marked a new era of prosperity and building work, of great monuments and planned city lay outs, of philosophy and literature—indeed, the Persian period is a golden age for the Greeks on the coast of Asia Minor (small wonder that so many of them joined Xerxes in his invasion of Greece). It is not often appreciated, for example, that such great figures of *Greek* culture as Anaximander, Hecataeus, Hippodamus, Pythagoras, Mausolus, Ctesias, Anaxagoras, Hippocrates, Herodotus and Heraclitus, were either born under Persian rule in Asia Minor or spent much of their lives as its citizens. A R Burn notes that of the twelve Greek historians writing before the Peloponnesian War, all but one were from east of the Aegean—usually writing under the Persian Empire.[7] Herodotus, to cite the best known of these 'Persian' Greeks, is naturally expressing the Greek viewpoint, but his ambivalence is apparent on many occasions. This becomes more explicable when one remembers that he grew up a Persian subject. This naturally raises the question: were such figures a part of the Greek or Persian worlds? Herodotus, of course, considered himself a Greek and wrote in Greek, certainly not a Persian and even less a Carian (although he might have had some knowledge of Aramaic, the administrative language of the Persian Empire). But Greek was a language first given literary expression by Homer—a language of both sides of the Aegean as we have stressed. Although it was Attic Greek rather than Homeric Greek that became standard, it was the Ionian form of the Greek alphabet that was adopted by Athens (after 403) and made the standard one for the Greek language. Herodotus' other characteristics—his curiosity, his breadth, his tolerance—could not have been possible without the *Pax Persica* and the freedom of movement within it that Herodotus obviously enjoyed. Herodotus, 'the father of history', is universally (and correctly) acknowledged as a Greek historian. But his Carian, Anatolian and Persian backgrounds are as relevant as his Greek.* In his introduction to the Penguin Classics edition

---

* Although note that Herodotus himself, in writing even handedly of 'the outstanding achievements both of our own and the Asiatic peoples', (p. 13) is making the point that he does *not* regard himself in the latter category.

of Herodotus, Aubrey de Sélincourt writes: 'Herodotus ... was the first Greek, the first European, to use prose as the medium of a work of art.' In contrast, it is notable that almost alone among historians, it is an historian of Iran who refers to Herodotus as an 'Ionian historian' rather than 'Greek'.[8]

Lydia in Asia Minor was Cyrus' first major conquest outside Iran and Babylonia, so it naturally became an important centre for the Iranians. Indeed, in the present context one cannot emphasise too much the importance of Anatolia for the Persian Empire, becoming a centre for the dissemination of Persian civilisation comparable to the heartland itself (the geographer Strabo, for example, writing in the first century BC, includes his description of much of Anatolia in his section on Persia), with cultural ramifications that were still felt over a thousand years later. The Lydian capital, Sardis, became an important centre of the Achaemenid Empire (although it is notable that Miletus became a part of the empire even before Sardis did in 546 BC), being the terminus of the Royal Road from Susa (Pl 26). Lydia also became a major focus of Iranian colonisation, not only in the capital but in the countryside as well. The 'Hyrcanian Plain' near Sardis was named after immigrants from Hyrcania to the east of the Caspian (modern Gurgan) and the 'Plain of Cyrus', also near Sardis, was named after the founder himself. In addition to Persian and Hyrcanian colonists there are references to Median and Bactrian colonisers in Asia Minor as well. There was presumably much intermarriage. Some of the Greek cities in Asia Minor, for example, were bilingual in Greek and Persian in 466 BC, and elsewhere in the empire mixed marriages are reflected in mixed personal names. Lydia also became an important stronghold of Iranian religion. This took root and long outlasted the empire that created it, with significant ramifications for subsequent Greek and Roman history as we shall see (Chapters 5 and 7).[9]

Accordingly, there is ample evidence for Achaemenid settlement in Anatolia, particularly in the west, still discernible well into Roman times. The Lydian satrap's palace at Dascylion has been identified, and other Achaemenid garrisons and gardens in Anatolia are known. Dascylion was known in antiquity for the large number of Persian hunting parks around it—known as 'paradises'*—and there was an attempt by the settlers to create an 'Iranian' landscape in western Anatolia. A Persian hunting relief has been found near Dascylion and another relief depicts an Iranian religious fire

---

* Derived from the Avestan Persian *pairadaeza*, becoming *firdaws* in modern Persian, coming into European usage via the Greek *paradeisos*.

ritual. Further east, the remains of a possible Achaemenid satrapal capital have been found near Erzincan. [10]

There was substantial Persian cultural presence in Lycia in south-western Anatolia. The 'village of the Kardakes' in Lycia, for example, was probably an Achaemenid settlement. The inscribed pillar at Xanthus (Pl. 29), capital of Lycia, contains the name of the local ruler Arppakku, the Lycian version of the Persian (or more correctly Median) name Harpagus. Harpagus was the Median general who figures prominently in Herodotus' account of the Persian conquest of the area. Hence, it was originally suggested that Lycia was settled by senior members of the Achaemenid court. However, more recent studies indicate that it is almost certainly not the same person, as the other family names in the inscription are purely Lycian. But it does at least indicate that the local Lycian rulers probably married into the Achaemenid royal house. Another inscription, the trilingual inscription of Pixodorus, satrap of Caria, at Letoön near Xanthus, was written in Aramaic (as well as in Greek and Carian), the administrative language of the Persian Empire.

PERSIAN IMPERIAL STYLES

The upper echelons of Lycian society certainly adopted Achaemenid ways. Achaemenid styles are reflected in the funerary architecture, and Achaemenid forms of audience scenes are depicted in Lycian art, such those as on the Harpy Tomb and the Nereid Monument (both in the British Museum). The 'Harpy Tomb' from Xanthus, for example, depicts a Persian audience scene in the spirit (if not the style) of Persepolis (Pl. 30), leading one authority to conclude that the satrapal family must have been educated at the Persian royal court, and Persians are depicted elsewhere in the art, in both paintings and sarcophagus reliefs (Pl. 20b). The characteristic funerary architecture of Lycia combines elements derived from Persian architecture (Pl. 31). In particular, the Lycian platform tombs, which evolved into the highly distinctive pillar tombs, are thought to have been inspired by the Tomb of Cyrus at Pasargadae (Pl. 6), and tombs marking the transition have been investigated at Taşkule near Phocaea and Ariassos in Pisidia. Fire altars, too, have been identified at Arycanda and Apollonia in Lycia, suggesting some possible Iranian religious presence. [11]

Further Persian influences can be discerned in the neighbouring province of Caria ruled, by the Hecatomnid Dynasty as satraps on behalf of the Persian Empire, particularly in its best known ruler, Mausolus. It is often overlooked that the monumental new 'Greek' city of Halicarnassus built by its ruler, Mausolus, was a part of the Persian Empire. The huge tomb for him that became one of the Seven Wonders of the World and gave language a new word, the Mausoleum, must be considered in this context. The Mausoleum is almost invariably viewed as a part of Greek history and culture, yet its architecture represents the culmination of the Lycian funerary tradition, that in turn was based upon Anatolian and Persian traditions (Pls 32-34). The Persian royal cities were planned and laid out entities revolving around the king. The Mausoleum, whilst certainly sharing many characteristics of Greek architecture, belongs more firmly within the rich funerary tradition of Anatolia, whilst its size, scope and eclecticism belongs within the Persian world. When describing the Mausoleum as 'Greek-built in Greek style'[12] the question must be asked how 'Greek' is a building in the Persian Empire with no counterpart in Greece? A building whose scale and grandeur (and not just the building, but the whole layout of new Halicarnassus which was subordinate to the grand design) conjures up impressions of Persepolis rather than of Athens. But the architecture of the Mausoleum is essentially eclectic. It combines both native Lycian and Persian funerary styles, such as the Nereid Monument on one hand and the Tomb of Cyrus on the other, but also reflects Greek, Carian, other Anatolian, Egyptian and Assyrian elements. Such eclecticism is wholly Achaemenid—it is the main theme throughout at Persepolis.

Mausolus also brought a new concept in town planning to the Aegean. This was the idea of self-glorification, central to the layout of the new monumental city of Halicarnassus. These new elements involved the introduction of visual priorities: monumental terracing, grand approaches, massive propylaea and a monumentality generally that was later to characterise much Hellenistic planning. Inspiration from the Persian Empire can be seen in these new elements, demonstrated so impressively by the monumental royal layouts of Pasargadae, Susa and Persepolis, or perhaps by the earlier Neo-Babylonian ceremonial centre of Babylon. Other cities of Asia Minor, such as Priene, Myndus, Alinda and possibly Cnidus were also founded by Mausolus, and these architectural works are invariably regarded as a part of Greek architecture and rarely, if ever, in the context of Persian culture (Pls 35-37). Mausolus' embellishment and expansion of the religious complex of Labraunda in particular elevated the cult of Zeus Labraundeus into an essentially non-Hellenic 'Carian national cult'.[13]

Mausolus probably remained loyal to Artaxerxes in the Satraps' Revolt of 366-59, hence one can view his works in a Persian context.[14] He also adopted Persian styles in his administration and court, with its emphasis on pomp and ceremony. The historian of Mausolus' Carian dynasty, Stephan Ruzicka, characterises it as above all submissive to greater powers: first of all to Persia, and then to Macedon following the rise of Philip the Great. A later member of the dynasty, Pixodorus, for example, pursued a marriage alliance with Philip when Persian power appeared at a low ebb, but repudiated it at Persian reassertion, and finally the last of the dynasty, Ada, courted Alexander. Even Mausolus' half-hearted support of the Satraps' Revolt was only to support what then appeared to be the winning side. But this policy was subordinate above all in maintaining the autonomy of the dynasty of Caria, entirely consistent throughout with Mausolus' creation of a Carian 'national identity'. Caria as a small state could never aim at total independence, and Mausolus was wise enough to realise that. Its only hope was to be on good terms with whoever's star was in the ascendant at the time.

A key site in Asia Minor for the transmission of Persian culture westwards was the city of Miletus (Pl. 38). Not only was it ruled by the Iranians for over two hundred years (indeed, it became Persian even before Sardis did—and of all Greek cities in Asia Minor, Miletus put up the stiffest resistance to Alexander's 'liberation'), but Miletus before that was the greatest of the Greek colonial powers, establishing a maritime and trading network throughout the Black Sea and elsewhere (Map 2). It was in Persian Miletus that one of the most important architectural innovations to affect the Mediterranean was developed. This was the ordered grid system of town planning, usually referred to as the 'Hippodamian' town plan after Hippodamus of Miletus. Hippodamus developed this new system in his rebuilding of Miletus as a fully planned city on a large scale, based on mathematical principles, in 479 BC following its revolt against Persia (Map 4). This is almost invariably cited as a Greek development and its subsequent adoption as evidence of Greek or (after later adaptations) Graeco-Roman influence. Not only does this ignore its origin, *within* the Persian Empire, but also the architectural precedents for planned cities elsewhere in the Persian Empire and beyond.[15]

The orderly layout of a town or city seems to have been a high priority of the Achaemenids. The native Iranian tradition was probably the circle, brought from their original homelands in Central Asia (and it

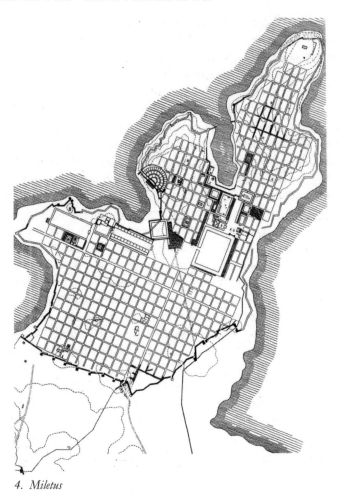

4. Miletus

is notable that Plato's 'ideal city' resembled a circle).* But this idea of a town plan based upon geometric principles does provide the mathematical inspiration behind Hippodamus' development. Although favouring the circle, occasionally Achaemenid town planning used the grid, such as at Zerneki Tepe in Anatolia and possibly at Hamadan and Kandahar. The grid system of town planning was, in any case, firmly established in Asia long before the Achaemenid Empire. It is seen in its fully developed form

---

* Note that when the town of Mantineia in Arcadia in Greece was rebuilt after its destruction by Sparta in 371 BC it was laid out in the form of a circle almost four kilometres in circumference. See Trümpler and Gerster 2003: Pl 31.

in places as far apart as Egypt, Syria and the Indus Valley. In this context it is worth stressing that the Achaemenid Empire included all of these widely spaced cultures where religious, architectural and other ideas were transmitted throughout Asia: Greek ideas travelling eastwards as much as Indian ideas westwards. Against this background, it is very easy to see how town planning ideas might have been transmitted, particularly with an urban based power like the Achaemenids (who ruled, remember, from no less than four capital cities). After the destruction of Miletus following the Ionian Revolt there was an exchange of populations (not the first in that region!) where Milesians were deported to Susa and Persians settled in Miletus.[16] Miletus was then rebuilt on the 'Hippodamian' plan. There can be little doubt, therefore, that Miletus received its idea of town planning from (or via) the Iranians, and whatever one says about the 'Hippodamian system', it is as correct to call it Persian as it is Greek.[17]

The Persian period corresponds with an upsurge in building activity throughout Asia Minor: a veritable Ionian renaissance. Not only the revolutionary new layouts at Miletus and Halicarnassus, not only grand new monuments such as the Mausoleum or Labraunda, but some of the greatest buildings of Greek architecture reached their peak at this time. The great temples of Sardis, Samos, Didyma and Ephesus were probably begun under Lydian rule, but their main period of construction was Persian (Pls 27, 39-41). There is even some suggestion in the layout at Didyma of assimilation with Persian cult practices.* The same architect who built the Mausoleum, Pytheus, went on to build the Temple of Athena at Priene, regarded by Vitruvius as the perfect ideal of the Ionic style and as such the inspiration behind a huge range of later Greek, Roman and ultimately European neo-Classical buildings (Pl. 35). Of the ancient so-called 'Seven Wonders of the World' it is notable that four of them are located in, or have close associations with, Ionia: the Temple of Artemis at Ephesus, the Mausoleum of Halicarnassus and the Colossus of Rhodes, while the Pharos Lighthouse of Alexandria was built by an architect from Cnidus. Even as late as the sixth century AD when the greatest building of its time—indeed, almost of any time—came to be constructed, it was two architects from Ionia, Anthemius of Tralles and Isodorus of Miletus, that Justinian called upon to design and build his cathedral of Haghia Sophia in Constantinople.

---

* Boardman 2000: 207-8. In this context it is worth noting that many features of architecture that are usually thought to be characteristically 'Greek', such as pointing, denticulation, or stepped architraves, were Persian architectural techniques *before* they occurred in the Greek. See Roaf 1983: 101-2. See also Cook 1976: 221.

It is difficult to see the origins of this Ionian tradition of 'giganticism' in the archaic architecture of the Balkan Greeks; in concept it owes more to the great religious and civil complexes of Persia, Mesopotamia and Egypt.

This immensely productive period of Persian rule in Asia Minor corresponds starkly with the period of Athenian hegemony, of which J M Cook writes, 'the fact remains that in the era of the Athenian league city life was at its lowest ebb. Archaeologically, it is virtually non-existent: no substantial new buildings seem to have been erected, Ionic art was at an end, and the sites of the eastern Aegean cities show scarcely any sign of urban habitation in this period.'[18] Ionia is often regarded as culturally an extension of Europe, but should one not describe the Halicarnassus of Mausolus or the Miletus of Hippodamus as 'Persian'? Like similar issues relating to Homer's or Thales' Herodotus' identity, the question is not so much one of language, geography or even ethnicity, but simply one of perspective.

Persia's initial contact with the Greek world, therefore, represented an intermingling, not a confrontation. We must now turn to the period when that contact turned to conflict—but remained equally complex.

Chapter 3

THE IONIANS BEYOND THE SEA
The Graeco-Persian Wars

X was King Xerxes, Who,
more than all Turks, is
Renowned for his fashion
Of fury and passion.
X
Angry old Xerxes!

X was once a great king Xerxes,
Xerxy, Perxy, Turxy, Xerxy, Linxy, lurxy,
Great King Xerxes!

X was King Xerxes,
Who wore on his head
A mighty large turban,
Green, yellow, and red.
X!
Look at King Xerxes!

From Edward Lear's *Nonsense alphabets*

In the fifth century BC, the Persians fought several wars against the tribes on the north-west frontier of its Empire, culminating in the campaign of Xerxes. The Graeco-Persian Wars (Map 5) are viewed by many as perhaps the most formative period of ancient Greek history. Indeed, some view it as the beginning of European history, a history defined by a perceived conflict between east and west that continues to this day. Hence, the Graeco-Persian wars have become iconic to Europe's self perception. On the broader level, such a view depends upon the 'invention' of an east or an Asia in order to define Europe. On the more immediate level this view is one-sided, depending solely upon the Greek viewpoint. In the fifth century

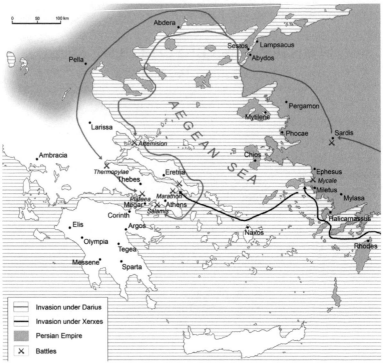

5. The Graeco-Persian Wars

BC, Persian historians—we know that they existed as Herodotus refers to them on several occasions—wrote up the history of their recent conflict with the Greeks to their west. However, these records are now entirely lost and we have little idea what they contained. But we can be reasonably certain that they would have been substantially different to the only version that has survived: the Greek one.

The former vilification of Persia as the ultimate embodiment of an 'evil empire' is no longer fashionable, at least amongst most modern scholarship (although there is still much cinematic mileage to be had, from the 1962 film *The 300 Spartans* by Rudolph Maté to the more recent 2006 Zack Snyder film *300*, based upon a computer game). But even among modern historians, one still finds innate prejudice as we shall see, whilst in the more popular literature the views of the Persians and Xerxes have hardly progressed beyond Edward Lear's caricaturisation, where Persians and Turks are conflated into a general image of the 'oriental other'. And it must be noted that both Persians and Turks are in quite a different category

1. Where it all began? The site of Troy, perceived as the beginnings of a perennial east-west conflict.

2. The North Jazira plain of Iraq, with the mountains of Kurdistan, the beginning of the Iranian plateau, rising abruptly beyond the Tigris River at its foot.

3. Relief at Pasargadae, once considered to be Cyrus but now thought to be of a deity.

4. Columned hall at Pasargadae. Note the Greek style workmanship of the columns.

5. *The so-called Zendan-i Sulaiman at Pasargadae*

6. *The Tomb of Cyrus at Pasargadae*

7. The inscription of Xerxes at Ganj Nameh, just outside Hamadan.

8. The Palace of Darius, the Apadana, at Susa.

9. *One of the bull capitals from the Apadana at Susa*

10. *The remains of the Ishtar Gate at Babylon, with the restored palace in the background.*

11. *General view of the great terrace at Persepolis*

12. *A lion capital at Persepolis*

13. The Persian mythical Homa *bird, used for one of the column capitals at Persepolis.*

14. A bull capital at Persepolis

15. *A composite style column at Persepolis (now in the Archaeological Museum, Tehran).*

16. *The 'Gate of All Nations' at Persepolis*

17. *Columns of the Apadana at Persepolis, the sunset evoking images of Alexander's conflagration.*

18. *Relief of Xerxes at Persepolis*

19. Tributary reliefs at Persepolis: a: Scythians, Ionians; b: Cilicians, Cappadocians; c: Babylonians, Syrians; d: Susians, Armenians.

20. *The continuation of the lion and bull motif from Persepolis: a: the original on the Apadana; b: 4th century BC tomb relief at Xanthus; c: 13th century Armenian monastery at Gladzor; d: above the entrance to the 11th century Great Mosque at Diyarbakır.*

21. The rock-cut Achaemenid royal tombs at Naqsh-i Rustam

22. The Tomb of Darius at Naqsh-i Rustam

23. *Relief of Darius at Naqsh-i Rustam*

24. *The so-called Ka'ba-yi Zardusht at Naqsh-i Rustam*

25. The relief and inscription of Darius at Bisitun

26. The beginning of the Royal Road in Sardis. (The pavement is Roman).

27. The temple of Artemis in Sardis

28. General view of Xanthus, with the 4th-century pillar tombs overlooking the Roman theatre.

29. The inscribed pillar at Xanthus

30. The audience scene on the Harpy Tomb at Xanthus (now in the British Museum)

to other peoples from the east who fought Europeans: both had invaded the one country that European sentiment has placed on a higher pedestal than any other: Greece.

We might think of the various Greek polities as model city-states and the birthplace of our democratic way of life, but from the Persian point of view they would have been regarded simply as a motley group of constantly feuding tribes (in much the same way as British imperial rule regarded the conglomerations of states, tribes and petty valley chiefdoms of the North-West Frontier) ruled by simple gatherings of tribal elders. As such the Persians would have viewed them as unmitigated barbarians given to blood-drinking and duplicity who habitually broke treaties, judiciously stoned women and children, venerated child-sacrifice, destroyed religious sanctuaries, murdered diplomatic envoys and left all state matters to the indecisions of a rabble.* But, like many a perceived barbarian on the fringes of a great empire (Germans, Turks or Scots spring to mind), these Greek 'tribesmen' were natural born fighters, a quality the Persians soon learnt to appreciate by incorporating Greeks into their own army.

THE BATTLE OF THE BOOKS

With the rediscovery of Classical Greece during the period of romanticism after the eighteenth century, western Romantics such as Lord Byron, Lord Lytton and others cast the Greeks into heroic mould,† and the Greek defence against Persia became part of a carefully nurtured myth equating it to the

---

* Cf the story of Greek mercenaries fighting alongside the Egyptians in Cambyses' invasion, who notoriously drank human blood just before the Battle of Pelousion. See Burn 1962: 85. The Athenians judicially condemned to public stoning the wife and children of a councillor who favoured terms with Persia. The Greek Bronze Age practice of child sacrifice had ceased by the Iron Age, but was still recalled in legends such as Agamemnon's sacrifice of his daughter Iphigenia, or the sacrifice of Polyxena to the ghost of Achilles. The murder of Persian envoys to Athens and the Athenian burning of the sanctuary of Artemis at Sardis were regarded by the Persians as shocking acts and one of the reasons for Darius' Greek campaign. Megabyzus described democracy as 'the wanton brutality of the rabble'. See Herodotus 210. By these examples I do not by any means imply that this is how one must view the Greeks; I am merely trying to envisage how they might be viewed from the banqueting halls of Susa.

† Lord Lytton, a famous Hellenophile, was even offered the throne of Greece on one extraordinary occasion by a group of Greek exiles in 1863 (see Leslie Mitchell, *Bulwer Lytton. The Rise and Fall of a Victorian Man of Letters*. London, 2003: 216-7) and Lord Byron remains a national hero in Greece to this day.

Greek War of Independence against Ottoman Turkey in the nineteenth century, and Greek resistance to Nazi Germany in the twentieth. Hence, the Greek resistance in the Second World War notably attracted the participation of European Classicists.* The two main histories of the Graeco-Persian Wars in English, A R Burns' *Persia and the Greeks* and Peter Green's *Graeco-Persian Wars*, were both written when the events of the war were still vivid in the minds of the authors (published in 1962 and 1970 respectively). Both works, for example, are scattered with references to the Second World War and its campaigns in Greece, and both authors compare Themistocles to Churchill.[1] A Persian campaign is even quite inappropriately referred to as a 'blitzkreig' on one occasion. By implication, the Persians are equated with Nazis and Xerxes with Hitler.

Such modern preconditioned ideas serve only to detract from the undoubted scholarship lying behind such works, with the contact between Greek and Persian simply becoming part of the baggage of anti-eastern prejudice, yet more ammunition in some perceived eternal war. Even the subtitle of Burns' work is emotively entitled as *The Defence of the West*, repeated by Tom Holland's subtitle in his more recent book on the same subject as *The Battle for the West*. In Green's account the wars are viewed in emotive, heroic overtones as an 'ideological struggle' by just a 'handful' of Greeks against 'the towering, autocratic figure of the Great King', while 'the recurrent Persian motif of flogging, mutilation and torture' and 'Xerxes' soldiers [being] driven forward to fight under the lash' are contrasted with 'the Greeks' … heritage of freedom'. Anthony Pagden's chapter entitled 'Perpetual Enmity' in his *Worlds at War* recycles the old image of Xerxes' army as merely slaves driven on by the lash versus a freedom-loving west. The war rapidly and grandly becomes a war 'of east versus west', 'the first great ideological conflict of European history' that rocked the Persian Empire to its foundations.[2] Green's work is liberally coloured with such emotive language, while throughout Holland's more recent work the rhetoric has overtones of Bush's 'War on Terror' or Tolkien's *Lord of the Rings* (which Holland cites on numerous occasions, both in interviews and in later works).

By introducing such highly-charged emotional expressions into the very first paragraph,† the tone is immediately set: 'west versus east' is the underlying theme, a state that is not only perceived as eternal, but one of

---

* Such as the archaeologist J D S Pendlebury, who was executed on Crete as a spy by the Germans. For Pendlebury and other romantic archaeologists, see Imogen Grundon, *The Rash Adventurer* (London, 2007).

† In Peter Green's book.

which most people are assumed to be self-evident and even to approve, requiring no justification. And in writing that the 'Greeks ... decided to stand out against the *Oriental* [my italics] system of palace absolutism,' anti-Oriental bias is immediately brought to bear.[3] By invoking the 'Orient', the absolute rightness of the Greek cause need not be questioned.

Both Anthony Pagden and Tom Holland take the theme further when they write: 'Had Xerxes succeeded ... Western civilization would never have happened ... one thing is certain. In the years between 490 and 479 the entire future of the Western world had hung precariously in the balance.' 'Much that made Greek civilisation distinctive would have been aborted ... Not only would the West have lost its first struggle for independence and survival, but it is unlikely, had the Greeks succumbed to Darius' invasion, that there would even have been such an entity as "the West" at all.'[4] Xerxes' war had become, grandly, not merely the war against Athens, which it was, nor even a war against Greece, but one against 'The West' and 'Western civilisation', and by implication a war against all that 'the west' is perceived to stand for: freedom, liberty and democratic values.

And so, by a process of collocation, Persia and the Orient in general become bywords for absolutism and despotism—all that is most hateful in a government. Frequent references to Persian 'theocratic absolutism' (applied to Cyrus in particular) are used to underline the difference between 'Oriental' and European civilisation. Cyrus is emotively called an 'Oriental autocrat' with all the derogatory implications of 'Oriental'. The reign—and character—of Darius is swiftly demolished as 'short-sighted avarice', 'delusions of grandeur' and 'In modern terms ... pure economic lunacy' (Darius was hardly twentieth century) while his personality is depicted as a blood-thirsty, murdering, usurping tyrant with 'paranoia on an almost global scale'. The character of Artaphernes is described as 'brutal hypocrisy' and 'the trumpetings of the "pax Persica" [as] a total sham'.[5] 'Palace absolutism' by definition must be 'oriental'. The Persian form of despotism was surely no more—nor less—'oriental' than, say, that of France at the time of Louis XIV—or the very occidental despotisms of Alexander of Macedon, Augustus, Ivan IV, Henry VIII or Stalin for that matter. In the end, Greek victory is explained almost in mystic, religious awe as 'an inexplicable miracle'.[6] For many historians, historical impartiality is discarded when it comes to the discussion of east-west conflict.

The concept of 'freedom' versus 'slavery' has become part of the standard package of prejudice in such views of Persia. The Battle of

Marathon, for example, has become a symbol of 'free men' versus 'imperial conscripts', i.e., Persian soldiers wielding 'scimitars'* who were little more than slaves.[7] For all Athens' (and modern writers') rhetoric of keeping the Hellenes free from the 'Persian yoke', Athens did not hesitate to subject fellow Greeks to their own yoke. By the fifth century BC Athens stood for the very enslavement and tyranny that Persia is usually meant to symbolise. The Peloponnesian War was as much a war for freedom as the Persian Wars were—but against Athenian 'enslavement'.† Even Thucydides specifically accuses the Athenians of 'slavery' on one occasion.[8] Athens at this time regularly conscripted slaves, and Athenian slaves were forced to fight at Marathon, while some at least of the Greek forces sent against Xerxes' invasion were 'conscripts'.[9] The appalling conditions of child labour working deep underground for long hours at the Athenian silver mines at Sunium is enough to emphasise that the Persians by no means had any monopoly of the lash or of cruelty.‡ By this I do not mean to denigrate the Athenian democratic achievement nor to hold up Persia as some embodiment of liberty: I simply mean to stress that slavery and suppression were fairly universal in the ancient world.

On the Persian side, its Greek allies were as much from democracies as the Greeks fighting against them were, while the core of the imperial army was made up of the 'Immortals' who were drawn from the free-born classes. There is little evidence that even the rest of the Persian army were 'conscripts' any more than building workers were: the evidence of the Persepolis tablets, for example, is clear that labourers in imperial building projects were paid wages, while the canal digging through Athos was carried out by paid levies, not slaves.[10] Yet the Graeco-Persian Wars have become a symbol of the 'free world' versus 'despotism' in vocabulary more reminiscent of Cold War rhetoric (and of equal nonsense, when one recalls that the post-War 'free world' included military dictatorships in South Korea, Greece, Spain, the Middle East and much of Central and South America). The point here is not to either down-play Persia's despotism nor

---

* The scimitar was not even invented, but provides yet another call to prejudice with reference to Saracens fighting Crusaders.

† Cf Starr 1989: 41-2, 'Stripped to its essence, the Athenian empire produced "slavery" (*douleia*), and in the Peloponnesian War the Spartans were able to raise the battle cry of liberation from the enslavement by an Athenian elite.'

‡ In this context it is worth recording the words of Edward Bulwer Lytton on the great hero of Thermopylae, Sparta: 'Sparta incorporated, under the name of freedom, the worst complicities, the most grievous and the most frivolous vexations, of slavery.' See Lytton 2004: 197.

to exaggerate Greece's, but simply to emphasise that the war does not have the glib explanation in terms of freedom versus slavery.

Of course, when looking back thousands of years at events that—by modern historiographical standards—are very poorly documented, it is impossible for even the most scrupulous of historians not to be dispassionate: reconstructions are necessary and are hugely inferential. For example, a recent foray into the Graeco-Persian wars by George Cawkwell, whose knowledge of the sources appears second to none (and furthermore argues the Persian perspective), must resort to such imprecise phrases as 'one may guess' or 'one may suggest' or 'it seems to have been' or 'there is no reason to suppose.'[11] Ultimately, it is the individual historian's own interpretations that are needed, hence such wide discrepancies.

In fairness to modern perspectives, it must be pointed out that the perceived east-west conflict of the Graeco-Persian Wars was a part of a carefully nurtured myth that goes back thousands of years, with Homer and the Trojan Wars retrospectively re-invented as the first episode in an eternal struggle of east versus west, Greek versus Asiatic barbarian as examined previously (see the Introduction). In *Iphigenia at Aulis*, for example, Euripides overtly recasts Homer's epic as a pan-Hellenic crusade against the barbarian, the Asiatic.[12] Even when writing of the Persian-Byzantine wars of the sixth century, Gibbon colours his account with such imagery, despite his anti-Byzantine bias. Hence, the Trojans became a part of the anti-Persian rhetoric, and the Persian became established as the stock image for slavery and barbarity that dominated history writing down to the modern era.

It is not intended here to cast doubt upon the greatness of Greek achievement which has been admired for millennia by the west *and* the east (Islamic civilisation, for example, was avowedly indebted to Greek learning, and the madrasas of Shiʿa Iran remained one of the last redoubts of a Classical education).* It is true that there are now several academic works on the Graeco-Persian conflicts which offer a corrective.[13] But the main works cited—by Burns and Green—are mainstream histories by well-known historians with impeccable credentials, both still in print and both the best known works on the subject in English, while that by Holland enjoys popular success. Josef Wiesehöfer writes of similar prejudice in modern German works.[14] Suffice to say that the prejudice is widespread.

---

* In addition to Qurʾanic studies, the traditional teaching of the Iranian madrasa consisted of morphology, rhetoric, grammar, jurisprudence, logic, philosophy, medicine, and mathematics, and included the study of Aristotle, Euclid and Ptolemy.

CAMPAIGN OVER THE DANUBE

The first Persian incursion into Europe was by Darius the Great (Pl. 22), when he built a bridge of boats across the Bosphorus in 513 BC. This was followed by the conquest of Thrace, carried out in alliance with Ionian Greeks, and a campaign deep into south-eastern Europe across the Danube (on another bridge of boats) against the European Scythians. The fact that Darius entrusted his whole line of communication in his trans-Danubian campaign to the Ionians demonstrated that Darius trusted the Greeks, and that Greeks and Persians worked together. Darius' Scythian campaign was not a signal success, but the campaign did result in Thrace and parts of Macedon becoming a part of the empire, Persia's first European satrapy. In about 505 BC the king of Macedon, Amyntas, submitted to Persian rule, marrying his daughter to the Persian ambassador.

Persian rule brought about a period of stability and prosperity to the warlike tribes of Thrace and Macedonia. It was the successor to Amyntas, Alexander I, who was mainly responsible for building up the Macedonian kingdom. Alexander ruled for some forty years (497-454 BC)—and for thirty of those years it was a part of the Persian Empire. It was thus a period of increasing stability and expansion under Persian rule, and this prosperity is reflected in a series of particularly rich royal graves containing Achaemenid vessels and other silver Achaemenid treasures— probably royal gifts—found in present day Thrace and Bulgaria. These included gold death-masks, bronze vases, gold and silver jewellery and magnificent armour, as well as objects from Syria and Egypt. The richest grave was from Trebenishte near Ohrid in Macedonia (although Ohrid may have been just outside Persian rule despite the Achaemenid nature of the burial objects). Persian satrapal 'paradises' and residences are also recorded in Thrace, and there is evidence of a state infrastructure being built including roads and bridges. Thrace and Macedonia were now encompassed within the international world of trade, prosperity, communications, urbanism and cultural contacts of the *Pax Persica*. From an essentially rural kingdom of transhumant pastoralists away from the mainstream of history, Macedonia became a country with a settled urban life and an agriculturally prosperous countryside, and Alexander's long reign reflects the *Pax Persica* as much as Alexander's personality.[15] It is an irony that Persia laid the basis of future Macedonian greatness that would later destroy it.

Darius' campaign also brought the Persians face to face with the Balkan Greeks. Darius returned to Susa after his first successful European conquest and there is no evidence that he intended to extend Persian conquests further into the Greek peninsula.* However, he did send an intelligence mission, consisting of fifteen Persian officers in Phoenician ships, on a reconnaissance of the coasts of Greece and even parts of southern Italy. This mission has been taken as evidence that Persian intentions towards Greece were warlike from the beginning, but the motivation might equally have been purely commercial—and gathering information about lands immediately beyond one's borders is sound strategic sense, whatever the agenda (in much the same way as Scylax of Caryanda's voyage down the Indus, again under Darius' auspices).

THE IONIAN REVOLT

Whatever Persian intentions were towards the Greeks west of the Aegean, they were soon distracted by those to its east with the outbreak of the Ionian Revolt in 499 BC. The ostensible reasons for this uprising were the imposition of pro-Persian (albeit Greek) non-elected governors ('tyrants'—although the term did not have the overtones that it does today) on the Greek cities and—that perennial bugbear—taxation. The Ionian Revolt was seen by the Persians as little more than a minor localised uprising; hence Darius saw fit to delegate its suppression to others, and did not regard it as a big enough threat to intervene personally. Even the Revolt itself did not have the wholehearted support of all the Ionian cities: Ephesus, for example, notably stayed neutral, as did others. Many Ionians sided openly with the Persians, recognising both the futility of revolt and the consequences of defeat, as well as the benefits of the *Pax Persica* (and Herodotus calls Aristagoras, the fomenter of the revolt, 'a poor-spirited creature)'.[16] Indeed, Herodotus leaves little doubt that the Ionian revolt and its aftermath was a disaster for all concerned.

The Revolt itself may well have been partially instigated—it was certainly exacerbated—by interference from Athens and other non-Persian Greek states, who had their own axes to grind (axes which have been well

---

* Despite Pagden's (2008: 2) claim that 'Darius I had launched the first full-scale attempt by an Asian power to subdue the whole of Europe.

and truly ground ever since).* This is not to say that there was no genuine resentment of the Persians by the Ionians—no people ever choose to be ruled by others, benefits or not. And the Revolt, when it was fought, was fought well and heroically by the Ionians and aroused strong emotions. For example, when a minor Athenian tragedian staged a play *The Fall of Miletus* in 493 BC after the Revolt, it produced such emotional reaction that the play was banned by the authorities (although probably more for cynical political reasons than genuine concern for the feelings of the masses).

The Ionian cities, it is true, revolted against Persian rule. But it would be a grave mistake to view this or Xerxes' later invasion of Greece as the simple Greek versus Persian/Asiatic/barbarian affair that many think. Many Greek cities supported Persia or stayed neutral as we have noted. Nevertheless, the Revolt tried the patience of the Great King, so crushed it had to be and crushed it was. Even so, Darius had the wisdom to be lenient: he had, after all, learnt his lesson in suppressing all the revolts that marked the beginning of his reign. Taxation was reassessed fairly, in some cases even reduced. More important, it was assessed on the basis of land rather than individual income, thus acting as an incentive to what the Ionians did best: trade. In 492 BC new governments were organised in all the Greek cities, but as a concession to their sensibilities—and to the reasons that sparked off the Revolt—Darius allowed these to be locally elected democracies in nearly all of the mainland cities rather than the previous form of strong-men installed by Persia. As in many such cases throughout Persian rule, the Great King was ready to listen and to respect.

With the settlement of Anatolian Greece, this only left Balkan Greece to be resolved. Whilst Persia probably had no previous ambitions there, as already observed, conditions had changed after the Ionian Revolt. To begin with, the Balkan Greek cities—notably Athens—had provided aid to the rebels during the Revolt: a group of freebooters led by Athens had even penetrated as far as the satrapal capital of Sardis and burnt the sanctuary of Artemis in 498 BC (Pl. 27). Such aid was admittedly half-hearted, and in any case self-interested (and Athens later withdrew its support for the Ionian Revolt, talk of Greek solidarity notwithstanding), so it might not have been enough to warrant Persia pursuing them beyond their borders.

---

* 'From bitter experience during decades of war, the Greeks who had been submitted to Persian hegemony knew very well that the slogans about their liberation were empty demagogic tricks and that the deeds of the politicians and generals of Athens were not directed by ideals of liberating their fellow-Greeks from the Persian yoke, but exclusively by the egotistical objectives of their state.' Dandamaev 1989: 251-2.

But from the Persian point of view was Athens, technically speaking, outside Persian imperial borders?

For there is the question of whether Balkan Greece was already a part of the Persian Empire *before* the invasion of Darius, let alone that of Xerxes. In 508 BC envoys of Cleisthenes from Athens offered the symbolic tokens of earth and water as submission to the Persian Empire to Darius' satrap in Sardis, Artaphernes.[17] Technically, therefore, the Persians would consider Athens to be at least a part of the empire (even though the Athenians themselves doubtless did not). And since Athens later revoked this, it was technically in revolt. The fact that Athens or even 'Ionia beyond the Sea' is not mentioned as a separate satrapy in the Persian records does not discount this, as it would naturally be considered a part of mainland Ionia: we have already noted how Persia considered the Balkan Greeks as an extension of the Ionians, so would hardly merit a separate satrapy. Greeks are thus depicted as part of the tributary procession on the Persepolis reliefs (Pl. 19). Hence, when Athens and Sparta subsequently revoked the symbolic tokens of earth and water to Persian envoys in 491, they were from the Persian point of view technically in revolt. Accordingly, the 'invasion' under Darius, would be viewed as a continuation of the suppression of the Ionian Revolt, an operation *within* territory it considered its own, rather than a new attempt to extend the Persian borders. Herodotus additionally makes the point that Athens attacked Persian possessions in Asia *before* the Persians attacked Greek when he emphasises that 'the sailing of this fleet [the Athenian fleet to attack Persia in Asia Minor] was the beginning of troubles not only for Greece, but for the rest of the world.'[18] From the Persian viewpoint, therefore, not only was Athens in revolt, but it was also the aggressor.

THE MYTHS OF MARATHON

Thus, as a continuation of the suppression of the Ionian Revolt, the direct intervention of the Great King was not required. The trans-Aegean campaign was delegated to Datis, the Satrap of Ionia, whose responsibility this was, and Datis landed an expeditionary force in Euboea in 490 BC. Many of the towns in Greece submitted to Persia. The city of Eretria was sacked, and Datis sent a detachment over to Athenian territory on the mainland, where it camped on the plain of Marathon. Here it faced an Athenian force of roughly the same number, but neither side at first was willing to initiate hostilities: the Persians because they were awaiting their main force, the Athenians because they were still in awe of the Persian army. When reinforcements failed to arrive, the Persians began to withdraw, prompting the Athenians to attack. This culminated in Persian defeat at the Battle of Marathon. Marathon has become one of the great icons of European history, a symbol of 'west versus east' and the perceived Greek 'Crusade' against the Persians, massively overstated as 'the mobilisation of his [Darius'] empire'.[19] Even the name 'marathon' (not to mention its perversions, such as 'walkathon') has entered our language as a race equivalent to the distance from Marathon to Athens after the entirely apocryphal run of the soldier Pheidippides in bringing the message of victory to Athens.

Even a superficial examination reveals a number of anomalies that run counter to the myth: Greek states, such as Sparta, stood back and took no action,* whilst other Greeks fought alongside the Persians *against* Athens. There was even an Athenian (Hippias) acting as a guide to the Persian forces—throughout all its wars with Greece, the Persians always had a plentiful supply of quislings at hand. Herodotus makes it clear that it was never an 'invasion of Greece' but simply a limited punitive expedition aimed just at Eretria and Athens. Pierre Briant downplays the Greek accounts of Marathon as being vastly exaggerated, both in the numbers involved and slain and in its importance, emphasising that 'in sum, from the Persian point of view, Marathon was nothing but a minor engagement that had no effect whatever on the Aegean strategy defined by Darius.'[20]

But Marathon did destroy the myth of Persian invincibility. For some Greeks at least it demonstrated that a war against a Persian force might be winnable. Even so, this was not enough to win over all or even most of the Greek states into an anti-Persian alliance. For Marathon also demonstrated something else to many Greeks: that it was possible after all to live with the Persians. Their tolerance and respect for others' religions and ways of life would already have been known from the Anatolian Greeks, and this was upheld in their brief incursion into Greece. For example, the Persian fleet under Artaphernes and Datis honoured the sanctuary of Delos with gifts and generous quantities of incense. Datis in fact made a point, even after his defeat at Marathon, of confiscating a gold-plated image from an allied Phoenician ship that had previously looted it from a Greek temple

---

* Sparta refused to come to Athens' aid before Marathon because of some religions superstition. Green (1970: 32) writes, therefore, that 'we have no right, without strong supporting evidence, to accuse them of practising religious hypocrisy for political ends.' There is no hesitation of accusing the Persians of precisely that without supporting evidence.

of Apollo in a raid, and deposited it on Delos with instructions to return it to the rightful owners (the Delians did not).[21]

THE INVASION BY XERXES

Whatever Persia had in store for Greece after Marathon, it was distracted by the death of Darius in 486 and a revolt in Egypt soon after, and it was not until about 483 BC that Darius' son and successor, Xerxes, was able to turn Persia's attention once more to affairs beyond the Aegean (Pl. 18). This time, it was to involve the Great King in person. Xerxes has been pilloried by later writers, amounting at times to ludicrous caricature (one recalls Edward Lear or the film *300*, but he has also inspired opera).* Briant stresses that 'We must renounce, once and for all, the Greek version of Xerxes' reign,'[22] although Herodotus at least gives a more balanced view (and one recalls that Herodotus grew up a Persian subject). Burn, therefore, rightly draws upon Herodotus when he writes:

> Xerxes lives in the Greek tradition as the arch-enemy, presented naturally in an unfavourable light. Herodotos, more generous to the enemy than later writers, alone presents him "in the round". His Xerxes has a Persian love of natural beauty; he enjoys being munificent on a princely scale; he can forgive surrendered enemies (even those surrendered in atonement for a "war crime"); he weeps for compassion over the mortality of mankind. But he is easily roused to rage by opposition; he is cruel when crossed, even to those lately favoured; he is uncontrolled in lust, and at heart a coward. It is a well-conceived literary portrait: the character of an Oriental Prince, born of good stock, brought up to rule, but not to tolerate opposition or endure a setback; there may be much truth in it.[23]

Our evidence suggests considerable ambivalence on the part of Xerxes towards an invasion of the Greek peninsular. The revolt of Egypt had to be put down, it is true: Egypt was the jewel in the Persian crown. But

---

* The *Grove Dictionary of Opera* lists a three-act musical drama, X*erse*, by Giovanni Bononiani, first performed in Venice in1654, which was revived in London in 1738 with Handel's *Serse* ('Xerxes'). Xerxes' successor, Artaxerxes, inspired more: Leonardo Vinci's three-act musical drama *Artaserse* in Rome in 1730, Johann Adolf Hasse's three-act opera of the same name in Dresden in 1746, and Thomas Arne's (best known for *Rule Britannia*) three-act opera *Artaxerxes* in London in 1762.

Greece was another matter—or rather hardly mattered—and the evidence of Herodotus suggests that Xerxes was reluctant to embark upon the campaign. Even after Sparta murdered Persia's diplomatic envoys, Xerxes still refused to be provoked but wished to uphold 'international law'.[24] It is questionable whether Athens actually belonged to the Persian Empire as we have seen, and Greece was so small and insignificant (from the Persian point of view), that subduing it would not add significantly to Persian prestige. But Xerxes' court was surrounded by a considerable lobby of self-interested Greek exiles, who hoped that Persian arms would return them to power in their own city states (Greeks had no hesitation in turning to Persia when it suited them, pan-Hellenic unity notwithstanding).* In the end, Xerxes was persuaded. But both the ambivalent attitude of Xerxes right from its inception, together with the dubious benefits that might accrue from invading Greece in the first place, was to spell the ultimate failure of the expedition.

Herodotus' vast figures are now almost universally rejected by historians— as mis-translations of his Persian sources, if not as his own exaggeration—and the figure of 210,000 for the invasion force (that included—notably—some 30,000 Greeks and Thracians) is the figure that seems to have gained wide acceptance. Of his figure of 1327 ships, an astonishing 427—nearly a quarter—were contributed by Greeks (including Lycians and Carians). Even if the figures are halved, the proportion of Greek ships would remain the same. In other words, the Persian invasion would have included almost as many Greek ships as the Greeks opposing them had.

Whatever the nature of the Persian army, it could hardly have been the rabble that had to be forced on by the lash, so beloved by later romanticisers. This was no rabble but a battle hardened army that had fought from Egypt to India, from the freezing Central Asian steppe to the baking Arabian desert. In the latest reconstruction, George Cawkwell ignores Herodotus' figure altogether and highlights Thucydides' reference to the Persian Wars where he states that the Persian numbers were in fact far *less* than the Greeks opposing them, and that Persian failure was due more to Persian mistakes than to Greek valour.[25]

Even so, preparations for the invasion were impressive. The Dardanelles was spanned by two bridges of boats, and a canal was cut through Mount

---

* The Persian court, before, during and after the wars, seems to have been continually home to Greek asylum seekers who defected to the Persian side. These defectors included senior Greek rulers and generals, such as Demaratus, Themistocles and Histaeus. But we do not know of a *single* Persian who defected the other way.

Athos, both remarkable feats of engineering.* This enabled Xerxes to march into northern Greece winning many over to the Persian side without even a blow being struck. Most Central Greek states, including Argos, Thebes, Thessaly and Boeotia, were on the Persians' side, as were of course most Asiatic Greeks. Notably so, too, was an ancestor of Alexander the Great: King Alexander I of Macedon (whose aunt, one recalls, had married into a Persian noble family). An exiled ex-king of Sparta, Damaritos, was with Xerxes even at Thermopylae as both adviser and collaborator. The idea that resistance to the Persians was some form of pan-Greek crusade does not stand up.

The Persians first met serious resistance at the Battle of Thermopylae in 480 BC. Like the earlier Battle of Marathon, this has become one of the great iconic events of ancient history—indeed, it has often figured as one of the great decisive battles of the world. Like so much else in this story it has been much obscured by legend—modern as well as ancient. The defence of Thermopylae is rightly regarded as heroic, but it was not just 300 Spartans who defended the pass: altogether there were some 2,000 Greeks. The figures given for Persian casualties are now regarded as exaggerated and Thermopylae, for all its heroism, did not seriously hinder the Persian advance towards Athens. Sparta, for all its military renown, was the most reluctant participant throughout the Persian wars—Leonidas and the Three Hundred heroes of Themopylae notwithstanding—with its army as often as not delayed under some pretext (usually religious) as committed to battle.

After the Persian victory at Thermopylae, Athens was occupied by the Persians but they came up against their first major setback with the defeat at the set-piece sea battle of Salamis. In fact after his victory at Athens, Cawkwell rightly points out that Xerxes had no need to fight Salamis at all, but was merely 'folie de grandeur' on his part—and a cardinal mistake.[26] But 'Greek' victory here has been the source of prolonged triumphalism ever since. Green writes that 'The conflict between Occident and Orient was nearing its climax' while Pagden describes Salamis as 'a Greek victory which would seal the fate … of the whole of Europe.'[27] But again, one must look carefully at exactly who were fighting whom at Salamis. The Anatolian Greeks remained loyal to Xerxes and fought tenaciously against Athens at

---

* With reconstructions of ancient achievements so beloved by television—the Great Pyramids, the Hanging Gardens, Hannibal's Alpine adventure and numerous others spring to mind—it is a pity that the story of bridging a wide body of fast-running sea such as the Dardanelles with flimsy boats has never been attempted; on casual observation, Xerxes' achievement looks *utterly* impossible.

Salamis, and so too did many Balkan Greeks. None of them deserted, despite Athenian efforts at persuasion. Indeed, at least a quarter of the 'Persian' fleet fighting at Salamis was Greek (mainly from Asia Minor) and remained loyal, despite Athenian propaganda trying to win it over. Occident versus Orient? Briant gives a more sober assessment when he writes that 'Salamis was a very notable achievement; it had saved Greece from a prolonged occupation and from the horrors of inevitable rebellions; but it had by no means made an end of Xerxes, nor yet of Mardonios and his army.'[28]

Classical historian Lynette Mitchell, in her book on Panhellenism, argues that out of all the Greek city-states that existed at the time of the Persian invasion, only a minority actually fought against Persia: only thirty-one, for example, were inscribed on the Serpent Column marking the victory, compared to up to a thousand Greek city-states estimated to have existed at the time (Pl. 42). Even if a thousand is an over-estimation, it is clear that the majority of Greek states either openly sided with the Persians or simply stood aside. She makes a further point when she stresses that 'rather than actually creating unity, the Persian Wars came to *represent* unity and the idealized condition of the Hellenic community.' [her italics] 'In fact, although the Greek states were transparently *not* united in their resistance to the Persian invaders, the Persian Wars were responsible for one of the most powerful Panhellenic themes: the war against the barbarian. Reinvented as a symbol of unity in the face of the common barbarian enemy, the Persian Wars were the basis of a unifying story which both glorified the past and looked to the future.'[29]

Throughout the war there was rarely, if ever, the diametrically opposed attitudes and ideologies that many modern interpretations suggest. The Greeks on the one hand were as much fascinated by the Persians as afraid of them, and even the most anti-Persian factions—especially in Athens— had 'Medizers' opposing them. The Greek term 'Medizer' is a curious one with few equivalents in other languages. It was used, of course, for those Greeks who sought accommodation with the Persians, but it had a stronger meaning than simply 'collaborator' as it implied an admiration for the Persians as well: 'Persophile' would be closer.* Persian attitudes, on the other hand, to the occupied territories and its people's sentiments and religion were marked on the whole by toleration and respect. The sanctuary of Delphi—and other Greek sanctuaries—remained consistently pro-Persian

---

* Curiously, one language where it does have an equivalent is modern Persian with the term *gharbzadeh*, which can be roughly translated as 'west-struck', a term that was coined in the seventies to apply to those who were captivated by Western (and particularly American) culture.

throughout in recognition of this: Xerxes in fact took particular care to spare Delphi during the Persian occupation. With the notable exception of the destruction of the Athenian acropolis and its sanctuary to Athena (which had a political agenda, possibly related to the destruction of the sanctuary of Artemis at Sardis by a band of Athenians during the Ionian Revolt—and Xerxes' conscience remained uneasy afterwards according to Herodotus),[30] Greek religion was not interfered with and no attempt was made to impose Iranian religions or cults.

For all that, the Persians did not remain long in Greece. They were defeated again at the Battle of Plataea in 479 BC—although not before Mardonius occupied Athens a second time in the same year—when the Persians were finally evicted and, with the loss of Thrace in c. 450 BC, they lost their one and only foot-hold in Europe. Iran's entire European adventure, therefore, lasted little more than sixty years.

Hostilities spluttered on a further fifty years after Plataea, ultimately with neither side achieving outright victory, although gains were made—and lost—by both sides. Athens even made an attempt to internationalise the war by invading Egypt to prompt an Egyptian revolt against Persia. Athens' foreign experiment ended in disaster. Cyprus changed hands several times, and in 454 BC Arsames, the Satrap of Egypt, decisively defeated an Athenian fleet. In the end peace was made with the Treaty of Callias in 412 BC when the spheres of influence on either side of the Aegean were mutually recognised.

WHOSE VICTORY?

Thus ended the opening salvos of what some have described as a part of the perennial war of west versus east. For the Greeks there was always ambivalence. During the Graeco-Persian wars the Greek attitude was never one-sided as we have seen, and even the most militant Greeks were marked as much by admiration for Persian culture as resistance to its supremacy. Xerxes' invasion was barely over when Pausanias, the commander of the Spartan forces and victor of Plataea, asked for the hand of Xerxes' daughter and offered in 478 to make Sparta and the rest of Greece subject to Persia. Themistocles himself, the hero of Salamis and architect of Athenian greatness whom twentieth century historians compared to Churchill,[31] illustrates this ambivalence more than most. His military prowess is beyond doubt, but very soon after Salamis he entered into secret negotiation with Xerxes. After the war he was exiled from Athens by political opponents. He made his way to Susa and sought refuge in Xerxes' court in 465, learning Persian and taking a Persian wife. He later became a confidant of Artaxerxes and lived out the rest of his life as an adoptive Persian on a handsome pension provided by Artaxerxes.

From the Persian point of view, Xerxes' invasion was hardly the major affair that is portrayed in the Greek histories, but a more minor campaign: a punitive expedition ending a revolt, unfinished business left over from Darius' reign. Herodotus himself states on a number of occasions that it was never more than a punitive expedition with the capture of Athens being the 'main objective of the war', his exaggeration of Persian preparations and numbers notwithstanding, and it is a moot point whether the conquest of Greece itself was ever an objective of Xerxes.[32] This was never an east versus west campaign, indeed it is doubtful whether such a concept even existed then, nor was it the free world versus tyranny, nor was it even Greeks versus Persians. With Themistocles entering into secret negotiations with Xerxes almost immediately after Salamis, one even wonders whether Greek victory was as complete as it appeared. Thus, within these limits, Xerxes 'grand invasion' was successful: the Greeks were taught a lesson, Athens was sacked, Persian rule over the Anatolian Greeks was reaffirmed.

Nonetheless, a defeat is a defeat: when all is said and done the Persian army had been badly bruised and the Great King himself had been personally humiliated. But Xerxes, for all his humiliation, was not lacking in wisdom and learnt much about the Greeks from the campaign. The first and most obvious lesson was that Greeks fought extremely well, and not only as opponents, but as allies: Greeks, remember, had fought alongside the Persians in all of the battles, from Marathon to Plataea, and had fought loyally and tenaciously. In other words, they made better allies than enemies, hence the increasing incorporation of Greek fighting units into the Persian army. In many ways the relationship of the Persian Empire with the various Greek 'tribes' on their north-western frontier is closely paralleled by the relationship of the Roman Empire with the Germanic tribes on the fringes of their northern borders. Like the Greeks, they were a constant source of trouble and the cause of punitive expeditions sent against them (with some Roman campaigns, like Xerxes' expedition, commanded by the emperor in person) with mixed results, some being successful, some utterly disastrous. There were few outright Roman victories, despite 'Germanicus' being added to many an emperor's title. Roman attitudes to the Germans were like Persian attitudes to the Greeks: untrustworthy barbarians who murdered diplomatic envoys. But they recognised the outstanding fighting qualities of these barbarians. Hence, the elaborate preparations that both Romans and Persians made for their forays into enemy territory. Such a complex 'empire-barbarian' relationship has a modern counterpart in British India's relations with the tribes of the North-West Frontier of India (and one recalls that it was those very tribes who suppressed the Indian Mutiny). Accordingly, in recognition of Greek martial qualities, Greeks were increasingly brought into the Persian army as cutting-edge fighting units, just as the Romans did with the Germans (and as the British did with the Pathan tribes). But natural born fighters have a tendency to be too good: just as it was fighting barbarians who eventually brought about the end of Rome, it was the barbarians who finished off Persia. The same relationship between great empire and barbarian fighters occurred between the Arab Caliphate and the Turks of Central Asia in the ninth and tenth centuries, and with the same result.

The second lesson that Xerxes and his successors learnt from the Balkan campaign was that the Greek tribes were inherently divided, divisions that were ripe for exploiting. As early as 480 BC, soon after Salamis, Athens received a Persian envoy in the person of the pro-Persian King Alexander of Macedon, with proposals to detach Athens from its Peloponnesian allies. The revolt of Chalcidice of 480 against the Persians was put down in a business-like fashion as much by Artabanus simply exploiting Greek rivalries as by military might. After their defeat at Salamis, Persian diplomatic efforts—backed up by hefty payments of Persian gold—accelerated the creation, widening and exploitation of these divisions. Where they could not win on the battle-field they could win in diplomacy. The war was not ended, merely the means had changed. The result was the Peloponnesian War.

This time the Great King did not have to lift a finger, but simply sit back and watch the Greeks tear each other to pieces, every now and then helping one side or the other by hurling cash instead of spears. There was a Spartan-Persian alliance, for example, in 412/11 BC, whilst in a war of 394 BC, a combined Persian-Greek fleet—that included Athens—defeated Sparta, and Persia even began raids on Balkan Greece once more.[33] Out of the Peloponnesian War, of all the Greek cities it was (for the Persians) the most detested of them all who lost: Athens (and it must be remembered that it was mainly Athens who demonised the Trojans/Persians). In Sparta's victory over Athens, Persian gold had been crucial. Chester Starr rightly points out that 'Persia was the hidden master of Greek politics until the rise of Macedonia.'[34] What victory Marathon now?

Despite remaining free of Persian military domination, Athens did not so easily escape Persian cultural influence. Possible Persian architectural influence upon Greek—especially Athenian architecture—has been much discussed. Persian inspiration has been seen behind the Acropolis itself, and parallels have been pointed out between the Persepolis procession friezes and the Parthenon friezes. The Odeon built by Pericles at Athens was widely believed to have been modelled on the royal tent of Xerxes that was captured at the Battle of Plataea, and archaeological excavations have demonstrated a similarity with Achaemenid columned halls—the Hall of a Hundred Columns built by Xerxes at Persepolis in particular. One might suppose that such architectural influences are as superficial as the Victorian English taste for Chinoiserie and other orientalist architecture such as the Brighton Pavilion: 'Perserie'. But it went deeper than mere passing fads. In discussing just one aspect of this 'Perserie', classicist Margaret Miller writes:

> The Odeion of Perikles shows not only the individual Athenian but also the state could look to the east for meaningful symbols of rank and status. In producing the Odeion, the Athenians deliberately adopted a building type developed in Iran to convey a specific message of imperial majesty for the Persian kings; and they modified it slightly to make it buildable using Greek construction methods. Resonating against its Persian models, it is a proud statement of empire.[35]

With such a template, it comes as no surprise that soon after the Persian Wars, Athens too embarked upon an empire. Athens' 'empire' never expanded much beyond the Aegean, but the next Balkan state to embark upon an empire did. It is to this that we turn in the next chapter.

Chapter 4

THE DEMON KING
Alexander of Macedon's Invasion

One world: an association of nations enriched by commerce, with facilities for intercommunication by land and sea, each member retaining its ancient learning and culture ... all subject to a single King—it was a grand conception.

Aubrey de Sélincourt

Right across the Old World Persia suddenly pulled peoples into a common experience. Indians, Medes, Babylonians, Lydians, Greeks, Jews, Phoenicians, Egyptians were for the first time all administered by one empire whose eclecticism showed how far civilisation had already come. The era of distinct units of history in the Near East was over. The base of a future world civilisation was in the making.

J M Roberts

Alexander of Macedon is generally regarded as one of the greatest figures in all of history (Pl. 43), with the foundation of internationalism, the creation of one world and the fusion of east and west commonly recognised as his greatest achievement. The two passages cited above appear to confirm this, and indeed the first one is taken from Aubrey de Sélincourt's introduction to the Penguin edition of Arrian's *Life of Alexander*. The second quotation, however, is from J M Roberts' *History of the World*, where he is referring not to Alexander's empire—but to Cyrus the Great's empire before him.[1] Was Alexander's greatest single contribution to civilisation his own, or was it the creation of the Persian empire that he destroyed?

Alexander undoubtedly created a great empire, but he destroyed an even greater one: Cyrus' empire lasted nearly 300 years, Alexander's collapsed upon his death. And it is important to remember that Alexander did *not* conquer all of western Asia as his reputation has it: he conquered a ready-made empire—Cyrus and his successors had already conquered it for him long before: 'Not an inch of territory conquered by Alexander had not been held before him by the Achaemenians.'[2] And without denying Alexander's undoubted military genius and charisma, it would be a mistake to allow this to degenerate into mere panegyric. After all, he did not always win: in Anatolia, for example, there were cities that he failed to take, such as Termessus or Syllium; in Central Asia the campaign was so hard fought that in the end he was forced to compromise and come to terms; the Indian campaign was such a shambles that it is likely that the surviving accounts cover up a defeat (he faced mutiny, he nearly lost his life, his army rampaged out of control, and in the chaotic retreat he nearly lost his army altogether). The empire that he inherited continued to be run on much the same lines: the former Persian system of provincial government remained virtually unchanged; indeed, many of the governors themselves were reinstated in office. After all, this was a great and ancient civilisation, the heirs of the Babylonian, the Assyrian and the Egyptian to the west and of the Central Asian and Indian civilisations to the east. How could a backwater prince from Macedonia (which even the Greeks regarded as barbaric) hope to match, let alone replace, this?

THE DOG THAT BARKED IN THE NIGHT: THE CASE OF THE MISSING SOURCES

Before we discuss Alexander's campaign, it is essential to examine the literary sources. For it is in literature that Alexander has left his greatest legacy. Writing in the early 1970s, the historian Robin Lane Fox—author of one of the best known biographies of Alexander—counts over twenty books on Alexander written by his contemporaries and 1472 books and articles on Alexander in the last 150 years alone.[3] The count is probably a conservative one, bearing in mind these are only works in English and do not include those in Arabic, Persian and other European languages written over the same period as well, not to mention the steady stream of literature that has appeared since.

King Alexander set up this temple to Athena Polias. (Pl. 44)

Above, I have just quoted the *sum total of all contemporary sources* for the person viewed as probably the greatest man in western history, and his life one of the greatest events of world history. It is an inscription from the Temple of

Athena at Priene in Turkey (now in the British Museum). There is nothing else. Of the twenty or so books on Alexander written by contemporaries, not a single one has survived. Brian Bosworth, one of the main Alexander historians, expresses a frustration common to all other Alexander historians when he emphasises the severe lack of source material for Alexander—and the woeful inadequacy of the little that we do have.[4] There was any amount of material—good and bad—written at the time. Peter Green writes: 'Once it became known that Alexander not only wanted his exploits written up, but would hand out good money for the privilege, a whole rabble of third-rate poets, historians and rhetoricians attached themselves to his train.'[5] *None* have survived. Much of it may not have deserved to survive, being rubbish not worthy of the name history as Green implies. The main sources that remain are the works written by Diodorus Siculus, Quintus Curtius, Plutarch and—most importantly—Arrian: his *Anabasis* or *Life of Alexander*, written in the second century AD. Book 14 of Strabo's *Geography* is an important source for the lands that Alexander conquered, Polybius' *History* contains important information (see below), and there is the fragmentary but important work of Pompeius Trogus. There is little else. However, these are hardly 'sources' in the strict sense: they were written hundreds of years after the death of Alexander, with the most important one, Arrian, written over *450* years after.* Arrian was as much a contemporary of Alexander as we are of Henry VIII.

The timing of these histories were of enormous significance. These main 'sources' correspond to the rise of Roman imperial power, when Rome was in turn busily carving out an empire in the east and Roman imperialism had its own axe to grind. Diodorus Siculus, for example, wrote between about 60 and 30 BC in the last years of the republic, at a time which saw Rome's most rapid expansion into the east under Pompey. It was, moreover, an era of larger-than-life military strong men: Marius, Sulla, Pompey, Caesar, Antony and Octavian, all of whom campaigned in the east, so it was an ideal time to resurrect an image of the ideal conqueror of the east. Quintus Curtius and Plutarch both wrote in the first century AD, when the republic had just been transformed into an empire so Alexander's empire provided the ideal—indeed logical—model. And Arrian wrote his *Life of Alexander* during the time of the Emperor Trajan (Arrian was actually governor of

---

* In fact Moses Finley (1985: Chapter 2) famously cautioned that ancient history has virtually no 'sources' in the modern history sense: i.e., no contemporary documents, *all* our literary sources are derivative.

Cappadocia under his successor Hadrian) whose conquests extended further east than any other emperor when he campaigned as far as the Persian Gulf. Indeed, the ghost of Alexander lay heavily on Trajan: he consciously thought of emulating him by campaigning all the way to India, and he visited the room in Babylon where Alexander supposedly died. Arrian's Alexander, therefore, was as much a product of his own era as Alexander's. What we know of Alexander, in other words, is very much a Roman construct—it was the Romans after all who made him 'the Great.'*

It is also significant that all of these Alexander sources with the exception of Quintus Curtius (and the fragmentary Trogus) were Greeks. As we shall see below, there was no love lost between Greek and Macedonian, and the Greeks at the time regarded Alexander simply as a brutal tyrant, so ostensibly there was little reason to present him as a hero to the Romans. But they were writing when the Roman conquests of Greece were still fresh in the memory—Diodorus in fact was a contemporary—and that conquest had been brutal, harsh and shameful, with Greece itself reduced by the Romans to a ready source of slaves. Indeed, Sulla's sack of Athens in the first century BC was far worse than Xerxes' in the fifth. The Greeks, therefore, felt the need for their own hero and their own imperial past, an empire that they could show to the Romans as greater than theirs. Adopting Alexander, therefore, provided a ready and an ideal model. As well as being a Roman construct Alexander became a Greek construct, both of them manipulated for political spin. In particular, it is the 'Greek Alexander' that has remained with us since. Hence, the historian Diana Spencer writes: 'From Trajan onwards ... we find a renewed interest in Alexander, as acceptance of one-man rule demanded a renegotiation of understandings of freedom and tyranny, and amongst Greek authors, we find Alexander revived as the embodiment of glorious, untarnished Greek heroism.'⁶

Alexander, therefore—surely the greatest event in Greek history—turns out to be far less well documented than earlier events, which had a

---

* It is interesting to note that when a modern imperial power first started extending its empire into parts of the east that overlapped with Alexander's conquests—Britain into India's Northwest Frontier in the later nineteenth century—there was an upsurge of interest in Alexander. This ranged from reports supposedly discovering descendants of his army (the Kafirs of the Hindukush), to works of fiction (Kipling's *The Man Who Would be King* is the best known), to archaeological investigations (such as Aurel Stein's *On Alexander's Tracks to the Indus*), to new academic studies uncritically extolling his virtues (the Alexander historian, W W Tarn, is essentially a product of this era, and his *Alexander the Great* (Cambridge 1948) is now regarded as over-eulogistic by most contemporary historians).

Herodotus or a Thucydides to chronicle them. We have more contemporary sources for Philip of Macedon than we do for his more famous son, let alone comparable exploits of later conquerors, for whom we can turn to either contemporary (or near contemporary) biographers—Belisarius had his Procopius, Pizarro his Zarate, even Genghis Khan had his Juvayni—or to the memoirs of the conquerors themselves, from Caesar's *Commentaries* to Babur's *Baburnama*. But for Alexander, perhaps the most famous of all conquerors, there is silence.

It is true that Arrian, generally considered to be the most reliable 'source', did have access to records that are now lost. The main lost source was Ptolemy, one of Alexander's generals, later king of Egypt. Arrian regards him as the most reliable because he believes that being a king, Ptolemy would have considered it unseemly to lie (if nothing else, it is at least a novel suggestion, that rulers and politicians never lie). But before he became a king, Ptolemy was a Macedonian freebooter turned warlord just like Alexander's other generals—and one wonders in any case just how reliable a source would be that relates how an army was led across a desert by two talking snakes! Bosworth rightly emphasises that just because Arrian cites Ptolemy, it would be a mistake for modern authorities in turn to cite Ptolemy as a source.[7] Arrian in any case admits to being a great admirer of the *Cyropaedia*, the fictionalised account of Cyrus the Great written by Xenophon to provide an idealised picture of the perfect prince. In modelling his account of Alexander on Xenophon's *Cyropaedia*, Arrian too is surely distorting the truth to idealise his subject. Richard Billows points out that 'One of the most prominent features of the biographical tradition of Alexander is its tendency to be apologetic and/or adulatory and to invent marvellous stories illustrating his superhuman nature: so far as we can tell this is true, to a greater or lesser extent, of all the "Alexander historians".'[8]

The sources for Alexander—or lack of them—is, therefore, a major issue. Like the curious case of the dog that barked in the night in the Sherlock Holmes story,* it is the conspicuous lack of *any* surviving direct sources that is one of the most significant points in the whole Alexander saga. Any

---

* It is so often cited that it has virtually become a standard metaphor without the need for explanation. It refers to an incident in one of Sir Arthur Conan Doyle's short stories, 'Silver Blaze', collected in *The Memoirs of Sherlock Holmes*, where Inspector Gregory asks Holmes, 'Is there any other point to which you would wish to draw my attention?' and Homes replies, 'To the curious incident of the dog in the night-time'. 'The dog did nothing in the night-time.' 'That was the curious incident,' remarked Sherlock Holmes.

number of ancient sources of course have long disappeared—the burning of the Library of Alexandria is often cited as a reason. But the events surrounding the life of Alexander appear to have been specially selected to be excised from history. It is significant that *all* of the contemporary books on Alexander (there were over twenty remember) have disappeared. Is this why no literary sources survive: to preserve only one version of Alexander?

It is important to appreciate that censorship and the suppression of evidence was as active in the ancient world as it is in our own. Even during Alexander's own lifetime, Alexander exercised a strict censorship of the truth by confiscating letters and other evidence, ensuring that only the version he wanted was left to posterity. He even executed the official campaign historian, Callisthenes (a nephew of Aristotle), whilst on the campaign. On another occasion, Alexander deliberately concealed a letter from Darius and forged another for political purposes, and elsewhere the forging of letters, wills and speeches was common. Ctesias' history of the Persian Empire was extensively re-written after Alexander in order to anticipate his conquest. Centuries later, Philip V of Macedon burnt the royal Macedonian archives at Pella after his defeat by the Romans at the Battle of Cynocephalae in 197 BC to avoid them falling into the hands of the Romans. This act demonstrates, of course, just how easily documents relating to Alexander have become lost to us. This adds to the picture of how censorship was exercised, how documents were suppressed and how records, quite simply, could and would be doctored. The image we have of Alexander, therefore, has been a carefully created and nurtured one for thousands of years. [9]

One of our main Alexander historians, Brian Bosworth, points out that there is 'no testimony direct or indirect from the peoples he conquered,'[10] and it is certainly true that all views we have of Alexander stem from the Greek and Roman panegyrists. Perhaps at this point it is worth drawing attention to the few sources that did escape the censors and which are not only far more contemporary than our Greek and Roman ones, but give the point of view of the conquered. We may start with one of the most frequently cited works in all the world's literature: the Bible. In the *Book of Daniel* the empire of Alexander is alluded to as the 'fourth kingdom' (the first three being the Babylonian, the Median and the Persian) in terms solely of death and destruction (*Daniel* 2: 40). This is further amplified in allegorical terms as the 'fourth beast, fearsome and grisly and exceedingly strong, with great iron teeth. It devoured and crunched, and it trampled underfoot what was left. It was different from all the beasts which went before it' (*Daniel* 7: 7; the 'fourth beast' is generally taken to represent the 'fourth kingdom', Alexander's empire). The *First Book of Maccabees* (1: 2-3) also gives quite a different view of Alexander: 'In the course of many campaigns he captured fortified towns and slaughtered kings, ... and plundered innumerable nations.' Of Alexander's successors, *Maccabees* (1: 9) is even less complimentary: 'They brought untold miseries upon the world.' Contemporary Babylonian documents on Alexander's invasion show a preference for Persian rule rather than Macedonian.[11] Interestingly, it was a Gallic historian who lived under Augustus, Pompeius Trogus, who paints Alexander as a brutal and unsympathetic tyrant. And to the Iranians, his is 'the evil reign' or, quite simply, he is the 'Demon King'.[12]

Perhaps our main 'source' for Alexander is one that is both the oldest of all and the one most often overlooked: Xenophon's *Cyropaedia*, his idealised life of Cyrus the Great. Of course, to cite this as a source is anachronistic: it was written before Alexander was born. But is it so ridiculous? Arrian, our main source, consciously modelled his life of Alexander on Xenophon's life of Cyrus as we have observed. Xenophon, in using a real historical figure to paint an idealised portrait of what a ruler *ought* to be as opposed to what he *is* set a biographical pattern that has had followers ever since. In this way, the ancient Greek and Roman biographers are doing the same: not the real Alexander, but an idealised icon. Diana Spencer rightly poses the question, 'Why should *The Alexander Trilogy* [the novels by Mary Renault] sit on a fiction shelf at a bookshop, while Arrian or Curtius on Alexander can be found in the ancient history section?'[13]

THE GREAT INVASION (MAP 6)

Macedonian rule in Persia itself lasted barely a century, and it passes fairly unnoticed both in Persian history and in the archaeological record (apart from the ashes of Persepolis): there are no great buildings, city foundations or even any substantial construction that can be definitely attributed to this period. The actual events of Alexander's campaign can be told briefly. Following the death in 336 of Alexander's father Philip the Great, who was largely responsible for the expansion of the Macedonian kingdom and building up its war machine, Alexander quickly consolidated his rule over Macedon and Greece, wiping out the venerable city of Thebes in 335

6. *The campaigns of Alexander of Macedon (after Roaf 1990)*

in the process. In 334 BC he crossed the Dardanelles into Asia to attack the Persian Empire. After an initial engagement against a minor Graeco-Persian force at the Granicus River, not far from Troy, he won his first battle against a major Persian force at Issus in Cilicia in 333, then more decisively at Gaugamela in Mesopotamia two years later. In the lull between these two battles he marched down the Levantine coast into Egypt, capturing all the Phoenician ports one by one: Byblos, Sidon, Tyre and Gaza. Tyre and Gaza were sacked, but Egypt, where he supposedly consulted the oracle at Siwa in the Western Desert, fell without a blow.

After Gaugamela, all of the Persian Empire lay open to him as he looted his way through the Persian royal cities of Babylon, Susa, Persepolis (which he destroyed) and Hamadan, hot in pursuit of the hapless Darius III, with whom he finally caught up on his death bed at Hecatompylos in north-eastern Iran in 330. The pursuit was not over with Darius' death,

however, as rival pretenders to the Persian throne, at first Bessus and then Spitamenes, drew him further east, deep into Central Asia, over the next two years. It was on this campaign that he married Roxana, the daughter of a Bactrian prince. Then, having completed his nuptials and mopping up operations after Spitamenes' death, he crossed the Hindu Kush in 327 and entered the easternmost provinces of the Persian Empire in India. The 'impregnable' fortress of Aornos on the Indus was taken and he fought the Indian king Porus, before finally turning westwards once more in 325, returning to Persia across the deserts of Baluchistan, where his army, its leader, and the legend almost perished. Alexander and the remnants of his army survived, however, to return in triumph to the Persian royal cities: Persepolis, Pasargadae, Susa (where he married the daughter of Darius III) and finally to Babylon. It is there that he died on 10 June 323 BC, eleven years and two months after stepping foot on Asiatic soil.

So ended Alexander's conquest of the world—and began the world's conquest of Alexander. The man was dead and the myth was born. Out of it emerged one of the west's greatest icons, a cornerstone of European identity—and one of the main icons of the east-west myth. Icelandic sagas and medieval legends celebrate the great man; the romance has grown out of all proportion as a plethora of Alexander legends have him do battle with monsters and demons, with Huns and Japanese, with Gog and Magog. He is a super-hero, someone more commonly associated with Greek civilisation than anybody else, someone whom Greeks ever since have looked upon as their own national hero—the ultimate Greek hero who outshone Hercules and Achilles. Even today, the purported discovery of his tomb in Egypt prompts official statements by the Greek government and a Hollywood film is threatened with official Greek litigation. He is depicted as the archetypal Helleniser, one who spread Greek civilisation throughout the known world and successfully launched a pan-Hellenic crusade against the great demon state to the east: liberation of the Greeks of Asia Minor from the Persian yoke and vengeance for Xerxes' destruction of Athens.

In writing of El Cid and the manufacture of national heroes in his *Europe: a History*, Norman Davies writes that 'It is a fair comment on the state of European identity to recall that, as yet, there is no national hero or heroine of Europe.'[14] Yet surely Alexander is precisely that. It is for this reason that European kings, from Scotland to Russia, have been named after him, and the name, or its variants, remains to this day probably the most popular pan-European boys' (and girls') name outside the Bible. But Alexander, like any national hero such as El Cid or Robin Hood or Tamerlane is distorted to suit the ideal model, and re-invented national heroes end up with little resemblance to the originals.*

---

* El Cid (or al-Sayyid, the original Arabic title from which the Spanish version derives), it must be emphasised, fought as much *alongside* the Moors as against them. Tamerlane in fact forms an interesting parallel to Alexander. Newly independent Uzbekistan, in search of a national identity after 1990, re-invented Tamerlane as an Uzbek national hero; yet the Uzbek tribes during the sixteenth and seventeenth centuries, as a part of their attempt to wrest Central Asia from the Timurid legacy, confined Tamerlane and the Timurid family to *damnatio aeternae* (destroying Timurid monuments in the process).

GREEK HERO OR MACEDONIAN WARLORD?

In the prevailing view of Alexander as the ultimate Greek hero, it is important to remember that Alexander was not a Greek, but a Macedonian, a people whom the Greeks themselves considered barbarians.* In itself, of course, this should occasion no comment: a 'barbarian' to the Greeks does not necessarily mean barbaric as we understand it but has more the connotations of 'outsider'. But the Greeks 'regarded Macedonians in general as semi-savages, uncouth of speech and dialect, retrograde in their political institutions, negligible as fighters, and habitual oath-breakers, who dressed in their bear-pelts and were much given to deep and swinish potations, tempered with regular bouts of assassination and incest'. For the society in which Alexander grew up in was 'a loud, clamorous male world of rough, professional soldiers, who rode or drank or fought or fornicated with the same rude energy and enthusiasm'[15]—the Macedonian court resembled more a Viking war camp than the rarefied world of Athenian enlightenment with which we more usually associate Greek civilisation.

Even before Alexander, his father Philip was regarded as much as— or more than—a threat to Greece as the Persians were. Demosthenes at least compared Philip to Artaxerxes and urged his fellow Athenians to join the Persians in an alliance against the Macedonians, with Philip the 'irreconcilable enemy of constitutional government and democracy.'[16] Upon Philip's death, Greece tried to break free from Macedonian rule, necessitating the young Alexander's campaign of re-conquest.

Certainly in Greece itself Alexander came as an outsider, with the sack and destruction of Thebes appalling in its savagery. According to Arrian 'They burst into houses and killed the occupants; others they cut down as they attempted to show fight; others, again, even as they clung to the temple altars, sparing neither women nor children. ... They decided to ... raze the city itself to the ground. All its territory ... was to be divided among the allies; the women, the children, all the men who survived were to be sold into slavery.' No previous invasion of Greece had ever been so ferocious. Thebes, it must be stressed was the city of King Oedipus and Pindar, a centre of Greek civilisation comparable to Athens itself: Alexander wiped it out. Not even the Persians had wreaked such devastation on Greek soil,

---

* Of course, it might be argued that Alexander considered himself Greek—but we have only the word of later Greeks for this, by which time it had become imperative to cast Alexander's success as a Greek success.

and Polybius at least amongst the ancient sources condemns it simply as an unjustifiable atrocity.[17] Alexander's destruction was supposedly because Thebes had sided with Persia in Xerxes' invasion—but so too had Macedon. Athens itself was next for Alexander to sack, and the citizens of that city braced themselves for a holocaust.

Perhaps centuries of patronising treatment of the Macedonians by Greek cultural snobbery had built up resentment. In the end Athens was not destroyed by Alexander, although not due to any pan-Hellenic ideals. The figures for Alexander's army alone bear this out: 43,000 infantry, only 7000 of whom were Greeks; 6000 cavalry, only 600 of them Greek; 160 ships, a mere twenty of which were supplied by Athens (who had over 300 at her disposal).[18] Hardly the 'Greek' army that conquered Asia. Indeed, the Persians had over *six times* more Greeks fighting on their side than Alexander did—and they remained loyal to the bitter end. Even those Greeks who did fight on Alexander's side were rarely used in full battle, but for garrison and communication duty only—and then were sent home as soon as possible. Alexander had them mainly for their value as hostages than for any real military value. Indeed, one gains the impression that Alexander was fighting Greeks as much as Persians: not only were there sizeable Greek armies in the pay of the Persians, but he was plagued by Greek revolts back home in his rear.

In 331 Sparta revolted against Macedon, raising an army of 10,000 that defeated a Macedonian army in the Pelopponese. Elis, Achaea and Arcadia joined the revolt and a general Greek uprising against Macedon seemed to be in the making—resistance that matched earlier resistance against Xerxes' invasion. 'This all took place more or less at the time Alexander was expected to meet Dareios in battle [of Gaugamela]; co-ordination was surely intended.'[19] The eventual death of Alexander was marked by open war breaking out between Greeks and Macedonians throughout the empire— notably in Bactria and in Greece—which the Macedonians suppressed, with extreme brutality in the case of Athens. In this context one must recall that in that most iconic of all wars between Greeks and Persians—Xerxes' invasion in the fifth century—Alexander's own ancestor, King Alexander I of Macedon, fought *alongside* the Persians *against* the Greeks. The massacre at Thebes and the butchery of the Branchidae (the Greek community in Central Asia discovered and wiped out by Alexander) begin to make sense.

The foundation of cities across Asia is often cited as one of Alexander's greatest legacies, supporting the oft made claim that he was bringing civilisation to a backward Asia. But aside from the fact that the Near East has the lead over Greece in cities and urbanism by many thousands of years, there is little real evidence that Alexander founded new cities. Even the many 'Alexandrias' and 'Alexandropoleis' that he allegedly founded turn out, upon analysis, to be almost all founded after his death, in some cases many hundreds of years afterwards (Alexandria in Egypt is the exception, not the rule) while the few that he did 'found' were merely re-namings of existing older settlements.[20] In the rash of new city foundations that sprung up in the wake of Alexander's conquest, it is notable that they are all either Macedonian dynastic names (Alexandria, Seleucia, Antioch, Philadelphia, Apamaea, etc) or cities named after places in Macedon, such Dium, Pella, Beroea, or Larissa. But it is notable that there is not a *single* new city named after cities in Greece. There would be new Pellas, but no new Athens or Thebes; many Antiochs, but no Themistocleias or Leonideias. In the mid-third century BC the author Herakleides of Crete excludes Macedon from the very definition of Hellas. As late as 200/199 BC the Athenians would formally 'curse and execrate ... the entire race and name of the Macedonians' according to Livy, and in the final showdown which brought an end to Macedonian independance at the hands of Rome in the Battle of Pydna in 168 BC, Athens fought on the Roman side.[21]

Posterity has made much of the Aristotle-Alexander relationship and his ensuing Greek credentials. In fact Alexander probably had less of a Greek education than his father, Philip, had who, at the age of fourteen, spent some years at the court of Thebes, at that time the most powerful of the Greek states. Philip was a hostage, admittedly, but hostages at that time were treated as honoured guests and given high education. Perhaps his father's better education at Thebes puts Alexander's later vindictiveness against that city in a new perspective.

Whilst not doubting that Aristotle might actually have acted as Alexander's tutor at some stage, it was doubtless just a labour from Aristotle's point of view, being exiled to a barbaric court a long way from the centres of learning in Greece where he was more at home. Philip presumably just cast around for the best teacher that money could buy to bash some manners into his raw, uncultured lad, and doubtless Aristotle had his price (indeed, a very heavy price to judge from the lands that Philip bestowed on his family). And a chance remark by a later historian[22] implies that Aristotle never really trusted Alexander—and Alexander himself later had Aristotle's nephew, the historian Callisthenes, executed. All that Alexander stood for—mainly, his totalitarian despotism—was in any case the exact antithesis of Greek political virtues of which he is the supposed torchbearer. And in the voluminous writings of Aristotle himself that have survived, there is not a single mention of Alexander. Like so much else, the relationship has been re-invented by posterity to make Alexander appear more 'Greek' than he really was.

GREEKS AND PERSIANS: ENEMIES OR ALLIES?

The Greeks also had a long tradition of fighting alongside the Persians in their army. There were even Greeks fighting alongside the Persians in those most heroically 'Greek' of all battles, Marathon in 490 BC and Thermopylae ten years later. In the subsequent naval battle of Salamis which saw the 'Persian' fleet decisively beaten, the battle was also one of Greeks fighting Greeks, with the Ionian contingent in the Persian forces putting up the stiffest fight against the Athenians. The most famous incident of Greek units in the Persian army—albeit on the losing side—was on the side of Cyrus the Younger's revolt against his brother, King Artaxerxes, with their subsequent epic escape across the mountains from Mesopotamia to the Black Sea under Xenophon in about 400 BC forming the subject of one of the most exciting adventure stories from Greek history. Greeks were involved in the Cyprus War of the 380s against the rebel Evagoras, in the Persian reconquest of Egypt in the 370s, and in the Satraps' Revolt in the 360s. This tradition showed no signs of abating in Alexander's invasion of the Persian Empire in the 330s. Quite the contrary: when Alexander first entered Asia Minor he faced a Greek army of 20,000 commanded by Memnon, a Greek officer in the Persian army. This army was defeated in the Battle of the Granicus and 15,000 of the Greeks were slaughtered by the Macedonians. Later, Alexander faced a formidable force of 63,000 Greeks fighting alongside the Persians in their army, and they remained faithful to the Persians to the end. Such was the frequency, loyalty and regularity of Greek units in the Persian army that it would be no exaggeration to say that Greeks formed as much a part of the regular Persian army as other nationalities did, such as the Bactrians or Parthians.

References to 'mercenaries' in the Persian army are always assumed to have been Greek. Whilst this was certainly true to some extent, they were not exclusively so, and the records refer to Arab, Carian, Armenian, Chaldaean and Indian mercenaries as well—there are even references to

Persian mercenaries. Clearly, the term never meant just Greeks nor even recruits from outside the empire, but were presumably paid troops hired for specific campaigns, as opposed to the more regular levies. To some extent the position of Greek 'mercenaries' in the Persian army is paralleled by the German units of the Roman army in late antiquity: situated both within and beyond the imperial borders, they were viewed as barbarians but appreciated for their fighting qualities, so incorporated increasingly into the army. In the end their fighting qualities were too good: they contributed to its collapse.

Hence, it was natural for the Athenians and Spartans to form alliances with Persia against Alexander even *before* Alexander's Asiatic campaign, while the Athenian generals, following Alexander's bloodbath at Thebes, promptly went over to the Persians.[23] The subsequent savagery of Alexander's destruction of Tyre was demanded not so much by the strategy of taking Egypt, but of safeguarding his rear against the still hostile Greeks. Alexander's anxiety to subdue or win over the Phoenicians with their mighty fleets had little directly to do with his war against the Persians, which was, like Macedon, a land based power. The only other sea-based power which posed a threat was Athens.

Clearly, there was no love lost between Greek and Macedonian—but a long and honourable tradition of Greek fighting alongside Persian. Already at the Battle of the Granicus Alexander had 7,000 Greeks, the Persians 20,000. Memnon, the commander of the Greek forces in the Persian army at Granicus had produced a plan for carrying the war into Macedonia. With such a long history of Graeco-Persian alliances on the one hand, and such a horrific recent history of Graeco-Macedonian enmity on the other, the answer to both Greek and Persian must have been an obvious one: an alliance. Alexander's Levant campaign, therefore, was aimed at driving a wedge between Greece and the Persian Empire.

Even one of Alexander's greatest legacies, the emergence of Greek kingdoms in Bactria and later in India, on analysis turn out to be as much a Persian legacy as Macedonian. For the Greek settlers who formed the core of Greek Bactria were not Greek veterans from Alexander's army, but Greeks fighting alongside the Persians *against* Alexander, said to number up to 23,000. These remained loyal to the Persians to the bitter end, following the lead of Spitamenes as he galvanised resistance to Alexander in his Central Asian campaign. It was only on the collapse of the Central Asian resistance that these Greeks fell to Alexander as prisoners of war. Alexander was ready enough to incorporate Persian prisoners of war into his army, as he did on numerous occasion, but could not rely upon the loyalty Greek soldiers. Rather than absorb them into his own army he settled these Greeks as garrisons in the newly conquered areas of Central Asia, and it was these 'Persian' Greeks who later formed the Graeco-Bactrian and Indo-Greek kingdoms.[24]

HIJACKING A MYTH

Nothing succeeds like success—and Alexander was nothing if not the most successful general whom the Greeks had ever experienced. Whilst despising the Macedonians as uncouth barbarians, the Greeks were quick to usurp Alexander once he had made good and claim him as their own, turning him into a Greek hero who rivalled Achilles. Just as the Greeks retrospectively reinterpreted the Trojan Wars in terms of a Pan-Hellenic crusade against the east, Alexander was similarly recast. 'Greeks fighting Trojans, Athenians fighting Amazons, or Thebans or Peloponnesians, or wars to recover wicked, and snatched, wives are reconstructed as Greeks fighting barbarians, so that then they can provide the appropriate example. For the orators, historical time is continuous. It moves from the present back to the past. As a result, the needs of the present change the past. ... Thus Alexander is the past come again. He is a Homeric hero, a new Achilles ...'[25] Hence, all the versions we have of Alexander are those of the literate Greeks.

The 'hijacking' of Macedonia and Alexander's legacy to Greek civilisation continues unabated today. The purported (and as it turned out, false) discovery of Alexander's tomb at Siwa in Egypt some years ago prompted official statements by the Greek government. In the valleys of Chitral in the North-West Frontier of Pakistan live a small religious and ethnic minority, the Kalash Kafirs. Erroneous British nineteenth century interpretations of the Kalash gave rise to the widespread—and still prevalent—myth that they are descendants of Alexander's army (Kipling's famous story and the subsequent film, *The Man Who Would be King*, are fictional interpretations of this myth). Imperial Britain, on treading for the first time in the footsteps of the great conqueror (the North-West Frontier was the only place where the Macedonian and British Empires overlapped) doubtless had its own axe to grind in such a fiction, but archaeological, linguistic and ethnographical researches on the Kalash have shown no connections either to Alexander or to the Greeks. To some extent the myth arose from some of the Chitralis being blonde and blue-eyed, which has led to the idea of blonds=Greeks=Nordics=us. Yet today there is an official Greek government aid programme in the Kalash Valleys of Chitral, where young Kafirs are given scholarships back to the 'home country' for re-education. The release in 2004 of Oliver Stone's epic film *Alexander* prompted a threat of legal action by a group of twenty-five Greek lawyers on the grounds that it presented Alexander in a perceived unfavourable light (the suggestion that he was homosexual). After the break-up of Yugoslavia into separate states, the Greek government refused Macedonia even the right to its name.* What is so astonishing about this extraordinary episode is not so much the Greek attitude, but that the corridors of power in Europe blithely accepted Greece's stipulation. One wonders whether Iran might have considered such a stipulation with the independence of the former Soviet Republic of Azerbaijan;† one is left with little doubt that it would not have been awarded even a moment's consideration in the international corridors of power if it had. Alexander of Macedon has indeed become the true European icon.[26]

FROM DEMON KING TO SIKANDAR THE TWO-HORNED

The very fact of the Persian Empire was an important element in Alexander's success: Alexander was merely conquering a ready-made empire—after all, apart from the Balkans, he did not make a single conquest *outside* the Persian

---

* Historian Eric Hobsbaum (1997: 8) writes: 'Greek nationalism refuses Macedonia even the right to its name on the grounds that all Macedonia is essentially Greek and part of a Greek nation-state, presumably ever since the father of Alexander the Great, King of Macedonia, became the ruler of the Greek lands of the Balkan peninsula. Like everything about Macedonia, this is far from a purely academic matter, but it takes a lot of courage for a Greek intellectual to say that, historically speaking, it is nonsense. There was no Greek nation-state or any other single political entity for the Greeks in the fourth century BC, the Macedonian Empire was nothing like a Greek or any other modern nation-state, and in any case it is highly probable that the ancient Greeks regarded the Macedonian rulers, as they did their later Roman rulers, as barbarians and not as Greeks, though they were doubtless too polite or cautious to say so.'
† Two-thirds of the territory of Azerbaijan lie within the borders of Iran—and the area of the present Republic of Azerbaijan was a part of Iran as recently as the nineteenth century, unlike the idea of a 'greater Greece' in relation to Macedonia.

Empire.* Nobody realised more than Alexander himself that the key to real mastery over the Persian Empire, lay not in victory in battle, not even in destroying the royal seat at Persepolis nor in seizing control of vast territories, but in the survival of the person of the Great King himself. Hence, his relentless pursuit of Darius halfway across Asia. When Alexander finally caught up with Darius he is killed. Greek sources dramatise Darius' death, supposedly at the hands of his officers, with Alexander's meeting the dying Darius and expressing regret at his death exhibiting all the trademarks of Greek drama. The fact is that Darius had to die.

Even after Darius' death, Alexander's further campaigns were not so much that of a conqueror adding to his domains, but of a new 'Persian king' pursuing rival claimants to the throne, at first Bessus, then Spitamenes, just as previous Persian kings had done on their accessions. In a sense, therefore, Alexander's campaign was a coup in much the same way as that of Darius I in his campaigns after the death of Cambyses and the suppression of the rival claimant Gaumata, or the civil war surrounding the rise and eventual suppression of the pretender Cyrus during the reign of Artaxerxes II. Indeed, Darius' and Alexander's 'coups' form a close parallel in view of the suggestion that Darius was replacing Cyrus' Elamite dynasty with his own Persian: Alexander replacing a Persian dynasty with a Macedonian one.[27]

As for the sacking of Persepolis, later apologists have attempted to gloss it over as, at best, an accident stemming from a drunken revel got out of hand or, at worst, an act of revenge for the burning of Athens by Xerxes (Pl. 17). Plutarch supports the latter view, and certainly Xerxes' buildings at Persepolis seem to have suffered particularly from the conflagration. There is also a story of some mutilated Greeks appearing at Persepolis to inflame Alexander's hatred of the Persians. But there can be little doubt that restitution for the burning of Athens meant nothing to the butcher of Thebes (not to mention one who stood poised to destroy Athens itself); Persepolis, one of the greatest palatial complexes ever built, surely makes sense as merely a mindless act by a barbarian invader.† Exploits of great

---

* Even the campaign in India was in what had formerly been a part of the Persian Empire, and whilst Arrian and other sources make much of Alexander's soul-searching in India to go onwards and forever eastwards in search of further conquests, the fact is that he did not.

† Fredricksmeyer (in Bosworth and Baynham 2000: 148-9) in any case rightly points out that Susa would have been the more logical city to destroy than Persepolis for any perceived 'revenge for Athens' or other supposed Panhellenic reasons. 'Indeed, given the state of the evidence, it is unlikely that a satisfactory resolution of the problem [the burning of Persepolis] will ever be achieved.' Bosworth in Bosworth

conquerors are the stuff of history: Qin Shih Huangdi, Genghis Khan, Babur, Augustus, Cyrus, Tamerlane, all conquerors, founders of great empires, even destroyers—but also great builders. Ultimately, Alexander was just a destroyer, nothing more.*

But whatever it was, Persepolis was a watershed for Alexander. Alexander was, after all, no mere Attila the Hun: in seeing what he destroyed at Persepolis, he seems to have learnt, and thereafter tried to emulate the civilisation that he had entered. After Persepolis, the acts of destruction diminished, and in civilising Alexander, Persia had finally taken captive its invader. Plutarch remarks that Alexander was fascinated by the Persians even as a boy, with the youthful Alexander's curiosity at the visit of Persian ambassadors to his father's court. Alexander's invasion was motivated as much by envy as covetousness. After Persepolis Alexander became more *Persian*: he adopted Persian dress, he adopted Persian court ceremonial (to the horror of his Macedonian officers), he reaffirmed Persian provincial rule, he incorporated more and more Persians into his army. Expediency or emulation? His first offer of a wife, by the Scythians, he turned down. But shortly after he married into the Iranian aristocracy of Central Asia with his marriage to Roxana—adopting a Persian ceremonial for the wedding. And later he married again: not to a nice young Macedonian girl from back home nor even to a Greek, but to the daughter of Darius III himself, Statira. In doing so he assumed the very mantle of the Persian king, ensuring that his descendants would be full, legal descendants of the Achaemenid kings by right of conquest, by right of law, by right of descent. In a famous 'what if' passage, Livy speculates what would have happened if Alexander's planned invasion of Italy had eventuated, 'then he would have come to Italy more in the manner of Darius than of Alexander, and would have brought with him an army that would have forgotten Macedonia and that was already falling into Persian ways.'[28] Alexander, in other words, was the greatest 'Medizer' of all.

We have already compared Alexander's invasion and the subsequent collapse of the Persian Empire to the Germanic invasions and the collapse of the Roman Empire. In the wake of Alexander came centuries

---

and Baynham 2000: 14

* 'Few commanders have been more expert than Alexander in creating the conditions for mass slaughter, and his troops developed a terrible efficiency in killing. ... For large areas of Asia the advent of Alexander meant carnage and starvation ... The conqueror created a desert and called it an empire.' Bosworth in Bosworth and Baynham 2000: 39 and 49.

of chaos—the Persian equivalent of the European Dark Ages—only to be restored in the first century BC by the Parthians and subsequently by the Sasanians—the Persian equivalent of the Renaissance. Indeed, the Persianising of Alexander has an exact counterpart with the Romanisation of the barbarian invaders, Theodoric and so forth. From the Persian point of view, Alexander's transformation is simply the older civilisation civilising the barbarian. In Iranian and subsequent Islamic tradition, *all* learning was derived from Iranian sources—even Greek learning was simply Persian that was stolen by Alexander and the originals destroyed, until recovered and retranslated by the Sasanians and ʿAbbasids.[29] The great fourteenth century Arab historian, Ibn Khaldun, thus writes:

> Among the Persians, the intellectual sciences played a large and important role, since the Persian dynasties were powerful and ruled without interruption. The intellectual sciences are said to have come to the Greeks from the Persians, when Alexander killed Darius and gained control of the Achaemenid empire. At that time, he appropriated the books and sciences of the Persians.[30]

Ibn Khaldun then describes how the Muslims, in becoming heirs to Greek learning, were ultimately able to recover the 'stolen' world of Persian learning. Of course, there is no evidence to suggest that Greek learning as we know it was 'stolen' from the Persians: it is the Persian and later Arab perception of how knowledge was derived that is important here. Thus, from the Persian point of view, Alexander is much the same as our images are for Atilla the Hun, and recall the Biblical image of Alexander that we have already cited. The *Ardashir Romance* refers to 'the evil reign of Alexander'. Alexander, the destroyer of Persepolis, the destroyer of books, the Zoroastrian equivalent of the Antichrist, becomes Ahriman, the exact opposite of Ahura Mazda and the personification of everything that is evil: quite simply, the 'Demon King'.[31]

But from about the tenth century, Persian historical tradition transformed Alexander from the Demon King to Sikandar, a great *Iranian* warrior. This is evident most of all in the Iranian national epic, Firdausi's *Shahnameh*, written in the eleventh century and since becoming for the Iranians much as Homer is for the Greeks or Shakespeare for the English. In the *Shahnameh* and other literary works of the Islamic period, Alexander is transformed into Sikandar *Dhu'l-Qarnayn*, the 'two-horned', the son of Darius III and a great conqueror and hero. This is derived from the conflation of two traditions. The first is the *Alexander Romance* written in the third or second century BC by pseudo-

Calisthenes, a translation of which might have entered Iran in the late Sasanian period. The second and the main tradition came with the Arab invasion under Islam: the *Qur'an*, which contains references (mainly *Sura* 18) to the great warrior and hero Dhu'l-Qarnayn, who came to be identified with the Alexander of the *Romance*. Although Dhu'l-Qarnayn of Arabian and Islamic tradition is most often associated with Alexander of the *Romance*, the two are more likely quite separate and unrelated traditions. The legendary prince Dhu'l-Qarnayn is a part of the pre-Islamic Arabian tradition, not Greek. According to the tenth century Central Asian historian and scientist, al-Biruni, Dhu'l-Qarnayn is possibly to be identified with the fourth century Tanukh tribal chief and warrior who became 'king of all the Arabs', Imru'l-Qays. Al-Biruni also refers to a tradition that Dhu'l-Qarnayn was the son of Bilqis, the name of the Queen of Sheba in Arabian tradition, although in the end he concludes that Dhu'l-Qarnayn is to be identified with one of the Yemeni princes of the pre-Islamic Himyarite dynasty.[32] An Iranian archaeologist, in dismissing the myth of 'Alexander's Wall', the immense Sasanian barrier to the east of the Caspian Sea, interprets Qur'anic Dhu'l-Qarnayn as referring to Cyrus and Darius.[33] In other words, of both traditions, the only one that can be definitely traced back in Iranian history to Alexander is that of the Demon King.

It must also be emphasised that even the *Shahnameh*'s view of Sikandar as the Iranian warrior-hero is not all positive. In several passages Sikandar is likened to the evil mythical kings Zahhak and Afrasiab, both the very embodiment of evil: of them and Sikander, Firdausi writes 'all that remains … is an evil name.' Sikandar's invasion is referred to in the *Shahnameh* as a 'sea of blood' that brought only 'pain and misery', and Sikander himself is described as a 'conquering renegade' who 'in recent times killed all the world's kings.' Ultimately, even the 'Persian' Alexander remains 'the Demon King'.*

In fact the transformation of Alexander from Demon King to Sikandar the Two-Horned does, in some way, reflect an actual transformation that Alexander underwent during his Persian campaign. Even before Alexander embarked upon his Asian campaign, 'all his ancestral domains in Macedonia and Europe he distributed amongst his friends, declaring that Asia was enough for him:'[34] he seemed to have no intention of returning home, and it is unlikely that Greece and Greek civilisation were ever much on the 'Pan-Hellenic Crusader's' mind at all. This was emphasised when he restructured his army in Central Asia: Alexander had his eye on a second generation army,

---

* Firdausi (Davis translation 2007): 463, 549 Firdausi (Davis translation 2007): 463, 549.

with no intention of returning to Europe (incorporating Iranians rather than Greeks into his army as we have observed). Persia and Persian civilisation was his object, not Greek. To the people on the eastern fringes of his campaigns, such as India, he would have appeared not as a new conqueror from Macedon, a country of which such people would never have heard, but simply as a Persian king reasserting his rule. Indeed, his return from this campaign—after his crossing of the notorious Baluchistan desert—resembles a triumphal return not of a barbarian invader any more, but of a Persian king returning after a successful campaign. He returns first to the dynastic seat of the Persian kings themselves: to Persepolis—regretting now, of course, that he had burnt it down (Pls 11, 17). He then proceeds to the Persians' first royal capital at Pasargadae, not to pillage any more, but to pay homage at the tomb of Cyrus the Great, a man whom Alexander by now not only tries to emulate, but whom he looks upon as his own natural forebear (Pl. 6). And the Persian imperial ritual triumphal progression continues: to Susa, the third Persian capital, where he marries Darius' daughter in full Persian ceremony, thereby becoming the son and heir of Darius himself (Pl. 8). And finally, to the fourth Persian royal capital at Babylon, in triumph (Pl. 10). Not having stepped outside Persian imperial borders, he regards his conquests as complete. There is no word of further conquests. There were rumours, perhaps, of a campaign into Arabia and a mention of Italy. But his troops were paid off, so there was presumably little truth in such intentions. And not a word of returning to Macedon. Alexander the Great, Great King, King of Kings, the Persian, had returned home. Both Richard Frye and Pierre Briant regard Alexander as the last—or at least the heir—of the Achaemenids.[35] It seems fitting that in Babylon, the fourth Persian capital, he should die. One is left wondering who had conquered whom?

DECLINE AND FALL

In reflecting at the ashes of Persepolis, one is left wondering how such a great empire fell with so little effort. There was, of course, Alexander's military genius: there can be little doubt that he was at least a great general. Related to this was his magnificent war machine, the Macedonian army, a creation of the father rather than of the son. In fact one ancient source, Polybius, emphasises on several occasions that much of Alexander's success was due to Philip's planning and preparation, and that Alexander merely put it into effect—and even then attributes the success of his conquests more to Philip's army than to Alexander, whose youth and inexperience Polybius is at pains to point out. Polybius attributes Alexander's success more to the favour of 'Fortune' than to inherent talent—or 'plain old good luck' in the words of one modern commentator.[36] The main reason for Persian defeat that has been widely accepted since ancient times is the theory of Persian decadence, vigorously refuted by Pierre Briant. In dismissing this theory, Briant writes of 'the well-known vicious circle: the Empire was conquered because it was in a state of profound structural crisis ("Achaemenid decadence"), and this state is "confirmed" by the defeat' and that 'the theory of "Achaemenid decadence" must definitely be relegated to a display case in the museum of historiographic wonders.'[37]

Ironically, it was the empire's very tolerance and pluralism that contributed to its downfall. The Achaemenids never tried to impose their own language or religion on the subject people. On the contrary, the Persian kings adopted a policy of encouraging the empire's diversity. This, of course, was its greatest legacy, the policy that subsequent generations so admired. But because of this, each individual component followed its own identity; there was no supra-natural identity to impose a common unity, such as the Greek language provided for the Hellenistic kingdoms or the Christian religion later provided for the Roman (and subsequent European) Empires. The key to maintaining and protecting both the multiculturalism and the unity was the Great King: without him the empire would easily break into component parts, each of which would negotiate with Alexander on an individual basis simply for their own patch as the best way of maintaining vested interests and protecting their own elite. Alexander had the genius to recognise this key to the Persian Empire. Hence his single-minded pursuance of the Great King: with him fallen, the empire too must fall.

In conclusion, who and what can we make of Alexander (Pl. 43)? In short, we cannot know, lost as he is behind thousands of years' of carefully nurtured images, with everybody re-creating their own 'Alexander' for different ends. There is the Greek Alexander, the Roman Alexander, the Persian, the Islamic, the Christian and the Victorian British. Or, as Diana Spencer concludes, 'Each Alexander reflects a figure that answers us in our own idiom.'[38] Of the original Macedonian Alexander, we have no way of knowing—the original has quite simply been erased from the record. We can only assume that there must have been something to erase.

A recent book provocatively entitled *Alexander the Great Failure* written by a historian of the Hellenistic world, John Grainger, probably contains the most damning indictment of Alexander. Grainger writes that failure 'is the most notable result of Alexander's life work: for all his military prowess, he was one of the world's great failures—and that failure spelt misery and death for countless thousands of people. Not only that, he brought that failure on himself.' Alexander destroyed a great empire, of course. But in doing so he substantially weakened his own Macedonia, which his father Philip had built, and so destroyed own country as well. Soon after, Macedonia was so weakened that it succumbed to invasion by Gauls. Most of all he destroyed Greece: Alexander's reign marked the end of the great age of Greek achievement as the Greek cities were repeatedly pillaged by groups of mercenaries commanded by one warlord after another.[39]

On the surface it seems quite astonishing that many in today's western world who unhesitatingly condemn the politics of imperialism, aggression and invasion, who openly disapprove of brutal tyrannies, will equally lionise Alexander the Great as one of history's noblest heroes. Why the contradiction? Whatever it was, Alexander's achievement was first and foremost that of Macedon, but his legacy was quickly usurped at first by Greece and subsequently by Rome, the two main fountainheads of European civilisation and European identity. Furthermore, Alexander's conquests were directed at the perceived other, at a power perceived not only as non-European but identified with the antithesis of Greek—hence 'western'—ideals. More than any other single historical figure, therefore, Alexander has become the pan-European hero, an icon who has come to stand for the image that Europe perceives itself.

Alexander is a flawed ideal. Sources as divergent as the Bible and Seneca describe Alexander as a 'beast'.[40] Alexander was, without doubt, a military genius, albeit not as great a one as he is generally thought. Alexander the great, all-round super-hero must at least be closely scrutinised. Alexander the great pan-Hellenist and torch-bearer of Greek civilisation, leader of an avenging pan-Hellenic crusade, is fabrication. Even as a western icon, idolising Alexander is as suspect as idolising Attila the Hun. But most of all, Alexander the symbol of west over east, as a western stick with which to beat the east, as justification for western superiority and a precedent for imposing the west on the east, must be rigorously rejected. In the end it is perhaps Alexander's final words that ring truest, when he left his empire 'to the strongest'—ultimately, the words of a mere warlord, not of a wise ruler: his legacy was simply more bloodshed.

Chapter 5

AN 'IRANISTIC' AGE
Neo-Persian Kingdoms
and a Would-be Empire

Scholars of ... the Roman period view Pontus as a background noise that caused a significant but manageable amount of distraction; consequently modern scholarship has regarded it essentially as a peripheral region.

Deniz Burcu Erciyas[1]

Alexander of Macedon is conventionally taken as a watershed in Near Eastern history. Most histories of the ancient Near East end with Alexander,* and probably rightly so. For the invasion marks the end of a cultural continuum that stretched back unbroken into the beginnings of ancient Near Eastern history with the first formation of cities and the beginnings of writing in the fourth millennium BC. Indeed, it is a sobering thought that Alexander is nearer to our own age than he was to the shadowy events marking the beginning of the cultural continuum that he ended. Of course, this does not mean that Near Eastern culture ended: far from it. But it did mark a huge change, whatever we make of the character of Alexander himself. For out of the ashes of Alexander's conquests emerged the Hellenistic age, a term that was coined in the nineteenth century to describe the ensuing fusion of Greek culture with the indigenous cultures of Egypt and the Near East, as well as, to a lesser extent, Iran, Central Asia and India. Ultimately, the greatest outcome of the Hellenistic age was probably Rome itself.

Strictly speaking, the Hellenistic age was not a creation of Alexander's but that of his successors. The immediate aftermath of Alexander's

---

* Michael Roaf's *Cultural Atlas of Mesopotamia and the Ancient Near East* can be taken as fairly representative in this respect.

death was simply more destruction, as huge armies fought for the spoils. Eventually, order was restored by the end of the fourth century with the division of the shattered Persian Empire amongst Alexander's generals to form separate kingdoms. The main beneficiaries were Seleucus Nicator, who claimed the bulk of the Asiatic portion, Antigonus, who claimed Anatolia and the Macedonian homeland, and Ptolemy, who claimed Egypt. Intermittent fighting, however, continued for several more decades, with another kingdom emerging in Asia Minor centred on Pergamon and eventually separate Greek kingdoms in Bactria (Central Asia) and India. The first seventy years or so following Alexander's death, therefore, was probably one of the more destructive eras in the Near East's history, bringing destruction on a scale probably only equalled in the Mongol invasions, with great armies inflicting untold casualties as cities were constantly taken and retaken. Small wonder there is little in archaeological remains, and both Babylonian and Judaic sources record the era in utter despair. The 'Hellenistic Age' only really begins in about 250 BC, some seventy years after Alexander's death, reaching its peak in the second century BC.

It was an age that is rightly seen as one of creative achievement, one furthermore which saw Hellenic culture flourish—indeed, many would argue that this was a greater age of achievement than that of Athens in the age of Pericles. But at the same time, over two centuries of Persian domination did not simply disappear overnight with Alexander's conquest. On the contrary, Persian legacy is as far reaching as that of the Greeks. For just as Hellenistic kingdoms in the east and a Hellenistic age emerged after Alexander, Neo-Persian kingdoms emerged in the west and Persian cultural influences permeated: an 'Iranistic Age'.

The Achaemenid presence in Anatolia was more than a superficial occupation of the upper echelons of administration as we saw in Chapter 2. This is demonstrated by the continued existence of Iranian kingdoms—survivals of the Achaemenid Empire—within the Graeco-Roman world as enclaves of Iranian culture and (most important) Iranian religion long after the collapse of the parent empire at the hands of Alexander of Macedon. With the collapse of Alexander's empire his Macedonian commanders turned upon each other. This was in marked contrast to the former satraps of the Persian Empire in Anatolia, who maintained a semblance of order and continuity and founded several 'Neo-Persian' kingdoms in Anatolia, ruled by Iranian aristocratic families. The

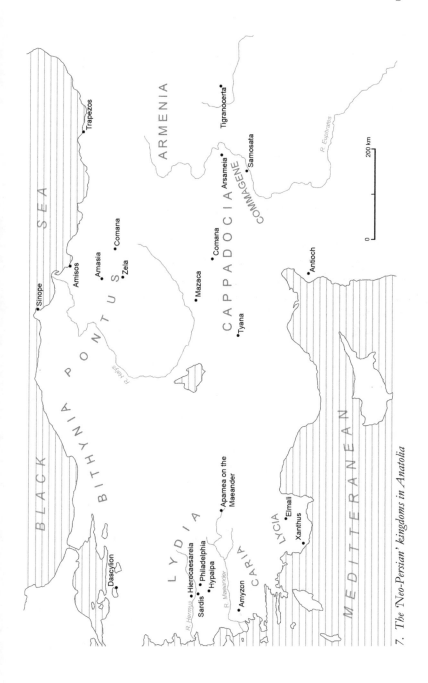

7. *The 'Neo-Persian' kingdoms in Anatolia*

93

main ones were the Kingdom of Pontus founded in 302 BC by Mithradates, the Kingdom of Cappadocia founded in 255 BC by Ariarathes, and the Kingdom of Commagene founded in about 163 BC by Ptolemaeus. There was also an Iranian element in the Kingdom of Edessa, on the Anatolian/Syrian borderland, and there were strong Iranian elements—both cultural and dynastic—in Georgia and Armenia as well. In fact Iranian communities existed throughout Asia Minor and the Zoroastrian religion survived there until the Islamic period. The religious aspects are discussed further in Chapter 7. All of these kingdoms survived into the Roman period (Map 7).

THE LEGACY OF PERSIA IN HELLENISM

Before examining these kingdoms in more detail, we shall glance briefly at the survival of ancient Persia elsewhere in the Hellenistic east. Most obviously, of course, this survived and revived in the Iranian homeland, at first under the Parthians and then under the Sasanians. But it is the survival within the Hellenistic world that is of more concern here (and we will be discussing the Parthians and Sasanians in the next chapter). Of all the Hellenistic successor states, it was the Greek kingdom of Bactria, isolated from the rest of the Hellenistic world, that incorporated the most Persian elements, but again this is outside the scope of our study.

I have examined elsewhere in detail the effect that the Achaemenid Empire had on the subsequent art and architecture of the Hellenistic and the Roman east, emphasising the immensely international and enduring influence of the Achaemenid Empire to explain such links as wide apart in time and space as Mauryan India and the Roman Near East, so it need only be summarised here. Indeed, behind the dissemination of Classical art throughout Asia, the 'remarkably durable arts of Persia' not only survived but underpinned other movements.[2]

Essentially, the legacy of the Persian Empire in the Hellenistic and Roman east took two forms: ideas that were imported directly from Iran and those that came from elsewhere but were disseminated by the common matrix of the Persian Empire. Of the former, one can include town planning, the four-way arch, monumental processional arches and circumambulatory temples, as well as other elements of form and style. Included in the latter category are colonnaded streets, dedicatory columns, decorative niches and various other decorative elements. Town planning—essentially the planned and gridded layout of streets—we have already glanced at in Chapter 2 above. Other elements that entered Hellenistic architecture either with or via the Persians, such as the monumental processional arch and dedicatory columns, became an element of the 'triumphalist' architecture of the Romans, eventually becoming a part of mainstream European architecture that continues to the present day.[3]

Perhaps the most impressive single standing Hellenistic building in the Near East* is the magnificent second century BC palace at ʿIraq al-Amir on the edge of the Jordan Valley to the west of Amman (Pl. 45). This was built by a little known Jewish dynasty, the Tobiads, originally governors under the Achaemenids. They maintained considerable wealth, status and influence throughout the Hellenistic period, constructing their palace and hunting park in the family estates in Jordan. Whilst the palace certainly exhibits some Greek architectural elements, it is like no other building in the Greek world. Some aspects of it probably derive from Ptolemaic Egypt (where the Tobiads had family ties), but the idea of the royal hunting park is probably one that came with the Achaemenids, and the overall effect of ʿIraq al-Amir with its massive portico and giant reliefs of leopards and other animals recall the smaller palaces of Persepolis, or Achaemenid provincial palace pavilions, such as that at Borazjan or those in the vicinity of the royal capitals of Susa and Persepolis. The idea of the country palace and hunting estate was later to achieve greater popularity in the region, at first under King Herod with his construction of such establishments at Herodion, Jericho and Machaerus and then later under the Umayyads with the so-called 'desert palaces' at Khirbat al-Mafjar, Mshatta, Qasr al-Tuba, Qasr al-Hayr al-Sharqi and elsewhere.

More Persian derived elements can be seen at Palmyra in the Syrian desert, as well as at is 'sister' trading city of Dura Europos on the Euphrates. After Palmyra assumed monarchical trappings, Zenobia and her son combined both Roman and Persian imperial titles, and there is the suggestion that Zenobia (or her sister) converted to Manichaeism. Palmyrene court ceremonial was Persian, and the Palmyrene army followed Iranian arms and tactics. There are also Persian overtones in the love of the hunt, so beloved by the Palmyrene upper classes, although this would be fairly universal amongst the desert Arabs without any Persian influence. Far more Persian influence is seen in the art of Palmyra and Dura Europos, where the styles of dress depicted in both painting and sculpture are Iranian—and there

---

* Albeit standing only since its very careful reconstruction in recent decades.

can be little doubt that many another cultural elements followed with the costume (Pl. 46).

THE CAUCASUS KINGDOMS (MAP 8)

Almost from the beginning of its history, Armenia entered into a special—but far from easy—relationship with Iran that in many ways still continues.* The first Armenian monarchy was a dynasty known as the Orontids, founded by the Persian satrap of Armenia, Orontes I, in 401 BC. It is uncertain whether Orontes was an Armenian or a Persian (although 'Orontes' is a Persian name). Orontes I married into the Achaemenid family with his marriage to Rhodogune, daughter of Artaxerxes II, and a strong Persian element was retained in the subsequent Orontid dynasty of Armenian kings, all of whom bore Persian names. Armenia enjoyed peace and prosperity under the Orontids with only very distant control from the Achaemenids, and remained loyal to Persia during Alexander's invasion, fighting tenaciously against him at the Battle of Gaugamela. The dynasty came to an end with the death of Orontes IV in 200 BC, but a minor branch of the family continued to rule in the smaller Armenian kingdom of Sophene on the upper Euphrates until 95 BC, when it was annexed to Greater Armenia by Tigranes II.

Antiochus III, the Seleucid king, installed his own puppet, Artaxias, as ruler of Armenia, but Artaxias proclaimed himself king in 190 BC and the Artaxiad dynasty ruled Armenia until 1 BC. Once again, whilst the dynasty was probably Armenian, their names were all Persian derived—'Artaxias' is a variant of Artaxerxes—and a strong Iranian element remained, particularly after they came under increasing Parthian influence. Their greatest ruler was Tigranes II, 'the Great' who, in the early first century BC, came close to establishing an Armenian empire in the Near East in alliance with his father-in-law Mithradates of Pontus, until both were defeated by Pompey in the mopping up operations following the Third Mithradatic War (see below). But whatever the Persian credentials of either the Orontids or the Artaxiads, the next Armenian dynasty was unambiguously Iranian. This was the Arsacid dynasty, belonging to the same Arsacid royal family of Parthians who ruled Iran. Ironically, it was a Roman emperor rather than

---

* For example, in the war between Armenia and Azerbaijan and its aftermath in the 1990s following the collapse of the Soviet Union, it is notable that the Islamic Republic of Iran followed a pro-Armenian policy against their fellow Muslims—and fellow Shia—of Azerbaijan.

8. The Caucasus kingdoms

a Parthian king who created the first Arsacid King of Armenia, when Nero crowned Tiridates I in Rome in 66 AD. The Arsacids of Armenia, however, long outlived the parent Arsacid dynasty of Parthian Iran, which was overthrown by the Sasanians in 226: Parthians lived on in Armenia until the death of Artaxias IV in 428, albeit in an uneasy relationship with the Sasanians (who had committed the memory of the Parthians to *damnatio aeternae*). The Parthian element in Armenia remained strong throughout subsequent Armenian history, probably stronger than in Iran itself. Many of the great houses of medieval Armenia traced their descent from Parthian and Sasanian aristocratic families (even Gregory the Illuminator himself, the evangeliser of Armenia, traced his descent from no lesser family than the Parthian Surens, whose greatest member was the hero Rustam), and to this day Parthian and other Iranian-derived names (such as Tigran or Anahit) remain popular in Armenia.

The Iranian element in Georgia was less prevalent, but still important. Historically and geographically, Georgia can be divided into two parts: Iberia in eastern Georgia, centred on the ancient capital of Armazi (Pl. 47), opposite modern Mtskheta not far from Tbilisi; and ancient Colchis or Lazica in western Georgia, facing the Black Sea. Being in the east, it was Iberia that came more under Iranian influence, although their early history is more shadowy than that of neighbouring Armenia. The name of its capital, Armazi, is itself a corruption of Persian Ahura Mazda, and its first king to emerge into history, Parnavaz in 302 BC, bore a Persian name. Many of the early Georgian administrative titles, furthermore, were Persian-derived, such as *spaset* from Persian *sipahi* meaning 'military commander', and *pitiakhsh*, 'satrap'. The last of Parnavaz' dynasty, Armazaspes (also a Persian-derived name), was replaced in the 180s AD by a Parthian dynasty related to the Arsacids of Armenia. The Georgian Arsacids were in turn replaced at the end of the third century by the Chosroids, another Iranian family related to the Mihranids, one of the noble families of Sasanian Iran. It was a member of this family, Miran III, who adopted Christianity in the fourth century, but the greatest of the Chosroids, the semi-legendary King Vakhtang Gorgasali (446-510), is often viewed as the most nationalist of Georgian kings, leading fierce resistance to Persian rule despite the Sasanian family connections. After his death Georgia came under direct rule by Sasanian Iran.

Persian dynastic connections in both Armenia and Georgia may mean little more than the German connections of most modern European royal houses: a Georgian king such as Vakhtang Gorgasali leading resistance to his fellow Sasanians in Persia would no more rule out his nationalist credentials than the Kaiser's were in declaring war on his first cousin George V of Great Britain. How deep, therefore, did Iranian culture penetrate in Armenia and Georgia? Zoroastrianism certainly penetrated under various forms—indeed, it was brutally imposed by the later Sasanians, who viewed Armenian and Georgian Christianity as a direct threat (or at least a potential fifth column) in the face of increasing conflict with the Christian empire of Byzantium. But there was probably more peaceful Iranian religious penetration much earlier under the Achaemenids. We have already noted how the Iberian capital, Armazi, is a derivation of Zoroastrian Ahura Mazda. In addition, the *Chronicle of St Nino,* the evangelist of Georgia, describes the worship of fire and the cult of Ahura Mazda. The Zoroastrian fire altar, often in association with a horse, which had sacred symbolism in Iranian religion, was also a popular motif in ancient Georgian art. Some elements of Iranian religion certainly took root, despite resistance to its later enforcement by the Sasanians, and it was to have important religious implications much later—it is significant that the very first monarchs to embrace Christianity, Tiridates III of Armenia in the early third century followed shortly after by Miran III of Georgia, had Iranian antecedents. This and the other religious implications of both the Caucasus kingdoms and Anatolia are explored more in Chapter 8.

Remains of Zoroastrian fire temples have been found in Armenia and Georgia, such as that at Nekresi in Kakheti in eastern Georgia (Pl. 48). The more extreme views of the art historian Joseph Strzygowski who, early last century, claimed that ancient Iran was the origin of European church architecture transmitted via Georgia and Armenia, are no longer widely accepted.[4] It has nonetheless been suggested that the distinctive circular form of many early Armenian churches, such as the famous seventh century cathedral at Zvarnots outside Echmiadzin (Pl. 49), derives from Zoroastrian fire temples.[5] This and other Armenian churches certainly incorporate many Sasanian architectural elements as well as earlier Achaemenid elements such as Persepolitan style column bases. A Persepolis-style bull capital has been found at Tsikhiagora in Georgia and Achaemenid motifs, such as the lion attacking a bull (derived from Persepolis), remained a popular one in Armenian Christian art (and was even adopted into Islamic art in the same region: Pl 21). Sasanian motifs such as the *senmurv* bird, gryphons and hunting scenes remained popular in mediaeval Georgian art (Pls 50-51).

THE RISE OF MITHRADATES THE GREAT OF PONTUS (MAP 9)

The region of Pontus lay outside the area of Alexander's conquests. Of all the Neo-Persian kingdoms it was to have the greatest future, coming close to establishing a 'neo-Iranian' empire based upon Anatolia and the Black Sea that seriously challenged Rome—indeed, it might have supplanted Rome as the main eastern Mediterranean power if Mithradates' grand plan had succeeded. It was the first time that an Iranian power—if not Iran itself—would occupy parts of Europe (Greece and southern Ukraine) since the time of Xerxes. Based in northern Anatolia, the kingdom was founded in about 302 BC by Mithradates I,* the son of Ariobarzanes and probably a

---

* The name—*Mihrdād* in its Persian form meaning 'gift of Mithra'—is a purely Persian one. Latin sources have Mithridates rather than the Hellenised Mithradates.

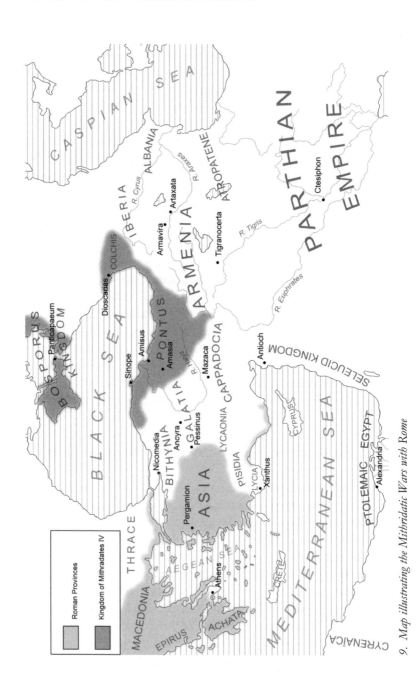

9. Map illustrating the Mithridatic Wars with Rome

former satrap. Ariobarzanes belonged to one of the seven great families of Achaemenid Persia and was related to the royal family. Pontus was bestowed on the family as a gift by Darius I as a reward for their support in the coup that brought him to power. Under the successors of Mithradates I, Pontus enjoyed stability and prosperity. This was partly due to wise rule but also, being tucked away in the mountains of northern Anatolia, because it did not become embroiled in the mainstream of Near Eastern and eastern Mediterranean history. This changed when Pharnaces I captured Sinope in 183 BC and transferred the capital there from Amaseia (Pl. 52). In gaining access to the Black Sea and its trade through Sinope, Pontus was able to expand. Pharnaces accordingly extended the influence of Pontus into neighbouring Paphlagonia, Galatia and Cappadocia.

The greatest era of the expanded kingdom was during the late second and early first centuries under its remarkable king Mithradates VI Eupator, or Mithradates the Great (Pl. 53). Mithradates was one of the most charismatic figures of ancient history whose exploits soon gained semi-mythical overtones. Of gigantic stature and strength (he was said to be able to drive a chariot of sixteen horses and to ride for several days without a break) he could also speak more than twenty languages. He gained an exhaustive knowledge of pharmacology and toxicology, which he used to build up an immunity to poisons (indeed, Mithradates' pharmacological knowledge was passed on to the Romans and formed the basis of much subsequent pharmacological science in Europe down to the Middle Ages). His knowledge of languages enabled him to travel incognito through his kingdom on several occasions (although one wonders how incognito somebody of his stature must have been!), enabling him to sound out the mood, feelings and opinions of the people he ruled at grass roots level. He was also a wise but pragmatic ruler, being able to judge the strengths and weaknesses of the powers around him, immensely generous to his friends and utterly ruthless to his enemies, with an almost uncanny talent for re-emerging as strong as before even after the most disastrous of defeats. To the Romans, he was one of the most persistent enemies they had faced.

Mithradates' first opportunity for expansion came from an unexpected quarter. During the course of the second century BC the previously nomadic Scythians of the northern Black Sea steppe established a strong Scythian state in central Crimea under King Skiluros, with its capital at Neapolis (now on the outskirts of Simferopol, the modern capital of Crimea). Eastern Crimea and the Taman Peninsula (in southern Russia facing Crimea) on either side of the Cimmerian Bosporus (the modern Straits of Kerch) had for some centuries been controlled by the Greek Bosporan Kingdom from its capital of Panticapaeum (Pls 54-55), originally established by Greek colonisation from Asia Minor (mainly Miletus) in the seventh and sixth centuries BC. This had resulted in a strong Greek presence all around the shores of the eastern and northern Black Sea.

Faced with the rising new threat from the Scythian kingdom, the Bosporan Greeks appealed to Mithradates for protection in 107 BC. But in avoiding one master they merely invited another. Mithradates seized upon the opportunity to expand his rule across the Black Sea, incorporating the Greek Bosporan kingdom and establishing garrisons in the other northern Black Sea Greek cities as far as Olbia (in southern Ukraine). He defeated the Scythians, but soon entered friendly relations with the Scythian kingdom, establishing a marital alliance with its king and so extending his influence deep into the southern Russian steppe. The Scythians are related to the Iranians (linguistically at least), and an element of ethnic kinship has been seen in this alliance. In due course, Mithradates would add Colchis in western Georgia as well as the Black Sea coast of Thrace and other parts of the western Black Sea to his kingdom. A new Black Sea empire seemed to be in the making, and from this power base Mithradates felt able to interfere increasingly into the affairs of the neighbouring Anatolian kingdoms of Bithynia, Galatia and Cappadocia, as well as Roman Asia Minor. It was soon to lead to direct confrontation with another emerging power.

THE 'MITHRIDATIC' WARS WITH ROME

The rise of Mithradates corresponds to the arrival of Rome as the new power in the eastern Mediterranean, following their entry into Anatolia after the Battle of Magnesia in 189/8 BC. The subsequent Roman colonisation of Anatolia caused huge resentment among the local population. At this stage in Rome's expanding empire there was little of the wise government that later characterised it, and the Romans in Anatolia were driven solely by greed, to milk the country dry as quickly, as thoroughly and brutally as possible—'the act of financial rape that passed for Roman governance in Asia Minor' in the words of Mithradates' biographer, Philip Matyszak.[6] Mithradates of Pontus was seen by the inhabitants of Anatolia as the one power who could withstand Roman misrule. Matters came to a head with a general uprising and subsequent massacre of the Roman communities of Anatolia in 88 BC with Mithradates' encouragement. This act was one of the most horrific of the ancient world and sent shock-waves throughout the Mediterranean. It has been likened to the 'Sicilian Vespers' after the Sicilian uprising against the French occupation in 1282 (and both events, one recalls, have inspired operas: by Mozart and Verdi respectively).*

There is no doubt that Roman rule was cordially loathed by the peoples of Anatolia, but even so the response seems to have been disproportionate: 80,000 Roman colonists and their descendants—some estimates were as high as 150,000—massacred over a single day, with no quarter given to women or children. Even the rights of sanctuaries that had been inviolate for centuries were disregarded. What does seem remarkable is that, first, no news of Mithradates' orders (which must have taken several weeks to put into place) leaked out to the Roman communities to alert them of their fate, and second, virtually none of the Greeks or native Anatolians made any efforts to secretly shelter any of the Romans (nearly all of whom were civilians, not soldiers): the loathing must have run deep. In this, Mithradates was shrewdly involving all in his revolt: henceforth they had little choice but to join him.

Mithradates had also carefully judged his time, for not only was Rome facing revolts in North Africa (the Jugurthine Wars) and Spain, but also civil war in Italy. Hence, Mithradates swept on with little opposition into Greece and Macedonia where he was welcomed as a liberator against the Romans. He seemed set to establish an eastern Mediterranean empire to rival or even to supplant Rome: Mithradates had made contact with insurgents in Italy wishing to overthrow Rome (there is some numismatic evidence for a common front),[7] and towards the end of his reign he was even planning an overland campaign from his Crimean base to invade Italy from the north via the Balkans. This may not have been a mere pipe-dream: it was no less realistic than Hannibal's trans-alpine campaign of a previous generation and, given Mithradates good relations with both his Scythian allies of the northern Black Sea area, as well as the tribes of the Balkans, it might have stood a good chance of success. This was, after all, the very direction whence came the invasions that did in the end bring about the collapse of Rome.

---

* See Steven Runciman's *The Sicilian Vespers* (Cambridge 1958). Mozart's *Mitradate Rei del Ponto* was his first opera, composed when he was just 14; both his and Verdi's more mature *Les vêpres sicilliennes* are now rarely performed. In fact Lâtife Summerer (in Højte 2009: 21) counts over 25 operas based upon Mithradates, most of them before Mozart.

Some of these invasions were of peoples who originated in the same region of the southern Russian steppe (such as the Goths and the Huns) whence Mithradates was plotting his own invasion.*

Rome's wars with Pontus—the three 'Mithridatic Wars'—were some of the more significant events in Rome's expansion into the east. At first, given the distractions of disarray in Rome and revolts elsewhere, the first Roman armies sent against Mithradates were essentially mercenary, whose main source of pay was loot (hence the spiral of more brutality against Greece and Anatolia, arousing yet more hatred of Rome) commanded by military strong men who were not always acting under the direct orders— or even approval—of the Senate. The Wars attracted the participation of many of the greatest Roman military leaders of the late Republic: Marius, Sulla, Lucullus, Pompey and Julius Caesar.

Conspicuous by its absence in the history of this Neo-Persian kingdom that so nearly became an empire is Iran itself: the contemporary Iranian empire of Parthia, by far the greatest military power in the east, whose ruler, Mithradates II (123-87 BC), even shared the same name. Mithradates of Pontus is entirely absent in Iranian historiography—and so far as we know remained largely unknown in his ancestral country. Although some sources do suggest connections between the two Mithradates—the two enjoyed good relations—there was never an alliance against Rome, even though Parthia was soon to replace Pontus as Rome's greatest threat. It is possible that Mithradates of Pontus, in boasting descent from the Achaemenids, might have viewed the Parthians—formerly subjects of the Achaemenids—as upstarts and usurpers. More likely, the 'Parthian card' would have been too dangerous a one to play for a shrewd politician like Mithradates, for Parthia was just as aggressive a new power as Rome was: bringing Parthia into the game might simply have been swapping one enemy for another, mutual Iranian sentiments notwithstanding. Mithradates of Pontus was wise, therefore, to keep on a friendly footing with Parthia, but also to keep his distance (apart from a last-ditch appeal for an alliance, preserved in some sources, when Pontus was already under Roman occupation and there was no longer anything to lose). There was also the delicate question of Pontus' ally Armenia, which the Parthians viewed as a client: bringing the Parthians westwards would risk upsetting

---

* Indeed, according to a medieval legend, Mithradates survived the coup in Panticapaeum that brought his son, Pharnaces, to power and escaped into the steppe to become the ancestor of the Goths, who eventually did conquer Rome. See Mayor 2010: 360-66.

the balance and might have led Parthia to annex Armenia directly, which would not have been in Mithradates' interest.

THE FALL OF MITHRADATES

The three Mithradatic Wars stretched over nearly thirty years. Although Mithradates undoubtedly nursed imperial ambitions, outbreaks of hostilities were almost invariably at Roman provocation, often beyond reasonable endurance (such as Murena's unprovoked attack upon and pillage of the sacred temple city of Comana in Cappadocia in 83 BC in flagrant violation of the Peace of Dardanis which ended the First Mithradatic War.) Despite vastly superior numbers who generally fought well and which were ably commanded, Mithradates' armies were ultimately no match for the highly trained and disciplined legions of Rome. At the same time, there were no easy victories for the Romans, and the reason that the wars continued over such a long time was that Mithradates could always regain his strength and regroup: the Roman victories were never unequivocal. Furthermore, each time that Asia Minor would revert to Roman rule, the Romans had not learnt the lesson of the 'Asian Vespers' and returned as much, if not more, venal, corrupt and repressive than ever before—so much so that it even attracted criticism from some Romans themselves. The Roman recapture of Athens from the Pontic forces during the First Mithradatic War was characterised by massacre and destruction of that venerable city on such a scale that contemporaries regarded it as far worse than Xerxes' capture centuries before. The areas of Greece and Anatolia controlled by the Romans was in contrast to Pontus, which was prosperous, well governed and stable. Hence, both the economy and population of Pontus could always be depended upon by Mithradates to withdraw and regain support. Roman mis-government also meant that resentment always provided a ready source of sympathy for Mithradates.

But in the end, Roman arms did prevail: the Romans were, after all, just as tenacious as Mithradates was in their ability to regroup and return, despite setbacks and their unpopularity in the region. After Mithradates' defeat at the end of the Third Mithradatic War he fled across the Black Sea to Panticapaeum, capital of the Bosporus kingdom, to rebuild his power and to plan an overland invasion of Italy (Pls 54-55). In the end it was not the Romans who finally defeated this indomitable old man, but his own family: faced with a Greek Bosporan uprising led by his own son, Pharnaces, Mithradates committed suicide in Panticapaeum in 63 BC (by falling on his sword, a lifetime of taking antidotes having made him immune to poison). Unlike the Anatolian—and to a lesser extent the Balkan—Greeks, the Bosporan Greeks had never warmed to Mithradates, seeing their future more bound up with the Romans than with a Scythian-Iranian alliance. Pharnaces in fact attempted to re-conquer Pontus from his Bosporan base, but was defeated in 47 BC by Julius Caesar at Zela in Pontus (Pl. 56).* Pontus was then annexed by Rome, but Mark Antony restored a token Pontic kingdom under King Darius which survived as a client of Rome until 37 BC—over five and a half centuries since a first King Darius appeared in the region.

POSTSCRIPT IN CRIMEA

Meanwhile, in the Bosporan Kingdom in Crimea, now separated from Pontus itself, Mithradates' son and successor, Pharnaces, was succeeded by his son-in-law Asandros. Real power, however, lay in the hands of his wife Dynamis, daughter of Pharnaces, who seemed to take more after her remarkable grandfather. Asandros was ousted—and divorced—in a palace coup in 17 BC, and we hear no more of him. Dynamis was now sole ruler, making several dynastic marriages and, by 9 BC, she was recognised by Rome as a client. On her death in about 8 BC her second husband Aspurgus assumed the throne, and subsequently married a Thracian princess, thus founding a new Bosporan dynasty (which lasted for the next four centuries) and bringing about the end of the remarkable line of Iranian kings, the last Iranian to rule a part of Europe.

Perhaps the most important result of the fall of Mithradates of Pontus was that it removed the final barrier to the emergence of Rome as the sole superpower of the Mediterranean world. Up until the time of Mithradates there was no inevitability in Rome's emergence: the only inevitability in the history of the last few centuries BC was that there almost certainly *would* emerge a sole Mediterranean power—but not necessarily Rome. For several centuries power struggles seemed evenly matched: Carthage and the Phoenicians came near to ascendancy,† but it could equally have been any of

---

* It was of this campaign that Caesar wrote his famous *veni, vedi, vici*, not of his British campaign as is commonly thought—*pace* Sellars and Yeatman, *1066 and All That*.
† See Vol. 1 of this series, *Out of Arabia*.

the other (mainly Hellenistic) strong men jockeying for pre-eminence in the region: Philip V of Macedon, Antiochus III of the Seleucid Empire, perhaps one of the Ptolemies of Egypt or even Pyrrhus of Epirus. Arthur M Eckstein in his *Rome Enters the Greek East* paints a picture of this period of essentially brutal, aggressive and opportunistic states and their war lords all vying for Alexander's legacy. Mithradates of Pontus was the last of these and, apart from Hannibal, probably the most ambitious and the most persistent—his plans, one recalls, included the invasion and extinction of Rome itself as a power. Mithradates' failure ensured that it would be Rome who ruled.

Mithradates' most recent biographer, Adrienne Mayor, writes: 'Mithradates' life had been a roller-coaster of sublime victories and harrowing losses, loyalties corrupted into betrayals, moments of divine happiness and terrible revenge as players both east and west jockeyed to choose the winning side, to make the best investment in a volatile market of alliances. The risks Mithradates took were never for mere riches or fame … but for the very survival of his Greco-Persian-Anatolian ideals and for freedom from Roman domination. Indomitable even in defeat, marvelled Appian, Mithradates "left no avenue of attack untried." Pliny praised him as "The greatest king of his era." Velleius eulogized Mithradates as "ever eager for war," a man "exceptional in courage, always great in spirit … in strategy a general, in bodily prowess a soldier, in hatred to the Romans a Hannibal." He was the greatest king since Alexander, declared Cicero.'[8]

HOW 'IRANIAN' WAS MITHRADATES AND THE PONTIC KINGDOM?

Most authorities, ancient and modern, discuss Mithradates in the context of the Hellenistic world—indeed, some modern Greek nationalists view him as the last champion of Hellenism in Anatolia and of his battles as a Greek 'war of independence' against the Romans.[9] Only occasionally has Mithradates been viewed as separate from the Hellenistic world, albeit still in terms of an ill-defined 'oriental'. Although Theodor Mommsen's famous vilification of Mithradates as the embodiment of oriental barbarism and the epitome of the barbaric east versus civilised west (indeed, Mommsen actually writes of him anachronistically as a 'sultan') is no longer fashionable, one mainstream work on the Hellenistic period refers to 'that thinly Hellenized Oriental monarch Mithradates', and throughout, Mithradates is simply referred to under that pejorative adjectival noun as 'an Oriental'.[10] More recently, biographies of

Mithradates have presented him in a more positive light, but he is still written about within a Hellenistic or a Roman context and seldom in an Iranian one (a notable exception being the *Cambridge History of Iran*).[11]

Mithradates VI claimed descent from Cyrus, Darius and Xerxes, but he also claimed descent from Alexander on his mother's side. Since Alexander had no descendants—they were all killed off by his successors—the claim is at best a spurious one, but one nonetheless that would have been deliberately promoted by Mithradates in order to gain support among the Greek populations of Anatolia and the Black Sea, as well as of Greece itself. Mithradates also married into the Seleucid dynasty as a part of his Hellenising policy (indeed, Mithradates married many times for political ends). One recent study downplays his Hellenism: because there was a large Greek population under his rule 'he emphasised his familiarity with the Greeks, but not necessarily his Greekness, by having his city mints use gods and goddesses who appear to be a combination of Greek and native; by using Sinope, a Greek city, as his capital; and by portraying himself on regal coins in a style known to the Hellenistic world.' In other words, his association with the Greeks in general and with Alexander in particular was a carefully manipulated image for political ends. Ultimately, it was his Persian royal ancestry that he spoke of most, emphasising the purity of his race in contrast to that of the Romans whom he contemptuously accused of impurity.[12] But both his purported ancestry and—most of all—the wars he fought against Rome were nothing less than a revival of the old alliance that existed between Persians and Greeks.

The early history and upbringing of Mithradates that is described in the sources is modelled on that of Cyrus the Great—or at least the version that is preserved in Xenophon's idealised biography. In fact Mithradates' infancy is in keeping with the traditional upbringing of a Persian prince: seclusion, training in truth, strength and the arts of war. At the same time he anticipates another, later great Persian warrior prince, Bahram V or Bahram Gur (421-439) of the Sasanian dynasty. Like Mithradates, Bahram was said to speak many languages, travelled around his kingdom in disguise and perform great feats of strength.[13] Mithradates' background thus belongs within a long Iranian tradition of kingship.

The population of Pontus would have been mainly indigenous Anatolians, at least in the countryside, presumably descendants of the Kashki and others whom the Hittites fought so hard to subdue. Their language remains unknown.* The towns were dominated by Greek settlers, who had been colonising the north coast of Anatolia since the seventh century BC, with many fresh Greek and Macedonian arrivals after Alexander's conquests, so they probably made up the majority of the urban population. There would also have been a small but significant number of Iranian settlers, mainly descendants of administrators from the time of the Persian Empire, as well as a sprinkling of other minorities. Many of these Iranians would have married into local Greek and Anatolian families: the Greek geographer Strabo's great-uncle, Moaphernes (a Persian name), was governor of Colchis under Mithradates Eupator, to take a prominent example.

The main language of communication in Pontus was Greek; there is no evidence that Persian was used, at least in any official capacity. However, Persian was rarely used in any case during the Achaemenid period, when Aramaic was the main administrative language: the Iranians were at pains to use the languages of the ruled rather than that of the rulers. It is notable that Mithradates Eupator made it a policy to learn all languages in his kingdom, suggesting that the royal family still spoke Persian amongst themselves, overt Hellenism notwithstanding (much as the Mughal rulers of India still spoke Chaghatai Turkish in the family right down until the dynasty was exiled after the Mutiny of 1857). This is in marked contrast to Greek and Macedonian rulers, who generally did not learn foreign languages (Cleopatra VII of Egypt being a notable exception). If direct evidence for the survival of the Persian language remains intangible, the remarkable tenacity of the Iranian religion in Anatolia is indirect evidence for its survival, at least as a liturgical language, as the sacred Zoroastrian texts were memorised and passed on in their original form as a principle of religious devotion. This is further discussed in Chapter 8. There were Perso-Babylonian and Zoroastrian prophecies and oracles forecasting Mithradates' rise and the fall of Rome, and there are many references to Iranian religious practices in Mithradates' family.[14] For example, Mithradates celebrated his victory over Murena in 83 BC by a massive victory fire at a mountain- top Zoroastrian sacred place of worship which had a sacred eternal flame. It has been identified with modern Mt Buyuk Evliya, and recalls the Iranian mountain-top sanctuary of Nemrut

---

* It might have belonged to the Kartevelo-Mingrelian group of the Caucasus, of which Laz, still spoken in the region today, and possibly ancient Urartian, belonged, as well as modern Georgian.

Dağ in Commagene (in spirit if not in form—see below). The Persian style ceremony was presided over by Mithradates himself as chief priest. Appian's description of this victory fire specifically alludes to it as 'the kind of sacrifice had been offered also at Pasargadae by the kings of Persia.'[15] The subsequent wedding of Mithradates' daughter to Ariobarzanes, the king of Cappadocia, was celebrated in the Persian fashion.

In summary, therefore, Mithradates and his family, together with the descendants of the Persian settlers who came into the region during the Achaemenid period, remained aware of their Persian roots. Whilst absorbing much of the Hellenic and Anatolian culture that they encountered, they retained their Persian names, some elements at least of their native religious beliefs and practises, and probably their language. Most of all, it was the Pontic kings' ability to adopt and adapt outside influences and thence to absorb them into their own underlying culture that was perhaps their most 'Iranian' characteristic.

PONTIC PLACES: THE MATERIAL REMAINS

Material remains of the Pontic period are remarkably meagre, with even fewer that are explicitly Iranian in character (although their paucity is probably due more to the lack of archaeological investigations in northern Turkey than to the non-existence of actual remains; current surveys in Paphlagonia and Sinope may alter this picture). Of all seven pre-Roman inscriptions for Pontus (excluding the Black Sea littoral), Cappadocia and Galatia, two are ascribed to Pharnaces I, two more are explicitly Iranian in nature, and the remaining three are Hellenised Iranian. An inscription found at Nymphaeum in the Bosporan Kingdom honours Mithradates with the ancient Achaemenid title of 'king of kings'. Pontic coinage depicts mixed iconography and royal imagery. The overall style of the imagery is Hellenistic, both to appeal to Greek subjects and to promote Mithradates as an equal to fellow Hellenistic and Roman rulers. But there is also imagery conveying native Anatolian messages as well as Colchian, Roman and Persian ones. In this way, Mithradates was continuing Achaemenid practice. Many (but not all) of the mints in the Pontic kingdom were of the Persian standard rather than the Greek.[16]

Architecturally there is little more. The Pontic region of Turkey today is littered with the remains of many impressive castles, some at least surely marking the Mithridatic Wars, but there have been few if any systematic surveys. Whilst these may well be of Pontic foundation, there would be much subsequent Byzantine, Georgian, Seljuk, Ottoman and other overlays. Neither of the Pontic royal capitals of Amaseia or Sinope have ever been excavated (apart from the Hellenistic Temple of Serapis in the latter), nor have the great religious centres such as Zela (Pl. 56) or Comana, despite substantial mounds marking their remains, particularly at the latter. According to Strabo, Mithradates had a palace, hunting pavilion and animal park at Cabeira, which is entirely in the Persian tradition of the 'paradise', but again this is unexcavated. A spectacularly wealthy early Hellenistic tomb dating nearly two centuries before the time of Mithradates VI at Samsun (ancient Amisos) was recently excavated by Turkish archaeologists, but whilst of an opulence befitting royalty, it belonged to the wealthy Greek aristocracy rather than to the Persian.[17] The one monument definitely attributed to Mithradates that has been excavated in its entirety is the victory monument he dedicated on Delos. This is unique in the Greek world, depicting both Greek and Persian elements alluding to his dual background.[18] But Mithradatic imperial imagery—his coins, his monuments and his portraiture—foreshadowed such imagery both of imperial Rome and Sasanian Persia. Delos was sacred in the Greek world to Apollo, but in Mithradates' homeland in Pontus, Apollo was equated with Mithras, Mithradates' own 'name deity'.

Little of the main Pontic capital of Amaseia, modern Amasya, remains apart from the magnificent rock-cut tombs of the Pontic kings cut into the cliff-face overlooking the river and the citadel above them (Pls 57-59). The second capital of Sinope still preserves magnificent ramparts as well as the ancient citadel, which may incorporate the royal palace, but this has only recently become accessible for archaeological study (having previously functioned as a prison) (Pl. 52). The Royal Tombs at Amasya, whilst belonging within the rich Anatolian tradition of rock-cut funerary architecture, could also be seen as distantly copying the Achaemenid royal rock-cut tombs of Naqsh-i Rustam (which may in turn have received inspiration from the Anatolian tradition). In the only architectural study to be made of the Amasya tombs, comparisons were made to Naqsh-i Rustam and it was noted that 'the high position of the entrances to the grave chambers … accessible only with a ladder … was chosen according to Iranian rules of purity.'[19] Whilst not overtly Zoroastrian, therefore, the Amasya tombs are at least consistent with Zoroastrian funerary practice.

The only Pontic capital that has been extensively excavated is the third one of Panticapaeum, on the Kerch Peninsula in Crimea (Pls 54-55). This is in a magnificent position on the slopes of Mount Mithradates (a modern name) overlooking the harbour and, more distantly, the Straits of Kerch (the ancient 'Cimmerian Bosporus'), the main strategic reason for its location. Just below the top of Mount Mithradates are the extensive excavated remains of the ancient city. These include parts of the city walls, a number of houses, the palace of the Bosphoran kings, a *pyrtaneion* and a Temple of Aphrodite. The palace is supposedly where Mithradates met his end, and Panticapaeum's Doric *pyrtaneion*—a place where a city council met and which held the sacred fire—might be suggestive of Iranian fire practice. There are also some non-Greek characteristics in the local Aphrodite cult. However, all belong firmly within the sphere of Greek—or at least Greek colonial—architecture and usage, and in any case have mainly been dated to the earlier periods of Greek colonisation and the Greek Bosporan kingdom (although many of the buildings doubtless were used by Mithradates). The magnificent burial tumuli surrounding Panitcapaeum (and for which the site is most famous) are all dated earlier.

THE KINGDOM OF CAPPADOCIA

South of Pontus was the Kingdom of Cappadocia, a land of greater—albeit different—Persian legacy than Pontus. The kings of Cappadocia traced their descent from the father of Cyrus the Great through an illegitimate line who had married into the Cappadocian aristocracy early in the Achaemenid period. By the time of Darius the family had become thoroughly Persianised, and it was one of this family, Otanes, who was a major conspirator in the coup that brought Darius to power. Otanes was accordingly awarded considerable powers and privileges by Darius, including the satrapy of Cappadocia.

Otanes and his descendants ruled Cappadocia as loyal Satraps from its capital of Tyana (modern Kemerhisar) until the invasion of Alexander (Pl. 60). The Cappadocians were amongst those offering stiffest resistance to Alexander: they fought him at the Battle of the Granicus, they fought him again at the Battle of Arbela, and they subsequently rose up against him in his rear. With the collapse of Alexander's empire the Kingdom of Cappadocia was one of the first to re-emerge in about 305 BC, with

31. Lycian house tomb at Kaş

32. Site of the Mausoleum of Halicarnassus in Bodrum

33. Scale model reconstruction of the Mausoleum of Halicarnassus in Istanbul

34. *Statues of Queen Artemisia and King Mausolus from the Mausoleum, now in the British Museum.*

35. *The Temple of Athena at Priene, designed by the architect Pytheus.*

36. *The agora at Alinda, founded by Mausolus.*

37. *The religious complex of Labraunda, embellished and expanded by Mausolus as a Carian cult centre.*

38. *The city of Miletus, rebuilt in the Achaemenid period as a planned city on a grid system (standing buildings visible are mainly Roman).*

39. *The Temple of Apollo at Didyma*

40. *The sole restored remains of the Temple of Artemis at Ephesus*

41. *A Persepolitan-Ionic composite bull capital at Ephesus*

43. Bust of Alexander in the Istanbul Archaeological Museum

42. The Greek Serpent Column marking the victory of Salamis, now standing in the hippodrome of Constantinople where it was brought from Delphi by Constantine.

44. Inscription of Alexander from the Temple of Athena at Priene, now in the British Museum. © Trustees of the British Museum

45. *The country palace of 'Iraq al-Amir in Jordan*

46. *Iranian style dress at Palmyra*

47. *View of Armazi-tsikhe, the site of capital of ancient eastern Georgia, on the Mtkvari (Kura) river opposite Mtskheta, the modern religious capital.*

48. *Excavated remains of a fire temple at Nekresi in Kakheti in eastern Georgia*

49. The 7th-century church at Zvarnots in Armenia

50. Detail of the 11th-century Samtavisi Cathedral in Georgia showing the Persian senmurv

51. A Sasanian style hunting scene on the 8th-century church of Ateni Sion in Georgia

52. The ramparts of Sinope on the Black Sea, which became the capital of Pontus in 183 BC.

53. Portrait of Mithradates VI Eupator (now in the Louvre) © Réunion des musées nationaux Agence Photographique

54. *Remains of the city of Panticapaeum, capital of the Bosporan kingdom in eastern Crimea. The building in the foreground is probably the 4th-century BC* pyrtaneion.

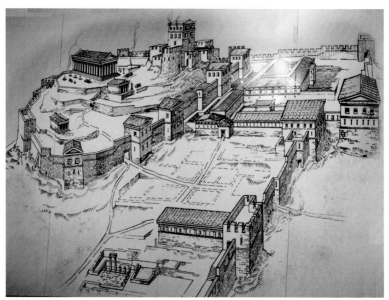

55. *Reconstructed drawing of Panticapaeum in the Kerch Museum*

56. *The citadel of Zela, modern Zile, site of one of the principal Pontic religious centres.*

57. *The rock-cut royal tombs of the Pontic kings at Amasya*

58. The three main royal tombs at Amasya

59. The citadel overlooking Amasya

60. *Site of the ancient Persian Cappadocian capital of Tyana, modern Kemerhisar. (The aqueduct is Roman.)*

61. *The mountain top dynastic complex of Nemrut Dağ in Commagene*

62. An altar at Nemrut Dağ

63. Orthostats at Nemrut Dağ depicting King Antiochus flanked by priests

its independence definitely asserted in 255 BC by King Ariarathes III, a descendant of Otanes. While wars raged throughout the Near East amongst the successors of Alexander throughout the third and into the second centuries BC, Cappadocia and the other Iranian kingdoms in Anatolia were islands of stability.

Cappadocia was also one of the kingdoms that was most Iranian in character: it is significant that Strabo, writing in the first century BC, included Cappadocia in his section on Iran rather than the section on Anatolia—it was considered, in other words, effectively a part of Iran. The coinage of the first Ariarathes (c. 280-255 BC), who led a revolt against Alexander, was in Aramaic, the administrative language of the Achaemenid Empire, but subsequent coinage was in Greek, albeit depicting the king in Persian dress. A devout population—part Iranian and part indigenous Anatolian—continued to worship at the great temples, both the old Anatolian cults and the new religion that had been brought in by the Iranians. Although never greatly urbanised, village and rural life prospered with the Iranian and native communities living peaceably alongside and eventually merging. The only other city we know about apart from Tyana was Mazaca (modern Kayseri); the aristocracy was mainly landed, living in wealthy estates that they ran from fortified manor houses—a variation of the *dihqan* system of ancient Iran, of landed aristocratic families owing allegiance to the king. This form of landed aristocracy was to characterise the Anatolian landscape until the collapse of the Byzantine Empire in this region in the eleventh century.

Much of the stability was no doubt due to Ariarathes III who enjoyed a long reign lasting some 25 years (c. 255-220 BC). His successors—all called Ariarathes—also mainly had long reigns, which argues for ordered successions. In the early first century BC Ariarathes VI married Laodice of Pontus, elder sister of Mithradates the Great, thereby becoming ensnared in the Mithradatic Wars with Rome. Indeed, Pontus, Rome and Bithynia (Pontus' rival kingdom to the west) all vied for influence in Cappadocia, leading to suspicion by all sides of complicity as it was swept between the three, even resulting in Mithradates personally executing his young nephew, Ariarathes VII, for suspicion of disloyalty on one occasion. The dynasty died out in about 96 BC with the death of Ariarathes VIII, a pawn of Bithynia. For a while Mithradates, was able to put his own puppet on the throne, his illegitimate son who became Ariarathes IX, but he was in turn replaced by Ariobarzanes, a member of the local Iranian aristocracy whom the Cappadocians elected as their king. Mithradates married one of his daughters to Ariobarzanes in order to keep Cappadocia within his orbit, but after his defeat Ariobarzanes allied Cappadocia with the winning side. Cappadocia became a client kingdom of Rome following Pompey's settlement of the east in 63 BC until it was annexed in AD 17 after the death of its last king, Archelaus.

There is some archaeological evidence for Iranian presence and colonisation in Cappadocia. A Persian relief stele depicting magi performing sacrifice has been found near Kayseri, and an inscription from Kanesh provides evidence for the density of the Iranian population, whilst other sources show the strong prevalence of Iranian surnames. At Meydançikkale, at the Cilician approaches to Cappadocia from the south, a rock relief in the style of Persepolis has been found. Numerous ancient accounts attest to the existence of large scale Persian hunting parks, or *paradeisoi* throughout Anatolia. Most of all, there is a considerable body of evidence of Iranian religion taking root in Cappadocia, and these religious elements are discussed further in Chapter 8.

THE MOUNTAIN KINGDOM OF COMMAGENE

Commagene, further south of Cappadocia, was the only one of these Neo-Persian kingdoms whose royal family bore mainly Hellenic names, despite their more visible claims to Iranian aristocratic descent, whereas both the Pontic and Cappadocian royal families retained Iranian names throughout. The origin of the Commagenian kings may well have been Achaemenid as they claimed—probably descended from one of the Anatolian satraps—but they were also connected to the Orontid dynasty of Armenian kings (who also claimed Achaemenid descent). Although the rulers of Commagene became increasingly Hellenised after the first few generations—it is unlikely that any of them spoke Persian in the end—they retained considerable Iranian sentiment and character, particularly in the field of religion. Significantly, members of the Commagene royal house married into the Parthian royal family and fled to Iran on the eve of the Roman annexation.[20]

The rulers of Commagene, despite their Greek names, practised an Iranian dynastic cult that incorporated Ahura Mazda, Mithras and Verethragna, equated with Zeus, Apollo-Helios-Hermes, and Heracles respectively. This extraordinary syncretic cult is depicted sculpturally, epigraphically and spectacularly at Antiochus I's (69-31 BC) great dynastic complex on the top of Mount Nimrod (Nemrut Dağ) in the middle of his kingdom, which was attended by Magi 'in the Persian fashion' (Pls 61-64). In addition to fusing both Persian and Greek religion, Antiochus also lists his own ancestors, tracing them back to Alexander on the maternal side and to the Achaemenid royal family on his paternal (hence primary) side. The Alexandrine ancestry is presumably fictitious as we have observed. Whether such a noble genealogy was correct or fictitious is not the point; the point is that Antiochus deliberately sought to create a fusion of the Hellenic and Iranian worlds. Alexander himself famously tried this at Susa and failed; it took an Iranian to put it into practice—the idea of combining different cultural elements was, after all, an Achaemenid one.

Nemrut Dağ, situated over two thousand metres above sea level, is one of the most impressive monuments of the ancient world. It consists of a central tumulus made up of small stones surrounded by three rock-cut terraces. The eastern terrace is dominated on one side by a row of seated colossal statues facing outwards with their backs to the tumulus, now all headless (the colossal fallen heads lie below in picturesque abandon), representing the royal family and the gods. On the rear of the statues is Antiochus' long inscription tracing his royal ancestry. The colossi themselves face a well-preserved stepped fire altar on the edge of the terrace. Both eastern and western terraces are lined with orthostats—upright stone slabs—carved with relief decorations portraying the Persian and Macedonian royal ancestors (mostly in Persian costume), as well as the gods.

At the foot of the mountain are the remains of the capital of Commagene, Arsameia (modern Eski Kahta), named after Arsames, one of the Persian royal ancestors (Pl. 65). The remains are scattered over a mountain slope with little surviving today apart from an important relief depicting Antiochus (dressed in the Persian fashion) shaking hands with a naked Heracles (representing the Iranian deity Verethragna). Alongside is a long inscription in Greek. At Karakuş nearby is another monumental tumulus mound, the burial place of the royal women (Pl. 66). It was originally surrounded by a circle of massive commemorative columns of which only three still stand, surmounted by an eagle, a bull and a lion.

Antiochus' extraordinary mountain-top complex belongs within a tradition of dynastic cult centres that stretches across the Iranian world. The royal proclamation echoes Darius' public proclamations in stone at Bisitun and Naqsh-i Rustam, and the depictions of Antiochus' associations with

115

the gods at Nemrut Dağ anticipates a whole range of Sasanian investiture scenes carved in rock throughout Iran (Pl. 68). The costume depicted at Nemrut Dağ and Arsameia is Iranian in style, with the distinctive pointed caps finding their closest counterpart in the stucco sculpted priests' heads at the near contemporary site of Dalverzin in Uzbekistan (and recall the pointed caps of the Central Asian Scythians). The commemorative columns at the funerary complex of Karakuş (Pl. 66), recall the Ashokan victory columns of Mauryan India and anticipate the victory columns of Rome. Whilst the language of Nemrut Dağ may have been Greek, the spirit was almost wholly Iranian. The tradition goes back to the greatest of Iranian dynastic centres at Persepolis, and anticipates later Kushan dynastic centres in Central Asia at Surkh Kotal in Afghanistan (also on top of a mountain), Khalchayan in Tajikistan and Mathura in India, and even the later Turk dynastic centre of Bamiyan in the sixth-seventh centuries.* Yet like the earlier great monument of the Mausoleum of Halicarnassus, it is almost invariably considered as a part of broader Hellenistic architecture: few studies consider it in the Persian architectural context.

*   *   *

We thus leave Anatolia and its extraordinary post-Achaemenid history that in some ways is as great as the Persian Empire that gave it birth. It bequeathed a spectacular monument at Nemrut Dağ that is among the greatest in Iranian architecture. It brought Iranian religion westwards that—as we shall see in later chapters—was to have an even profounder influence than the ideas of kingship embodied in Cyrus the Great. And it saw a Persian king having greater success—and equally greater failure—in establishing a foothold in Europe than either Darius or Xerxes did. We may return, therefore, to take up the thread once more in Iran itself.

---

* This is discussed further in Volume 3 in this series.

Chapter 6

TWO SUPER-POWERS
Recovery, Expansion
and the War That Changed the World

The wind of the East, that is the kingdom of Persia.

John of Ephesus[1]

Alexander's conquest was a humiliation for the far older Persian civilisation that took centuries to recover. Macedonian rule in Iran lasted barely a century and passes almost unnoticed in the Persian historical record: for Iran they are the equivalent of the dark ages. Despite some suggestion (supported by a few inscriptions) that Greek colonies were established in Iran with supposedly all the trappings of a Greek *polis*, none have been found. There is nothing found in Iran comparable, for example, to either the Greek city of Ai Khanum on the Oxus or even to Seleucia on the Tigris. Even if excavations were carried out where inscriptions suggest there might be a colony—such as at Nihavend in western Iran—it is unlikely that it would be another Ai Khanum exhibiting Greek-style architecture. The extensive excavations at Susa, where the sources most indicate the existence of Greek culture, have failed to find any real evidence: no Greek temples, agora, gymnasium or theatre.* Neither are there any traces of Greek institutions surviving in post-Seleucid Iran: no gymnasia or theatres (the report by Plutarch of the Parthian King Orodes watching Euripides when he heard the news of Crassus' defeat smacks of dramatic embellishment). The very rare Hellenic-style columns such as at Parthian Khurheh or Sasanian Kangavar must be viewed as exceptions, not the rule and are in any case superficial and debased elements that overlie the basically Iranian character of the architecture.

---

* And the Greek institutions and the Greek language of Susa, which survived until well into the Parthian period, probably ultimately goes back to Greek communities settled there by the Achaemenids rather than by Alexander. See Wiesehöfer 1996: 110.

THE PARTHIAN REVIVAL

The recovery of Iran's humiliation, when it did come, began in the northeast. This was the arrival of the third—and last—movement of Iranian tribes from Central Asia: the Parthians. Like the Medes and the Persians before them, the Parthians were initially little more than a tribal confederation, until in about 238 BC they seized control of the trans-Caspian territories of the Seleucid Empire under the founder of their dynasty, Arsaces. Building up a power-base in what is now Turkmenistan and Khorasan, ruling first from Nisa (near Ashkhabad) and then from Hecatompylos (near Damghan), by the middle of the second century the Parthians were ready to invade Seleucid Iran. By about 141 BC the Parthian king Mithradates I ruled an empire almost as large as the former Achaemenid one. It was the beginning of an Iranian revival.

Parthian conquests in Syria soon brought them up against a new power in the west which their Achaemenid predecessors never had to face: Rome. The two powers collided head-on only eleven years after the Romans had entered Syria, at the Battle of Carrhae in 53 BC. The Roman army was annihilated, suffering its greatest defeat since Hannibal; the Proconsul Crassus himself was killed and most of the army were either destroyed or taken off into captivity to the eastern fringes of the Parthian Empire. Subsequent history was one of many conflicts between Rome and Parthia, sometimes with one or the other in the ascendant (Trajan advanced as far as the shores of the Persian Gulf in 116 AD, for example, and dreamt of following in Alexander's footsteps to India), but an equilibrium was generally maintained with the Syrian desert kept as a buffer zone between the two powers.

The Parthian Empire was a very vigorous one. Parthian sculptures convey an aggressive image: proud looking warriors, barely removed from their Central Asian steppe roots, sporting beards and long hair, masculinely clad in trousers and carrying broad-swords (Pl. 67). Such an art conjures up images of warlords and campfires rather than the poetry and rose-gardens more often associated with Persian culture. Such vigour and such victories against the west's greatest power re-established the self-confidence of Persian civilisation after its humiliating set-back at the hands of the Macedonians. The Parthians, therefore, paved the way for a new dynasty of Persian kings to emerge from the same historic heartland of Persia as the Achaemenids did. These were the Sasanians, whose first ruler, Ardeshir I, overthrew the last

Parthian king, Artabanus V in 224 AD, to proclaim a glorious new Persian empire that was to last for the next 400 years (Pl. 68).

THE SASANIAN RENAISSANCE

Members of the Parthian royal family remained as rulers of Armenia to the west (discussed in Chapter 5) and in India to the east. But it was the Sasanian royal family who came nearer to reviving the Achaemenid glories of old, particularly when Ardeshir sent ambassadors to Rome demanding the return of the old Achaemenid provinces of Egypt, the Near East, Anatolia and Greece as an historic right. This resulted in an indecisive war against Rome under Emperor Alexander Severus, but it was Ardeshir's successor, Shapur I, who came nearer to living up to the names of Cyrus and Darius: he re-established much of the ancient borders, he reformed and re-organised the administration, he allowed religious toleration but at the same time re-affirmed Zoroastrianism as the state religion. He defeated Emperor Gordian III, who was killed in battle, and enforced humiliating terms on his successor, Emperor Philip the Arab in 244. Shapur's greatest triumph was at the Battle of Edessa in Syria in 260 when the greatest prize of all, the Roman Emperor Valerian himself, was captured and brought before Shapur. Never before had Persia been greater, and the event is proclaimed with understandable triumph in great rock reliefs that can still be seen throughout Persia depicting three Roman emperors: one dead (Gordian), one begging for mercy (Philip) and one captive (Valerian)—no greater depictions of Roman humiliation have ever been made (Pls 69-71).

The world of Sasanian Persia was in many ways a revival of the great days of ancient Persia (although it is doubtful whether the Sasanians consciously evoked the Achaemenids). It was certainly a new golden age, of opulent courts, of flourishing arts, of immense building activity, and of increased wealth from Persian control of both land and sea trade (Pls 72-75). The areas corresponding to much of present day Central Asia, Afghanistan and Pakistan formed an important hinterland of the Sasanian Empire, where Persian art forms were able to fuse with Greek and Buddhist to eventually influence the art of China and the Far East. Sasanian Persia was able to take back—albeit briefly—the historic lands of the Achaemenid Empire to the west as well: Anatolia, Syria and Egypt—even, for one brief heady moment (in 626: discussed below), crossing the Bosphorus into Europe like

Darius a millennium before. Beyond the imperial frontiers, Persian merchant ships were putting into ports as far away as East Africa and Indo-China. It seemed that a new great age was dawning for Iran.

The history of both the Parthian and the Sasanian dynasties, totalling over eight and a half centuries, is far longer than the Achaemenids at just over two. The contact with the west was correspondingly greater, particularly as this contact was mainly with Rome, a civilisation as intimately bound up with European identity as that of Greece. The contacts were greater, but so were the conflicts: Graeco-Persian relations were dominated by just two wars, but the wars between Rome and the successive Parthian and Sasanian Empires of Iran were many, from Crassus' debacle already mentioned to Heraclius' more heroic, but ultimately equally futile, campaigns still to be recounted. Along the way we witness Trajan's spectacular advance, Hadrian's cautious retrenchment, Septimius' aggression, Caracalla's duplicity, Julian's quixotic experiment, and a host of other characters and motivations in between. Leaders and motives are more shadowy amongst the Iranians, although the two Shapurs and the two Khusraus loom large. Much as the story is worth telling, these pages must be limited to just how these contacts and conflicts affected and changed our view of the west.

Whilst the early years of the Sasanian period in the third and fourth centuries when Sasanian Persia was still expanding were characterised by several wars with Rome, the fifth century was one of relative peace between the two great powers. This was to change in the sixth century.

THE GREATEST WAR IN THE HISTORY OF THE WORLD (MAP 10)

At the same time it would be a mistake to characterise Sasanian-Roman relations entirely in terms of war. There were long periods of peace, particularly by the fifth century, when a state of uneasy but stable equilibrium existed between the two powers, and many of the frontier defences in the Near East were allowed to deteriorate. But the sixth and early seventh centuries were shattered by a series of wars lasting a hundred years that ended up devastating both Rome and Persia. This hundred-year war sees some of the greatest kings of both sides: the Emperor Justinian of Rome and the Shah Khusrau Anushirvan of Persia saw its beginning while Emperor Heraclius and Shah Khusrau Parviz saw its end. Both sides produced equally great generals: Justinian's general Belisarius and Khusrau Parviz'

10. *The Near Eastern theatre of the wars of the sixth century*

generals Shahin and Shahrvaraz. Great valour was seen on both sides and great armies fought great battles. Few apart from specialist historians now know of the siege of Constantinople by the Persians in 626 or the battles that surged round the fortress of Petra on the Georgian coast overlooking the Black Sea in the 540s and 550s. But these events were part of a much

121

broader war between the two super-powers of the ancient world that had a far longer-term effect than the wars of the twentieth century. In one way it changed nothing: both powers reverted to virtually identical borders that they had at the beginning. At the same time, it changed everything.

The exact beginning and the exact end of this conflict is difficult to pinpoint, but two significant dates, 529 at its beginning and 629 at its end, mark exactly a hundred years. It is often regarded as two main wars in the earlier and the latter part of this period and several minor ones in between. But effectively, this was a single war punctuated by cease-fires and proxy wars which the historian James Howard-Johnston has rightly dubbed 'the last great war of antiquity'.[2]

It might appear foolhardy—or at least overstated—to label this hundred year war 'the greatest war in the history of the world' or even 'the last great war of antiquity'. But to a large extent, any major war is a retrospective construct. It still is disputed, for example, whether the 'Peloponnesian War' was a single war or a series of wars between the Greek states with a period of peace in between. The meaning and duration of any war might also differ enormously to the various participants, particularly those that involve great powers. To take the First World War as an example, its conventional dates are 1914-1918, but on war memorials throughout Britain the dates are inscribed 1914-1919; for an American they are 1917-1918; for a Turk 1912-1923. For Great Britain the issue was the challenge of Germany; for Italy it was the last war of unification; for the Balkans it was the war of Ottoman succession; for Japan it was a war of conquest in the Far East; for the Arabs it was a war of national independence; for Armenia it was genocide. The Second World War was the 1939-45 War to most of the European protagonists, but it was the 1941-45 War to the Americans and the Russians, or the 1939-1974 war according to the Helsinki Agreement which formally recognised the post-war borders. For many, both were part of a greater war that ran from 1914 to 1945—or to 1989, that included the Cold War.

Our 'great war' under discussion between Byzantine Rome* and Sasanian Persia is similarly amorphous, with many variant dates, issues and perspectives involved (all of them disputed). What makes this conflict

---

* For this period, there is no neatly defined difference between 'Roman Empire' and 'Byzantine Empire'. It still officially called itself the 'Roman Empire', as it remained right through until its end in 1453. By that time, however, it had changed radically from the early empire of the Caesars, hence the term 'Byzantine', but the events related here still form a part of an unbroken history from Rome's earlier expansion into the Near East. To some extent, therefore, I use the two terms interchangeably.

essentially a single war is not so much its beginnings or its issue, but its effect. It was a far greater watershed than the conquests of Alexander of Macedon earlier had been—indeed, it probably brought about more changes than any war in history. The effects are still felt today.

THE GREAT WALL, THE HUNS AND THE CAUCASUS PASSES

The beginning and causes of this 'Great War' are not easy to define against the background of the wars that characterised the first five hundred years of Rome's presence on Persia's western border. What changed was the formation in the middle years of the fourth century of an important—and menacing—nomad confederation on the northern borders of the Persian Empire whose name both Rome and Iran soon had cause to dread. These were the Huns (also known as the Chionites and Hephthalites). The Huns were new to the Roman Empire, but the Iranians already had some experience of these incredibly mobile—and ruthless—steppe nomads. Shapur II had managed to halt their depredations in Central Asia in the first half of the fourth century, but this merely served to deflect them around the Caspian Sea to their north-west frontier in the Caucasus. In 395-7 the Huns broke through the Caucasus passes and entered the Near East for the first time (Pl. 76). Hence, both super-powers for once were distracted by invasions from the north rather than by each other.

Who were these ruthless nomads who seemed to contemporaries to be only semi-human and to have appeared out of nowhere? Many have seen the origins of the Huns in the *Hsiung-nu* of Chinese sources. This was a particularly warlike nomadic nation on the northern and western borders of China, who formed a huge nomadic empire in northern Central Asia in the second century BC. Chinese imperial policy—it amounted to an obsession—in the last few centuries BC was aimed at evicting the Hsiung-nu from their borders by diplomatic and military means; the construction of the Great Wall was one of the results of this policy. As a result, the Hsiung-nu were driven away from China and back into the immense Central Eurasian steppe belt towards the west. The identification of the Hsiung-nu with the Huns, however, is disputed. But whether or not the Hsiung-nu of the Chinese sources are the Huns of the western sources is not important here. What is important is that the Chinese defeat of the Hsiung-nu resulted in a huge, long-term displacement of the steppe nomad nations, a chain reaction that would have a knock-on effect right across Eurasia. The Huns, whether or not they are related to the Hsiung-nu, were initially displaced by these events and would be beating at the gates of both the Persian and Roman Empires many generations later so that by the middle years of the fourth century an important—and menacing—nomad confederation had formed on the northern borders of the Persian Empire. Further west it was to result generations later in an avalanche of 'barbarian' tribes into Europe: not only Huns but those driven before them as well.*

In 484 a Sasanian army was wiped out whilst on campaign against the Huns to their north. Iranian-Roman relations were subsequently dominated by the need for Iran to maintain their defences against the Huns. This was first recognised in the treaty between Jovian and Shapur in 363 following the humiliating end of Emperor Julian's eastern campaign, when a clause referred specifically to the defences of the Caucasus passes. Then, beginning with Anastasius (491-518), Constantinople agreed to contribute to the upkeep of the defence of the Caucasus passes (mainly Dariel, in present Georgia, and Derbend in Daghestan) which Iran controlled, in the form of regular payments made to Ctesiphon; safeguarding the passes stopped the Huns from coming into Roman territory as much as into Persian. The great defences at Darband in Daghestan still stand today as mute evidence of the importance of this policy. Recently, British and Iranian archaeologists have re-dated the 190 kilometre long Gurgan Wall that stretches eastwards from the Caspian Sea across the Turkmen steppe of northern Iran to precisely this time—visible proof indeed that the Sasanians were spending Roman tax-payers money wisely.[3] Roman defaulting on these payments contributed more than anything else to the gradual deterioration between the two powers throughout the fifth century—and with good reason, for the Gurgan Wall demonstrates that the Sasanians were spending massively on these defences. Ultimately, however, halting the Huns at either Gurgan or Dariel merely deflected them around the Black Sea to the Roman west.

JUSTINIAN AND KHUSRAU ANUSHIRVAN

In 527 a new Roman emperor assumed power in Constantinople whose ambitions hearkened back to the great empire-building days of the earlier

---

* The Huns, their antecedents and their effect upon Europe are discussed further in Volume 4 of this series.

Caesars. This was Justinian, who sought to restore the ancient might—and the borders—of the Roman Empire. He first fortified the eastern borders with a string of gigantic fortresses along the Euphrates, including the construction of an entirely new fortress city at Dara (Pl. 77). Dara was a deliberate affront to the Persians. Whilst it was within Roman territory, it was beyond the agreed limits of fortification, thus in contravention of the existing agreement. Most important, Dara was aimed like a sword directly at the Persian garrison city of Nisibis, a city which the Romans had ceded to Iran in a humiliating treaty of 363 that rankled with the Romans ever since (Map 10).

Hence, in 529 open war broke out. The Sasanian Emperor Kavadh sent an army of 30,000 into eastern Anatolia. Justinian responded with a large force, but hostilities were suspended by both sides on the onset of the harsh eastern Anatolian winter. It resumed in 530 with a Roman offensive, this time under the command of Justinian's general Belisarius. The Iranians attacked Roman positions at Dara with a force of 70,000 but were forced to retreat to Nisibis. A peace treaty was duly negotiated—the 'Endless Peace' of 532—but the indecisive war continued intermittently with further battles still being fought along the frontier.

Faced with stalemate on the eastern frontier, Justinian embarked upon a diplomatic offensive that broadened the war to a new front. Some years previously a relatively minor king, Dhu Nawas of Himyar in the central highlands of Yemen, converted to Judaism. Dhu Nawas immediately embarked upon a pogrom against the Christians of Yemen, culminating in a massacre of the Christians of Najran. Accordingly, Justinian sent envoys to the court of the Christian king of Ethiopia in Aksum, King Kaleb, promising Roman aid in an Ethiopian invasion of Yemen in return for Ethiopian aid in blocking Indian Ocean sea routes to the Persians. With the neutrality of Roman Egypt thus guaranteed, Ethiopia began its expansion out of Africa. Kaleb sent an Ethiopian army commanded by his general Atsbeha across the Red Sea, which successfully occupied Yemen, Atsbeha remaining there as viceroy. The Red Sea became an Ethiopian lake with Roman backing, and Persian control of the Indian Ocean trade began to be challenged.

Meanwhile in Iran, a new emperor had ascended the throne in 531 after Kavadh's death, the legendary Khusrau I Anushirvan ('Of the Immortal Soul'). For Iranians, Khusrau Anushirvan is remembered as one of their greatest kings. Often referred to as 'the Just King', his long reign remained a model for kingship, lordly virtues and wise rule that was used as a mirror for subsequent rulers of Iran down to the Islamic middle ages.* Khusrau was also a scholar who knew the culture of the Greeks to his west thoroughly. As well as having a sound knowledge of Christianity, he had supposedly read all of Plato, Aristotle, Demosthenes and Thucydides in translation according to Agathias (indeed, he was believed by some ancient sources to have converted to Christianity).⁴ At the same time in Constantinople, Justinian had begun his ambitious programme of conquests in the west to reinstate the ancient Roman Empire—North Africa and Italy—in a series of wars lasting through the 530s. This had two effects. First, it turned Constantinople's back upon the east, leaving much of it relatively unguarded. Second, and more important, it demanded vast resources which had to be paid for. Under the terms of the peace treaty of 532, Justinian had agreed to pay 11,000 pounds of gold to Persia for safeguarding the Caucasus passes against the Huns, a huge sum. In desperation for more funds, Justinian defaulted on these payments. Accordingly, the peace was broken with a surrogate war fought by both empires' Arab allies, the Lakhmids of Mesopotamia and Ghassanids of Syria. It was during the 'cold war' of the 530s that Emperor Khusrau Anushirvan received a curious embassy from far to Persia's west.

This was the secret embassy of Vitiges, king of the Goths, to Khusrau in 638/9 to propose an alliance between Sasanian Persia and the Ostrogothic kingdom in Italy in order to encircle the Byzantines. The two envoys themselves were not Goths, who would have been far too conspicuous travelling through Byzantine territory, so Vitiges sent two Ligurian priests, who recruited a Syrian interpreter in Thrace, and managed to travel through Byzantine territory successfully avoiding discovery. Vitiges had become king in 636 and the following year launched a campaign from Ravenna to recapture Rome from Belisarius. It failed, and Vitiges' envoys warned Khusrau that Justinian's aggressive ambitions would inevitably turn against Persia as soon as the war in Italy was resolved. Vitiges urged Khusrau to pre-empt any move by Justinian and open up a second front against the Roman Empire. Thus warned, Khusrau used the pretext of accusing Justinian of provoking the Huns into invading Iran and, taking advantage of Constantinople's preoccupation in the west, Persia invaded the Roman Empire in 540.⁵

---

* E.g., Nizam al-Mulk's *Siyasat Nama* where he is held up throughout as the ideal king of the past for modern kings—in this case Sultan Alp Arslan—to emulate. The position of Khusrau Anushirvan in many ways echoes that of Cyrus.

Khusrau's triumphal progress through Syria was facilitated by desertions to his side by Roman subjects in Syria. Indeed, Khusrau was careful to comply with local religious sensibilities by replacing the unpopular Chalcedonian bishops appointed from Constantinople with local Monophysites. Apamaea surrendered peacefully, and Khusrau's subsequent capture of Antioch was a foregone conclusion. He went on to the port of Seleucia by the Mediterranean, the dream of Iran's emperors ever since they lost the Mediterranean seaboard to Alexander some eight and a half centuries previously. Emulating Shapur's precedent three centuries before, Khusrau founded a new city settled by captured prisoners from Antioch, naming it *Veh Antiok Khusrau* or 'Khusrau's Better than Antioch'.

Justinian's general, Belisarius, had some success in recapturing Syria for the empire, but he failed to recapture Nisibis and was recalled to Constantinople in 543. Edessa in its turn was besieged by the Sasanian army, but held. Faced with the stalemate at both Nisibis and Edessa, a five year armistice was established in 545.

THE CONFLICT EXPANDS: BLACK SEA AND RED SEA FRONTS

The war then shifted to a new front: Georgia and the Black Sea. Georgia at this time was divided between the two powers. The eastern part, known as Iberia* with its capital at Armazi (modern Mtskheta near Tbilisi), was a part of Persia. The western part, the kingdom of Lazica, was allied to the Roman Empire. The main Roman stronghold was the great fortress of Petra, modern Tsikhisdziri, on a dramatic bluff overlooking the Black Sea, as well as the nearby huge legionary fortress of Apsarus, modern Gonio, one of the largest and best preserved Roman legionary forts in the Roman world (Pls 78-79). Resentment of Roman rapaciousness by the troops forced Gobarzes, the king of Lazica, to appeal to the Persians, who advanced in 541 and captured Petra, bringing the two powers into direct confrontation. The 'Lazic War' as it was called dragged on throughout the 540s and 550s, with Petra withstanding sieges from both sides and exchanging hands on several occasions. Much of the territory of Lazica was laid waste by the two armies, until eventually a truce was declared in 547 following the successful

---

* The Caucasus can cause geographic confusion with ancient place names such as Iberia and Albania, the one having no connection with Spain and the other similarly not remotely connected to the country of that name in the Balkans.

Roman siege of Archaeopolis (modern Nokalakevi). In the end, the two sides had fought themselves to exhaustion on all fronts, and Iran was faced with a different threat from the newly established Western Turk Empire (or Kaganate) on its eastern frontier. Accordingly, a 'Fifty Year Peace' was finally declared in 556/7 to end a war that had lasted 31 years.

But hostilities were resumed under Justinian's successor, Justin II, in 571. This time, the war was to expand to an even wider stage. The events began when a delegation from the Western Turk Empire, led by the Soghdian ambassador Maniakh, entered Constantinople in 568 or 569 (a first contact between the Turks and the city that they would eventually make their own). Justin responded by sending his own mission under Zamarchus back to the Turk Kagan in Central Asia, and several further diplomatic exchanges are recorded. The reason for such extraordinary long distance shuttle diplomacy was the Turk proposal for a grand alliance with the Romans to crush their mutual enemy, Sasanian Persia, in between.[6]

Faced with the threat of an encircling alliance, Khusrau acted quickly and mounted a successful naval campaign against Rome's Red Sea ally, Ethiopia, which resulted in the invasion and occupation of Yemen in about 570 (Theophylact of Byzantium in fact explicitly linked this to Justin's embassy to the Turks).* Yemen hence remained a part of the Persian Empire until the Muslim conquest the following century. There is some suggestion that Khusrau may also have conquered Ceylon in a related naval campaign, as a part of a pincer movement to block Rome's access to the lucrative Indian Ocean trade through both the Persian Gulf and the Red Sea, whilst in the other direction Sasanian traders dominated the markets down the East African coast as far as Zanzibar.[7] Iran was becoming a major maritime power with a world reach.

Meanwhile, Roman diplomacy had not been idle either, and the Caucasus once more became the focus, this time moving from Georgia to Armenia, then a part of the Persian Empire. In 570 Rome made a secret pact with Armenia to foment revolt in order to open another front. The revolt took place the following year led by Vardan Mamikonian, who killed the Persian satrap, Suren (a relative of Khusrau's), and fled to Constantinople. Justin then defaulted on the subsidies sent to Iran. The 'Fifty Year Peace' of 561 was in tatters.

---

* A fragment of a tapestry woven at the end of the sixth/beginning of the seventh century was found at Antonoë in Egypt, now in Lyon, probably depicts this campaign. It depicts mounted Sasanian archers fighting black—presumed Ethiopian—soldiers with a Sasanian king—presumed Khusrau—observing the battle. See Dignas and Winter 2007: 113-4.

Khusrau responded by invading Syria and Armenia in 575. Both sides suffered defeats, Rome in Syria and Iran in Armenia, and so a peace between the two exhausted powers was negotiated in 576 and renewed two years later. The following year, Khusrau I Anushirvan died after a reign of forty-eight years.

KHUSRAU PARVIZ AND HERACLIUS

An intermittent and indecisive war of attrition resumed in 579 and continued until a new peace was negotiated in 591. Meanwhile, a vigorous new king had ascended the throne in Iran. This was Khusrau II Parviz, who was destined to outshine his namesake and become one of Iran's greatest kings (Pl. 80). In 603 Khusrau II Parviz resumed the war. This time, Iran not only finally realised its dream of reinstating the ancient borders of the Achaemenid kings, but advanced to Constantinople itself.

Khusrau Parviz's successes were nothing short of spectacular—not since the heady days of Cyrus and Darius had the world witnessed such conquests by a Persian king. The initial pretext for Khusrau was the overthrow of the pro-Persian Emperor Maurice by Phocas. Maurice had helped Khusrau gain his throne at the beginning of his reign, even marrying his daughter to Khusrau to cement the friendship.* But his father-in-law's overthrow and death at the hands of the usurper Phocas provided Khusrau with the pretext he needed. The Roman Empire's Anatolian fortress-cities fell to the victorious Iranians one by one and, by 606, Khusrau's armies had occupied Cappadocia. The way to Constantinople lay open and virtually unguarded. In Constantinople itself the city was undergoing one of its periodic bouts of blood-letting, as the rival political factions, the Greens and the Blues, fought each other in pitched street battles. Out of the rivalry the unpopular Emperor Phocas was deposed in 610. He was replaced by Heraclius, the seventh century's most capable emperor—but the one who tragically was to end up losing the most.

In the meantime, the Iranian army under Khusrau's general Shahin was able to advance virtually unopposed to Constantinople, pitching their tents on the Asiatic shores of the Bosphorus opposite the capital in 614.[8] The holy city of Jerusalem was captured in the same year, an immense

---

* This led some sources to describe Khusrau as Christian.

moral blow to the Romans. Not since Darius in the fifth century BC had the Bosphorus seen a Persian army. Shahin's huge force threatened Constantinople and, in desperation, Heraclius crossed to Shahin's camp in 615 to negotiate personally with Khusrau's general. Shahin treated the humiliated emperor with courtesy, but emphasised that only his king had the authority to negotiate with a fellow king. Returning to his capital empty handed, Heraclius even considered the momentous step of ditching Constantinople altogether and, in emulation of Constantine, moving Rome's capital once more: to Carthage.

Khusrau's initial campaigns against the Roman Empire had the direct effect of thinning Iran's eastern defences. This prompted the Kagan of the Western Turk Empire of Central Asia to invade in 616, broadening the war into Central Asia—and beyond. The Turks advanced as far as Rayy in northern Iran and, in response, Khusrau sent a hastily assembled force of Armenians (who might otherwise be pro-Roman) under Smbat Bagratuni to his eastern border. Khusrau was in a 'win-win' situation here: if the Armenians were defeated it would have ridden himself of a force whose loyalty was suspect; if they won it would have ridden himself of a dangerous new threat to his eastern front. The Turk Kagan died, however, and his successor turned away from Iran when faced with this unexpected new resistance from the Armenians and focussed his attentions further east, where the Kagan of the Eastern Turks, Shih-pi (609-19) was instrumental in eventually bringing about the end of the Sui Dynasty of China and establishing the new T'ang as its successor in 618. Thus were the beginnings of medieval Chinese civilisation. This gave a much needed reprieve for Khusrau, who was able to turn his fullest attentions to the west once more.[9]

Meanwhile, we see the war extending to another unexpected front in the opposite direction. With such major distractions to their east, the western defences of Constantinople and its vital hinterland in the Balkans were left unguarded. With a beleaguered Constantinople promising easy pickings, combined forces of Avars and Slavs crossed the Danube and stormed down through the Balkans in 618 devastating everything in its way, besieging Thesalonika that year. Their arrival was to eventually bring about a profound ethnic change: the Slavicisation of south-eastern Europe. Constantinople itself—the very existence of the Roman Empire—hung by a thread.

The final outcome of the war seemed about to be decided. Elsewhere in the Near East Khusrau's victories had been equally impressive. Tarsus and Damascus had been taken in 613, then in the following year Khusrau entered Jerusalem. The Christian buildings of the city were ransacked and the holy relics taken off to Iran. Persia then swept on to the greatest of its victories: in 619 they took Alexandria, extending their conquest to all of Egypt by 621 and a Persian fleet occupied Rhodes in 622. Thus, in Alexander of Macedon's city, Khusrau II Parviz, Great King and King of Kings, finally laid to rest the ghost of the 'Demon King'.

HOLY WAR

Khusrau made a cardinal mistake when the Persians seized the Christian holy relics in Jerusalem. More than anything else, this spurred the Christian empire of Rome into response as nothing else would, and in 622 Heraclius went on the offensive. In particular, Heraclius unleashed a demon that has continued to haunt the world ever since: he formulated the concept of Holy War whereby killing could be justified as a religious act and those who perishing in doing this would ascend directly to heaven. Heraclius first safeguarded his rear from the Slav threat by using Byzantium's greatest single weapon, money: he simply bought them off. Then, armed with religious zeal, these first Crusaders were able to penetrate deep into Iran in 622 where they plundered the Iranian holy city of Shiz, partly to seize back the holy relics, and partly to avenge the plunder of Jerusalem.

In 624-5 Heraclius moved the war to Transcaucasia once more: the Caucasus remained a strategic factor throughout. Accordingly, Khusrau sent his three best generals into Transcaucasia, including Shahin, the legendary besieger of Constantinople. Faced with such opponents, Heraclius wisely avoided open battle. In the meantime, Khusrau's diplomatic intelligence had been as busy as his military, and as successful. The following year his agents formed an alliance with the Avars, Slavs and Bulgars of south-eastern Europe in a move to encircle Constantinople. Acting in concert, the Sasanian army, commanded this time by Shahrvaraz, advanced in 626 once more to the Bosphorus, laying siege to Constantinople from Chalcedon, while the Avars laid siege on the landward side. Indeed, according to one source, Shahrvaraz actually crossed the Bosphorus and surrounded Constantinople, laying siege 'from the west' as well.[10] For the first time since Xerxes, an army from Persia occupied a part of Europe. Constantinople's massive defences, however, held.

Faced with encirclement, Heraclius used the same tactic himself, and in 626 opened negotiations with the Khazar Turks of the Caspian to outflank Iran in the east. Accordingly, a Khazar army commanded by their king advanced through the Caucasus passes and joined forces with Heraclius under the walls of Tbilisi, which was still held by the Persians.* Betrothing his daughter Eudocia to the Kagan (the first but by no means the last time that Byzantine and Turkish royal families would be united by marriage), the combined force entered Iran in 627, leaving a smaller Turk force to continue the siege of Tbilisi (Pl. 81).

Heraclius advanced to the historic battlefield of Nineveh in 627, whose capture by the Medes in 612 BC had first signalled the arrival of the Iranians upon the Near Eastern stage. This time the Iranians were defeated and a combination of both luck and secret intelligence work began to work in Heraclius' favour. The Persian general Shahin had died of illness the previous year, removing one of Khusrau's military geniuses from the war. This left only Shahrvaraz, still besieging Constantinople. Heraclius' agents, however, were able to show him a letter of Khusrau, which Roman agents had intercepted, ordering Shahrvaraz' execution as a potential challenger to his throne. Accordingly, Shahrvaraz entered into secret negotiation with Heraclius and withdrew his forces from Constantinople—the Persians 'evacuated Europe and returned to Asia' according to John of Ephesus.[11]

The following year Khusrau II Parviz was murdered, possibly at the instigation of his son Kavadh acting in concert with Shahrvaraz. His successor, Kavadh II, sued for peace in 629. Heraclius was able to negotiate an evacuation of Egypt directly with Shahrvaraz (now connected by marriage ties: Shahrvaraz' daughter married Heraclius' son) and a withdrawal back to previous borders.

THE END OF ANTIQUITY

Peace, like countless previous ones, was established once again. Many regard the wars between Rome and Sasanian Persia between the third and seventh centuries as 'endemic', as both empires claimed universal rule, hence leaving few options apart from war.[12] Others regard it as just another

---

* The history and legacy of the Turk Khazars is explored further in Volume 4 of this series.

chapter in a Manichean war between east and west that we have reviewed in the Introduction. Both views overlook the long periods of peace between the two powers when trade and cross-fertilisation of ideas—particularly religious—went both ways: relations between any two powers are always complex and can never be described in simple terms. More important, both views obscure the real significance of this particular century-long war.

After a century of war the borders remained exactly as they had been at the outbreak: the war, it seemed, had changed nothing. At the same time it had changed everything. Ultimately, it was not a peace like the previous ones, for the war had awoken a new giant from an unexpected quarter. Throughout the war, monotheistic religion had not only become arms of the state of both superpowers, but for the first time was used as offensive weapons: militant Persian Zoroastrianism versus militant Roman Christianity. The period also saw militant Judaism in the hands of an Arab prince in Yemen with Dhu Nawas' religious offensive against the Christians. Furthermore, both powers used Arab allies to fight each other in proxy wars: Persian Lakhmids versus Roman Ghassanids. This combination of militant monotheism with resurgant Arab power was to have profound implications, particularly when we realise that Heraclius' proclamation of holy war has its exact counterpart in the Islamic concept of *jihad*, first traditionally articulated by Muhammad in the very same year—622—when Heraclius formulated his.

In one of the most spectacular recoveries fought by any Roman emperor, Heraclius was able to save the tottering Roman Empire from the brink of collapse. It appeared that out of this increasingly bitter conflict one or other of the powers would fall. But in the end both Iran and Rome were defeated at the hands of an entirely new power from the fringes of the civilised Near East who wielded the same concept of Holy War that Heraclius had formulated: the Arabs under Islam. The two great powers of Persia and Rome had fought each other to exhaustion, making conquest easy for the Arabs, and less than a century later these unknown desert Arabs with their revolutionary new monotheism ruled an empire that stretched from the borders of China to the Atlantic, an empire far greater than Cyrus or Shapur, Caesar or Alexander, could ever have conceived. The age of Islam had arrived.

While the peace of 629 appeared to change nothing, this war to the death between the two great powers of Rome and Iran in the end actually changed everything. It changed the two main protagonists themselves. The

Roman Empire changed from the ancient empire of the Caesars that it had been up until that time to become the Byzantine empire of medieval history. Iran changed more radically, seeing the end of the ancient Persian civilisation of antiquity and the beginning of the great ages of Persian Islamic civilisation. The formulation of holy war by Heraclius and his contemporaries, turning killing into an act of sacred piety sanctioned by the almighty himself, unleashed hell, a spectre that still haunts us today. The period ushered in the beginning of what was probably the biggest single factor in world history for the next millennium: Islamic civilisation. It saw entirely new peoples beginning to move towards the eastern Mediterranean arena: the Slavs from one direction resulting in the Slavicisation of the Balkans, and the Turks from the other to result, centuries later, in the Turkification of Anatolia and culminating in the rise of Turkish power in Europe. It saw the Huns being deflected from the Near East around the Black Sea to enter Europe by the back door, the last and the most savage of the barbarian invasions that finally brought about the end of antiquity in the west and ushered in the European Dark Ages. The war had a ripple effect right across the Eurasian continent and beyond, affecting countries as far away as Italy, North Africa, Ethiopia, Ceylon and even China, where it affected the beginnings of the T'ang Dynasty.

It has, therefore, been rightly dubbed 'the last great war of antiquity'. But it was more: it was also the first war that involved countries and events well beyond those of the actual protagonists. It was the first war that used grand encircling tactics on a global stage to outflank the enemy in territories well beyond their own: from Persians negotiating with Avars of Central Europe to Romans negotiating with Turks of Central Asia; from Ostrogoths sending secret envoys to Ctesiphon to Romans sending envoys to Aksum. It was a war that used religious propaganda as a weapon; a war that intercepted and used secret intelligence; a war that used proxies on both sides in a 'cold war' when both powers were theoretically at peace. A war that brought about profound ethnic changes—Slavs, Turks, Arabs—over much of the known world. A war that was fought on fronts in the Near East, Anatolia, the Balkans, Italy, North Africa, the Red Sea, the Caucasus, Iran and Central Asia. Not quite a 'first world war'—that would have to wait until the sixteenth century—but certainly the first war to be fought on a world-wide stage. As well as the last great war of antiquity, it was equally, therefore, the first great war of the modern era. Most of all, it was a war that probably brought about more long-term changes than any other in history.

Nothing demonstrated more the central position of Persia as a world power. With this war we see the end of a succession of ancient empires in Iran that began with Cyrus. It was also the end of over a thousand years of a complex interaction with the west. Persian civilisation was, of course, soon to demonstrate its resilience by emerging phoenix-like out of the ashes into the brilliance of medieval Islamic Iran. But that would be a changed new Persia and a changed interaction with the west: with the ending of the old Persia, the old world also ended. In assessing the legacy of this interaction we leave the historical narrative to examine perhaps the single most powerful idea bequeathed by the Iranians to the world.

Chapter 7

LIGHT AND DARKNESS
Iranian Religious Ideas

If the world had not become Christian it would
have become Mithraic.

Ernst Renan

These often quoted remarks by the nineteenth century French philosopher and historian of Christianity are not now regarded as prophetic as they once were. But they do nonetheless underline how important the impact of Iranian religious ideas has been. Like any civilisation, the Iranian one has created a huge pantheon of gods, goddesses and demons, and a rich mythology of heroes, villains, tales, legends, beliefs, religions and philosophies. Indeed, it is through religion that Iran probably has its greatest effect upon the world today—or at least its policies in the name of religion. But Iranian religious ideas affected the world long before the birth of the Islamic Republic in 1979. This has mainly been through Zoroastrianism in its various forms and derivations, probably the world's oldest creedal religion, which has influenced the Judeo-Christian religions in often surprising ways.

Before outlining the main elements of Zoroastrianism, however, we will examine briefly some of the pre—or at least—non-Zoroastrian elements within Iranian religion. Chief of these are the gods and goddesses of ancient Iran, some of which percolated into the Graeco-Roman pantheon, albeit in different guises. Of course, to some extent Zoroastrianism incorporated these gods and goddesses, particularly the supreme god, Ahura Mazda, all of which came to be viewed as manifestations—or emanations—of the supreme deity. But Ahura Mazda was also invoked independently, such as in the Achaemenid royal inscriptions in whose name all of the kings nominally ruled. Hence, the mere mention of Ahura Mazda may not necessarily be evidence of Zoroastrianism (although equally it is not necessarily evidence of its absence). Ahura Mazda entered Anatolia where he was naturally equated with Zeus, and we have already observed (in Chapter 5) how he also entered Georgia, and neither occurrences were necessarily Zoroastrian. The Zoroastrian Ahura Mazda—along with his opposite Angra Mainyu, or Ahriman—is discussed further below.

Other significant Iranian deities that became familiar in the Graeco-Roman world were Anahita, Verethragna and Mithra. Anahita was the goddess of the waters (the one main female deity of the Iranian pantheon), hence the source of rain, springs and the ocean: her cults were often located at springs and other water sources. She entered Anatolia as Anaïtis, where her worship was often assimilated with that of Artemis, herself a far older Anatolian mother-goddess cult rather than the more familiar Graeco-Roman goddess of the same name. Verethragna was the warrior god, hence in Zoroastrian terms a manifestation of the struggle against evil rather than a separate deity. Verethragna was assimilated (unsurprisingly) with Heracles—and the Heracles cult was particularly popular amongst the Greeks of Central Asia because of this. Mithra is discussed further below.

There were also numerous semi-divine or mythical demons and fabulous creatures. Pre-Zoroastrian religion in Central Asia had divine beings known as *daevas*. Under Zoroastrianism these beings were changed into personifications of evil, but those Indo-Iranian tribes who migrated to India before Zoroaster's message retained the original meaning of these beings, and in India they are known as *devs*. These two diametrically opposite meanings of the same word—good and evil—are reflected in English, where the root word *daeva/ dev* has evolved to mean both good ('divine', 'deity', 'devotion', etc. and further back Greek 'Zeus', Latin 'deus', 'theus', hence 'theology' etc) and bad ('devil', 'diabolic', etc). Although perhaps not explicitly intended by Zoroaster, this dual meaning does nonetheless appropriately reflect the opposite pulls within Mankind that lie at the root of Zoroaster's message.

Of particular significance in Iranian mythology was the *senmurv*, the 'great all-seeing all-knowing bird' who sits on top of the *Saena* Tree, the 'Tree of All Seeds' or 'Tree of All Remedies', which grows in the middle of the Vorukasha Sea. As such it is seen to offer protection, but is also the giver of life as well as knowledge. To some extent this was assimilated into various tree of life symbols, and the Senmurv also became a popular motif in art, pre-Islamic as well as Islamic and Christian (Pl. 50). There is also a huge range of myths, legends and great tales, both semi-historical and legendary, that are gathered together in Firdausi's great eleventh century epic, the *Shahnameh*. This is one of the great classics of world literature that has certainly found its echoes in later literature, but this influence is more cultural than religious.

THE AGE OF ZOROASTER*

Perhaps the single most important cultural element that the Iranian tribes brought with them from Central Asia was an idea that had a profound effect upon subsequent history. This was the Zoroastrian religion. The main historian of Zoroastrianism, Mary Boyce, has written that 'Zoroastrianism is the oldest of the revealed credal religions, and it has probably had more influence on mankind, directly and indirectly, than any other single faith.'[1] Zoroastrianism was first transmitted orally but later written down in the *Avesta*, revered by Zoroastrians as a sacred revelation. Many Zoroastrians now believe the original homeland of Zoroaster to be Azerbaijan; perhaps there is an association with the sacred fires that emerge naturally from the ground because of the vast oil and natural gas deposits there (Pl. 82). Azerbaijan, therefore, has assumed the status of a Zoroastrian 'holy land', but this is now regarded as a later interpolation.[†] Another Zoroastrian 'sacred landscape' is associated with Mt Damavand in the Alburz Range (Harburz in the *Avesta*) of northern Iran (Pl. 83), which is identified with the first mountain in the Zoroastrian creation myth. However, Central Asia is now more generally accepted as Zoroaster's homeland. Much of the discussion has centred on Bactria (southern Uzbekistan and northern Afghanistan); Chorasmia in the region of the lower Oxus near the Aral Sea has also gained

---

* Zoroaster is the usual form of the name in English, but Nietzsche and Richard Strauss have made the German form of Zarathustra almost as familiar. The modern Persian form is Zardusht. The film director John Borman may have derived the name of his 1974 cult science fiction film *Zardoz* (Sean Connery's first major film since James Bond) from this, the name of a god in a post-apocalyptic world. Although any resemblance to Zoroastrianism is unintended, a central theme of the film is the perceived evil of sexual regeneration which finds its echoes in Manichaeism. The name also re-emerges as Mozart's Sarastro, the enlightened sovereign in *The Magic Flute*, famous for its Masonic rather than Zoroastrian references.

† The association of Azerbaijan with Zoroaster's homeland received a curious tribute with the exploitation of Azerbaijan's vast oil resources in Baku in the late 19th century by the Swedish Nobel brothers, amongst the world's first oil tycoons (whose wealth still underpins the Nobel Prize today). This resulted in the launch in Gothenburg of the world's very first oil tanker in 1878, which they named the *Zoroaster*. The *Zoroaster's* maiden voyage was from Gothenburg to Baku via the Volga River and the Caspian Sea later that year, where it entered service at Baku carrying oil to Astrakhan.

wide currency, although one recent study places his homeland in Margiana in southern Turkmenistan, while another in the Pamirs on the Upper Oxus. Others have placed Zoroaster as far north as southern Kazakhstan or even the southern Urals, prior to the migration of the Iranian tribes southwards in the Bronze Age. Whatever the exact location, a Central Asian origin of Zoroastrianism—the same original homeland of the Iranian peoples themselves—is not seriously in doubt.[2]

The date for Zoroaster is similarly widely divergent. The main dating evidence is the language of the sacred texts themselves, the *Avesta*. The texts were probably first written down in about the ninth (or perhaps as early as sixth) century AD, and the earliest surviving manuscript fragments are thirteenth century.* However, the form of the language that had been orally preserved bore little resemblance to the Sasanian Middle Persian of the time but was an archaic form of Persian. The language of the oldest portions of the *Avesta* (the *Gathas*, which is the only part that may be ascribed to Zoroaster himself) appears closest to the sacred Vedic texts of Brahmanism, and possibly even older. Max Müller's dating of the Vedic texts to about 1400 BC are still generally accepted; hence, this suggests that Zoroaster may have lived before the Indo-Aryan migrations into Iran and India. However, these portions contain no geographical indicators; the only portions that do are later portions of the *Avesta* written in a language closer to the Old Persian of the Achaemenid inscriptions, which contains specific references to places located in Central Asia and the Indo-Iranian borderlands. Hence, some studies have put the date of Zoroaster as late as the sixth century BC and others as early as about 2000 BC; Mary Boyce, probably our main authority on Zoroastrianism, dates Zoroaster somewhere between about 1700 and 1500 BC, although this might be an extreme view. Most modern scholarship now regards Zoroaster as having lived in about 1000-900 BC, but there is no consensus.

Oral tradition is a powerful method of recording history and it has particularly flourished in Iran. This has already been remarked upon in relation to the Achaemenids in Chapter 1 and even today Iran still maintains a high oral tradition (where professional travelling story-tellers will recite the *Shahnameh* and other tales from the epics). The suggestion that such a huge body of religious literature could survive for thousands of years purely by being transmitted orally is, therefore, a convincing one—indeed, the oral

---

* There is now a quasi consensus on the sixth century AD as the date when the *Avesta* was first put into writing (Frantz Grenet, pers. comm.)

transmission of religious belief was regarded as a sacred Zoroastrian duty (and the tradition continues in Islam where it is considered meritorious to be able to recite the Qur'an by heart). Religious precepts were only written down when they diverged significantly from the mainstream (such as Manichaeism, discussed below) or when its preservation became threatened in the face of the increasing challenge from Islam in the ninth century. This lack of historical record has presented scholars with a similar dearth of original sources that plagues Alexander studies that was discussed in Chapter 4 (and scholarly debate over Zoroaster is almost as heated as that which rages over Alexander). It has also led to the suggestion that by the time the texts were set to paper—in the ninth century—they must have absorbed a considerable amount of Christianity, Islam and a whole range of other beliefs as well. But even though the texts are thousands of years after the events and beliefs that they describe (making the four and a half centuries separating Arrian and Alexander a mere moment), the fact that the archaic form of the language was regarded as unalterable does indicate that the message it was expressing was similarly regarded.

In support of an early date for the birth of Zoroastrianism has been the excavation of some fire temples dating to the early first millennium BC. The most significant is that at Tepe Nushijan near Hamadan in western Iran, dated to the Median period (Pl. 84). The site appears to have been a sacred one with two fire temples: an older one that was replaced by a much larger newer one, standing to a height of eight metres, that still preserves its inner fire altar together with a spiral ramp leading to the roof (presumably for the display of the public fire), in keeping with Zoroastrian practice. Its extraordinary state of preservation (it is one of the best preserved ancient mud-brick buildings in Iran) was due to its having been ritually closed and the entire temple encased in brick. Both the fully developed architecture of Nushijan and its date in the Median period (eighth-sixth centuries BC) suggest that some form of fire cult arrived with the Iranian migrations and was a mature religion by the time of the Median Empire. It is difficult to believe that this was not Zoroastrianism. Another, probably slightly earlier, fire temple has been excavated at Gonur Tepe near Merv in Turkmenistan, belonging within a tradition of similar Central Asian temples going back to the Bronze Age. However, while the identification of these buildings as fire temples is established, there may have been a form of fire cult not associated with Zoroaster.[3] Suffice it to say that the Central Asian origins and very early date for Zoroaster are not seriously in doubt.

ZOROASTER'S MESSAGE

Zoroastrianism was the first religion with a concept of a hopeful hereafter offering a day of judgement, salvation, resurrection and paradise, rather than the amorphous netherworld of Greek or Judaic traditions. It was the first to articulate the idea of an ascent to a form of heavenly existence after death. It was the first religion to introduce an entirely abstract notion of deity representing the concept of purity and goodness, of the universal single god, of god the creator.* The idea that 'God is good' has become so much an accepted part of the Christian and Muslim faiths that it is now taken for granted, but it must be remembered that the idea was quite revolutionary in the Mediterranean world in antiquity: the pagan gods—the gods of the Greeks and Romans—were both good and bad; they could be philanderous or chaste, vain or modest, generous, moody or cruel—in fact gods reflected the full range of human behaviour, their only difference with Man being their immortality. They were rarely, if ever, *good*! Even the god of the Old Testament was to some extent a severe, vengeful deity; the Christian concept resembles more the Zoroastrian than the Judaic one.

Zoroaster taught that women as well as men, slave as well as master, rich as well as poor, may all enter Paradise. After death, all are required to cross a bridge, called in the *Avesta* 'the Bridge of the Separator', leading to Paradise. The righteous were able to cross and directly enter Paradise; for those who were not, the bridge would narrow to razor-sharp width and they would be seized by a demon and fall into Darkness. The tradition has survived into modern Iranian popular belief: nineteenth century shrine paintings depicting the martyrdom of Husain, for example, show the bridge to Paradise which Husain enters, but his enemies falling off into the clutches of a monster and Hell. According to a variant of this tradition, the after-world involved the crossing of a river or lake guarded by four-eyed hounds—a possible origin of the River Styx and Cerberus in Greek tradition. Dogs in Zoroastrianism were regarded as the intermediary with the dead.[4]

Zoroaster's message is essentially dualist: the concept of good and evil, light and darkness, the truth and the lie. The two concepts are known as *Ahura Mazda* and *Angra Mainyu* (or *Ahriman* in its better known Middle Persian form). These two concepts are entirely distinct, unrelated and

---

* 'Second Isaiah, brought into contact in Babylon with Persian propagandists, developed in striking ways the belief in Yahweh as God alone and Creator of all, thus, it seems, both vying with Zoroaster's concept of Ahura Mazda as Creator of all that is good and at the same time rejecting his dualism'—Boyce and Grenet 1991: 361 and fn. 2.

uncreated, unlike the Christian concept of good and evil where they are ultimately related (in the tradition of the fallen angel—although Zoroastrian tradition did include three fallen deities: Indra, Nanhaithya and Savra, who became devils). Central to the message is the idea of three times. The 'first time' was a state of perfection created by Ahura Mazda comprising one man, one animal and one plant in a perfect world. This, however, was invaded by Angra Mainyu who destroyed the first man, thus bringing about the 'second time', or present time. Ahura Mazda therefore created the first man and woman, from whom all of mankind are descended, to battle Angra Mainyu, but the perfect world by this time was polluted by Angra Mainyu: the first man and woman had lost their innocence through temptation, pure water had become polluted by salt, fire by black smoke, life by suffering, and so forth. In other words, all of creation had become a mixture of good and evil. Zoroaster's message was to make mankind aware of their inner, unpolluted perfection and offer redemption: an escape from suffering. This could be brought about by the practice of good thoughts, good words and good deeds in the battle against 'the lie'. (It is notable that telling the truth was the one quality of the ancient Persians that was particularly emphasised by Herodotus).

The conflict between good and evil was not indefinite, for it was believed that right worship and good actions would ultimately usher in the 'third time', aided by the *Saoshyant*—literally 'one who will bring benefit,' i.e., 'saviour' or 'redeemer'*—who would ultimately appear and overthrow the forces of darkness, beginning a new era of rule by the forces of light. The *Saoshyant*, moreover, was to be born of a virgin from the family of Vishtaspa, the prophet Zoroaster's own family and the name of a mythical king of Bactria. The *Saoshyant* would then oversee and judge all the living and the dead, with the righteous sent to the highest heaven and the wicked

---

* The term *saoŝyant* is the future form of the word *savah* in Avestan, meaning 'benefit'—see Boyce 1996: 234. It is interesting that a variant of this word, *Sāvah*, is the name of the town in central Iran where, according to tradition, the Three Magi began their journey to Bethlehem. Boyce and Grenet 1991: 448-56. According to Friar Odoric, the Three Magi began their journey from 'Cassan': Kashan in Iran. According to Marco Polo it was from Saveh. Both locations, and their associations with Zoroastrianism, are discussed by Yule and Cordier. It is possible that Saveh/Sava might be a mis-identification with Saba in South Arabia, the Sheba of Psalms lxx11.10. Yule/Cordier *Cathay*: 106-7. It has also been suggested that the origin of the Christian tradition of the journey of the magi lay in the Armenian King Tiradates' journey to Rome to receive his crown from Nero: Tiradates was believed to be a practising Zoroastrian priest, or Magus. See Redgrave 1998: 2.

cast into hell. This third and final time would be a state of perfection where evil is finally destroyed, lasting for eternity.[5]

Zoroastrians regard the basic elements of earth, fire, water and air as the sacred creations of Ahura Mazda, hence not to be polluted by corruption or uncleanliness, regarded as the work of Ahriman. This has given rise to the Zoroastrian practice of exposure of the dead, a decomposing cadaver being regarded as corrupting the sacred earth if buried or fire if cremated (Pl. 85). Once a cadaver has been de-fleshed the bones are regarded as clean and can be disposed of in ossuaries. In fact the practice of exposure was far more widely spread in ancient times than it is now, Zoroastrianism being practically its only remnant.* Their regard for the sacred fire—as a manifestation of the forces of light—has led to Zoroastrians being erroneously labelled 'fire-worshippers' (Pls 82, 86), but Zoroastrians are no more fire-worshippers than Christians are crucifix-worshippers (although popular practice and beliefs vary enormously in all religions).

Zoroastrianism was governed by a priestly hierarchy, termed the magi. A priestly hierarchy is a perennial theme in Iranian tradition. Its exact origins are uncertain: it may antedate Zoroaster, going back to early Iranian origins in Central Asia. When Indo-Iranian tribes migrated to India in the second millennium BC the idea of an hereditary high priesthood went with them and became the Brahmans, the Indo-Iranian overlay on Hinduism. The institution of the magi followed Iranian migrations to the Iranian plateau too, becoming a specific religious caste (possibly originally Median rather than Persian) who became the guardians of Zoroastrian tradition. To some extent the magi were a priestly caste independent of Zoroastrianism, so their presence does not necessarily indicate the existence of Zoroastrianism. The magi are attested in the Achaemenid period at Persepolis. The caste soon broadened greatly, in both ethnic and religious terms, and the magi even presided over Elamite rituals according to Achaemenid documents.[6] There is overwhelming evidence for a priestly hierarchy by the Sasanian period, integrated into the state apparatus. If there was not a priest or high priest breathing down the neck of a Sasanian official it was because the official himself was a priest.[7]

The idea of the magi remained an integral part of Iranian society: many important Iranian dynasties, such as the Sasanians, the Barmakids, the Samanids and the Safavids, began as hereditary priestly families or were

---

* The practice was outlawed in Iran for hygienic reasons, and Zoroastrians now dispose of their dead in concrete lined burials.

at least founded by priests, and the tradition continued unbroken into the Islamic period. Papak, the founder of the Sasanian dynasty and the father of Ardashir, its first king, was a hereditary warden at the temple of Anahita at Istakhr near Persepolis. The Barmakids were a family of prominent viziers and governors under the early ᶜAbbasids of Baghdad who in origin were a family of hereditary wardens at the great Buddhist temple of Nau Bahar at Balkh. Another Buddhist allusion (although this is less certain) is contained in the Samanid dynasty of Bukhara, the first independent Iranian rulers to emerge in Central Asia after the Islamic conquest: the Samanids derive their name from the village of *Saman*, a word that means 'Buddhist priest'.* Perhaps the greatest of the Iranian dynasties of the Islamic period, the Safavids, was founded by Shaikh Safi, a Sufi mystic and priest. Today, it is notable that Iran is the only country in the Islamic world which has a structured priestly hierarchy (the mullahs and ayatollahs).

Needless to say, any outline of Zoroastrianism is of necessity speculative. That it predates most of the world's great religions is fairly certain. However, its extant sacred books do not predate the ninth century (or perhaps the sixth century) when contact with Judaism and Christianity had become established. There is, therefore, much disagreement over what influences went which way, among both scholars and practising Zoroastrians themselves. Up until the ninth century the Zoroastrian sacred traditions had only been transmitted orally, and it was the challenge from Christianity that probably created the need for a less ephemeral repository. In setting down these oral traditions into text, the priests preserved more than the traditions: they preserved a language that had already been dead for some two thousand years. One cannot imagine, therefore, that in preserving the language the message would be lost: that the one would be as old as the other.

MITHRAIC MYSTERIES

The ancient Greeks and, to a lesser extent, the Romans appear to have had only a vague—and often confused—understanding of Iranian religion. Often their knowledge came via—and was influenced by—the Hellenised climate of Babylon, where it became mixed with magic (a word which ultimately is derived from the Persian 'magi') and astrology. But the one

---

* From the same Sanskrit root that English gets its loan word 'Shaman' or Hindi *Ashram*. 'Bukhara' itself might derive from the word *bahar* meaning 'Buddhist monastery'.

'Iranian' religion which was familiar to the Romans was Mithraism, the architectural remains of which have been found throughout the Roman world from the Euphrates to Hadrian's Wall, particularly along the northern frontiers (Pl. 87).[8] Several emperors, from Nero to Galerius, toyed with Mithraism, and so popular did Mithraism become in the Roman world—particularly in the army—that Ernst Renan famously stated 'if the world had not become Christian it would have become Mithraic' which would have been a triumph of Iranian religion indeed.

For all its popularity, Mithraism could never have pre-empted Christianity: it specifically excluded women which, whilst not necessarily a prerequisite for a major religion, does not exactly help if one is to exclude fifty percent of the population—and the triumph of Christianity was to a large extent a triumph of women.[9] Mithraism was also probably less popular than is often thought: Mithraeums were extremely small, which hardly suggests a large congregation. Indeed, it is unlikely that it was practised much outside the Roman army. But more important, how Iranian was Mithraism?

Mithra was certainly one of the most ancient of Iranian deities—indeed, it probably pre-dates the emergence of Zoroastrianism, for the name first occurs in Mitanni inscriptions in the Near East in the mid-second millennium BC, along with other ancient Aryan deities such as Varuna and Indra.* Mithra also entered the Indian pantheon very early. The name occurs in the *Avesta* where it means 'pact' or 'covenant' as a guide towards the truth, i.e., light in the Zoroastrian religion. For this reason Mithra became associated with the sun, becoming a sun god in both Iran and India and associated with Helios in Greece. The earlier associations also meant that Mithra came to be seen as a protector against evil, or Ahriman, armed with a club or a mace. Hence, it was a particularly popular theophoric name for warrior-kings: both Parthian and Pontic kings, for example, were named Mithradates, 'given by Mithra'. A solar disc discovered on the tomb of Cyrus suggests that Cyrus himself might have been a devotee of Mithra. The mace of Mithra itself came to symbolise the struggle against evil, and to this day a symbolic mace of Mithra is a part of Zoroastrian priestly accoutrement. The festival of Mithra was celebrated at the autumn equinox, and today

---

* Mitanni is the name of a second millennium BC kingdom of the middle Tigris-Euphrates region—roughly northern Syria and Iraq today—that, after about 1450 BC, became a major power in the Near East who subjugated the Assyrians and challenged both the Egyptians and the Hittites. Their language was known as Hurrian, of uncertain linguistic affiliation, but some documents of the kingdom's elite are in an Indo-European language, which numbered Mithra amongst the gods.

the month in the modern Iranian calendar when this occurs (September-October) is still called *Mihr*, the modern Persian form of Mithra.

There are practically none of these observances in the Mithraism that came to be practised in the Roman Empire. Here, it was an esoteric mystery cult attended by small numbers of initiates, each one of whom had to undergo seven grades of initiation (perhaps a reference to the seven heavenly bodies in Zoroastrianism). Mithraeums were either in caves or built to appear like caves, perhaps symbolising the cosmic cave. Rituals were preceded by a sacred meal and culminated in the sacrifice of a bull, symbolising Mithra himself slaying the bull. Almost none of this would have been remotely familiar to a Zoroastrian from Iran. It is notable that there are no records of magi presiding in Roman Mithraism, even though they were apparently willing to preside in other Roman cults (such as, on one occasion at least, even the official cult of Rome and Augustus—see below, Chapter 8). This suggests magian contempt for a heresy.

However, it must be said that we actually know very little about either the beliefs or the practice of Roman Mithraism. As Robert Turcan rightly points out in his study of Roman cults, it is as if future knowledge of Christianity could only be based upon the Old Testament and the carved iconography that had survived on the occasional cathedral. It may have incorporated more Iranian elements than we now know, however obscurely. The bull was, after all, a popular motif in Achaemenid art and may well have had religious meaning (we simply do not know), and images of either a bull being slain by a lion or the king slaying a beast recur frequently at Persepolis, and almost certainly conveyed a religious message (Pl. 20). The excavator of the Mithraeum at Dura Europos, Clark Hopkins, recognised more of an Iranian element there, and Mithraism was particularly popular among Roman troops of eastern origin: Syrians, Palmyrenes and Commagenians.[10]

THE TEACHINGS OF MANI

However Iranian Mithraism might or might not have been, it bore virtually no trace of any of Zoroaster's central messages: the universal creator, the struggle between good and evil, redemption and a hopeful hereafter. Zoroastrianism, therefore, did not enter the west through Mithraism, but a derivation from it did. This was Manichaeism, a syncretic religion proclaimed by the prophet Mani in the third century. Since Manichaeism was to have an enormous effect upon Europe—indeed, the word 'Manichaean' has entered our language—it is important to outline the religion in some detail in order to appreciate fully this effect.

Mani was born of Iranian parents in southern Mesopotamia in 216, a region that was wide open to many diverse religious elements. Hence, Manichaeism incorporated many elements of Zoroastrianism and acknowledged Zoroaster, Buddha and Jesus as the predecessors of Mani. Manichaeism also incorporated elements of Gnosticism and neo-Platonism. Its main sacred book was the *Shabuhragan*, written by Mani for Shapur I, but there are various other works, mainly the 'Seven Scriptures', also written by Mani. Mani himself was a noted calligrapher who encouraged calligraphy as a sacred task in order to revere the sacred texts. These texts have survived only in fragmentary or derivative forms (and mainly only recovered in modern times through archaeological investigations in places as far apart as Egypt and Chinese Central Asia).[11]

Like Zoroastrianism, Manichaeism teaches a basic dualism of light and darkness, the 'two principles'. There are in addition the 'three times' or 'conditions': Primeval time, when good and evil are separate, Present time, when both are mixed, and Future, or eschatological time, when they separate again. The dualism is Iranian, i.e., evil is an entirely separate, uncreated entity and not derived from good (such as the Christian fallen angel).[12] Evil is the exact antithesis of good from the very beginning: light and darkness, spirit (good) and matter (bad); these are the two 'natures' or 'substances'.

Both substances exist in Man in opposition: hence Man is the battlefield of good and evil. Physical nature—matter—is in constant struggle with the spirit or soul, the substance of which is divine light. Man's present state is determined by the mix; the mixture of the two led to unhappiness and suffering in the world. The aim of both human and divine activity is to recreate the original 'time' or condition by distilling and separating the light from the matter.

To help in this aim, the divine world (the world of light, or world of original condition) sends 'Man the Nous' to both reveal the knowledge of original 'home' (condition or time) and the final destination (the Third Time or condition) and to teach how to achieve this, for Man is in a 'sleep of forgetfulness'. The purpose of human life or existence, therefore, is redemption or salvation to achieve unity with the creator, or ultimate condition, and to help to save other souls of 'light elements' that are bound in matter.

The highest godhead is the 'Father of Light', not expressed in images but in emanations. The Father of Lights is the embodiment of light, beauty, perfection, and all that is good. In order to recapture the Light that is captive in Darkness, the Father of Light (or 'Lord of Greatness') evokes the Mother of Living, the First Man, and other supporting deities. These 'deities', therefore, are strictly speaking just emanations of the Father of Light, not separate beings or gods, thus preserving an abstract monotheism. The 'Evocation' of these emanations is important; they were evoked rather than created, there is no hint of reproduction or generation out of union (which is regarded as the work of darkness, as it was through procreation that Darkness made captive the particles of Light). Hence, sexual reproduction is regarded as the work of darkness.

THE TWO PRINCIPLES

The concept of 'two principles' was the fundamental message of Manichaeism, and it was this idea above all that was to remain with the dualist religions down to the Middle Ages. Hence, it is worth examining it in detail in order to understand the background of the Medieval dualist religious movements in Europe discussed in Chapter 9. The Realm of Light is the exact antithesis of the Realm of Darkness. It is ruled by the 'Father of Light' or the 'Father of Greatness', Zuraon. He has five attributes: Reason, Mind, Intelligence, Thought and Understanding. Figuratively, these attributes are called 'limbs'. The Father of Light is both the origin and the sum total of all that is divine, including other deities: the concept is both abstract and monotheistic. It has three other attributes: Light, Power and Wisdom. The Realm of Light is also inhabited by the Great Spirit, a 'twin' of the Father of Light.

The Realm of Darkness has five corresponding attributes: Dark Reason, Dark Mind, and so forth, corresponding to the five Light attributes. This is also referred to as the five dark elements: smoke, fire, wind, water and darkness. From this spring the five 'trees of death'. These are related to the five animal-demons who inhabit the five dark worlds: bipeds, quadrupeds, flying creatures, swimming creatures and crawling creatures, which are characterised by bestial urges and all that is abhorrent. There are male and female in each category, arousing sexual urges (which are evil) in each other. Animal demons are represented by the demon, lion, eagle, fish and dragon. These are the kings of the five dark worlds, who represent their inhabitants.

The king of the dark realm is Satan, combining all the five hideous forms in one. It personifies matter (evil), equivalent to Zoroastrian Ahriman.

THE THREE COSMOLOGICAL ACTS OR CREATIONS

In 'First Creation' in the beginning of time, the Realms of Light and Darkness were completely separate. Darkness saw Light and wanted to partake of it, so did battle with Light. To help in the battle, the Father of Light called forth the 'Mother of Living'. This is the 'First Evocation'. The Mother of Living (or 'Mother of All') created the 'First Man' or 'Primal Man' *(Ohrmizd)*, who was armed with the 'Five elements of Light' or the 'Five Bright Elements' of Ether, Wind, Light, Water and Fire. The Primal Man is defeated and the forces of darkness devoured the Elements of Light resulting in a mixture of Light and Darkness. This mixture is the present world. Having tasted Light, Darkness becomes addicted and does not relinquish it.

In the 'Second Creation' the First Man is thus defeated, lying in Darkness. He asks the Father of Light for help. Therefore the Father of Light evokes, or sends forth, more 'Beings of Light' to help in this struggle. This is the 'Second Evocation': the 'Friend of Light', who in turn sends forth the 'Great Builder', who in turn sends forth the 'Living Spirit', who, like the First Man, has five 'sons' or 'limbs' or characteristics: King of Splendour, King of Honour, the *Adamas* of Light, King of Glory and Atlas. The First Man is roused by a series of 'calls' and 'answers' by the Living Spirit and the Archons of Darkness are defeated. He is led back to Light by the Living Spirit and the Mother of Life. This represents salvation. The Living Spirit then created the world, after saving the First Man, as a means of recovering the Light that was still in captivity in the Realm of Darkness. To create the world, therefore, it was necessary to use mixed Light and Darkness. There are eight earths and ten heavens, all stacked. The Sun and the Moon were created out of the pure Light that had been saved. The Stars were created out of Light still contaminated by Darkness (which is matter, evil). Cosmic 'wheels' were created of fire, water and wind to purify and process Light that was redeemed or saved from Darkness and return it to the original Realm of Light.

In the 'Third Creation' the Father of Greatness, through the Third Messenger which he calls into being (this is the 'Third Evocation'), extracts the remaining Light still retained by Darkness. There is a rather convoluted myth involving sexual lust (equated with darkness) which brings forth five kinds of living creatures. Then a path to Paradise is created, visible as the Milky Way, to conduct redeemed Light to the New Paradise. This New Paradise is separated from the original Realm of Light to be a halfway house for redeemed Light, so that the Realm of Light remains completely untouched by all the disruption caused by welcoming redeemed Light back into the fold: the Realm of Light must remain absolutely pure and uncontaminated. This New Paradise is ruled by the First Man. The world is then set into motion: day, night, the seasons, etc., by making the Sun and Moon assume their motions. These two celestial bodies also fulfil their redeeming functions: the moon waxes as it fills up with Light redeemed from the world, and wanes as it passes it onto the Sun. From the Sun it passes to the New Paradise. Hence, the Sun and Moon are the residences, or thrones, of the redeeming bodies, or deities. In the Sun resides the Third Messenger (of the Third Creation), the Mother of Life, or the Living Spirit. In the Moon resides the Light Messenger Jesus, known as 'Jesus the Splendour', as well as the Maiden of Light and the First Man ('Lord of the New Paradise'). These are the saving or redeeming bodies (beings or deities). Other deities are called to life: the Great *Nous* ('Reason' or *Vahman*), and the Just Judge. The five 'limbs' or attributes of the Great Nous are the same as the Realm of Light and every soul, namely: reason (*nous*), mind, intelligence, thought, understanding.

In order to halt the process of extracting the Light back from Darkness, Darkness imprisons the remaining Light in Man, which it creates. It must be emphasised, therefore, that Man is a creation of Darkness, not of Light or of God, and this is the fundamental difference with the Judeo-Christian religions. The Light is the soul; Darkness is the body (equivalent to matter), which is created by Darkness (or matter). By the process of reproduction, the Light remains constantly imprisoned by the body from one generation to the next. Sex by definition is equivalent to evil: the concept of female and male (sex), therefore, is the creation of Darkness in order to retain captive Light. Man, however, is oblivious of his own soul, or the divine Light within him. In order to redeem Man's divine self, Jesus is sent.

'Jesus the Splendour' is an emanation of the Third Messenger. He is a redeeming emissary from the World of Light specifically for Man. He brought forth knowledge *(gnosis)* of his origin, his soul (Light) and ultimate salvation to Adam. Adam was created by Darkness to keep Light imprisoned; Light—ones' soul—is within Adam. Darkness also created Eve. Note that

Darkness creates by *generation*; Light creates by *evocation* or emanation. Eve was seduced by a demon, bringing forth Cain and Abel. Eve and Adam brought forth Seth. Mankind, therefore, is created from Darkness, but containing particles of imprisoned Light: Mankind is a compound of Light and Darkness. Jesus continues to bring Man redeeming knowledge. The Maiden of Light and the Great Nous fulfil the same function. Jesus also appears at the end of the world as the judge. Jesus is also the Messiah, as Jesus of Nazareth, who lived and died a man. There are, therefore, three Jesuses. Jesus the Messiah is the embodiment of suffering caused by the mixture of body and soul, or Darkness and Light; he is the immediate forerunner of Mani the prophet; Mani is the apostle of Jesus. The Great Nous is an emanation of Jesus the Splendour. The Great Nous is the inspiration of all great religious leaders, including Zoroaster and Buddha. He is also, therefore, called the 'Father of Apostles'.

The End of Time

Salvation is achieved through knowledge of the soul's origin and through a perfect ethical code. Perfect life leads to conditional salvation (through continual confession) and full salvation after death. Those who achieve conditional salvation are the 'Elect' or the 'Perfects'. Laymen who are merely good, but do not reject the material life, can hope for reincarnation as the Elect.

The task of winning back Light or Good from the world inevitably and logically means that only evil will be left remaining in the material world. This leads to a last great war, which leads to the end of the world. Jesus reappears as the judge between salvation and damnation before returning to the Realm of Light. Since all light is now restored, all other supporting deities, or emanations, merge back into the Realm of Light. The world collapses and fire consumes it. The last remaining redeemed Light returns; everything else, including Ne (temporary) Paradise merges back into the Realm of Light now that the work of redeeming captive light is done. Matter or Darkness once again becomes completely separate as it was at the beginning of time, collected into a vast mass or 'lump', sealed off from the Realm of Light, and this state remains for eternity.

Manichaeism is in many ways the most rigidly logical of all the great religions, that sought to explain all of creation and to follow existence

151

through to its ultimate conclusion in a manner that in some ways anticipates modern theories of the beginnings and end of the universe. It is probably the most cerebral of revealed religions, an appeal which perhaps explains its enormous success: its spread not only into Europe (see Chapter 9) but also into Central Asia and China, where it was even adopted as the state religion of the Uighur Empire in the tenth century. This same reason also probably explains its ultimate failure: whilst offering hope and an explanation for existence, it was perhaps too cerebral: despite its almost becoming a world religion in the past, today it is extinct. Only tiny derivative enclaves of the religion survive, such as the Yazidis of Kurdistan or the Mandaeans of southern Iraq, where elements of Manichaeism have been recorded. The impact of dualist ideas upon Europe, however, was immense and is to form the subject of Chapter 9.

ISLAM AND IRAN

Since the Islamic Revolution in Iran in 1979, Islamic extremism is more often associated with Iran than with any other Muslim country. However, it is important to emphasise that the Islam practised in Iran is very different to the way Islam is practised elsewhere in the Islamic world. It is also important to recognise that the Iranians have probably had almost as much influence on the practice of Islam as the Arabs, who saw its birth, have. Whilst this book is concerned mainly with ancient Persia, there was a certain amount of religious continuity from ancient into Islamic Iran.

The branch of Islam practiced in Iran is Shiᶜa Islam. This, of course, is by no means exclusive to Iran, as there are greater or lesser minorities throughout the Islamic world. But there are elements of its practice that are peculiar to Iran—or at least originate in ancient Iran. In its essentials, the differences between the Shiᶜa and the mainstream Sunni in Islam were initially political, a division that opened not long after the death of the Prophet. This was the question of who would lead the faith. The Sunni favoured an essentially elected line of leaders, or Caliphs, to be chosen amongst the Prophet's companions, whilst the Shiᶜa insisted that leadership should pass down the Prophet's bloodline through his cousin and son-in-law, ᶜAli, who had married Muhammad's daughter, Fatima. This soon led to open warfare between the two sides, with the early Shiᶜa leaders, or Imams, being killed by the Sunni: at first ᶜAli himself followed by his two sons, Hasan and Husain. The death of Husain and his followers is particularly mourned by the Shi'a because of the shockingly brutal nature of his martyrdom.

The mainstream branch of Shi'ism recognises twelve successors, or Imams. Many of the Imams were persecuted by the Sunni, and Shi'a minorities as a whole have suffered discrimination and persecution. This has introduced a cult of martyrdom into Shi'a Islam, comparable to that in early Christendom. The Twelfth Imam, however, never died but became *mahdi*, the 'guided one', who disappeared, to reappear at the ultimate triumph of Shi'ism upon judgement day. Hence, there is a messianic element to Shi'ism, comparable to that in Christianity but more likely derived from the idea of the *saoshyant* in Zoroastrianism (as indeed the Christian idea may have been). The Shi'a emphasis on the Imams has also meant that throughout its history there has always been a cult of religious leaders: not only the twelve Imams themselves, but a huge range of religious teachers, saints and leaders, often venerated in countless major and minor shrines and tombs—*imamzadehs*—found throughout Iran. The biggest of these—indeed, almost the largest religious complex in the world—is the Shrine to the Eighth Imam, the Imam Reza, at Mashhad. Again, this finds its parallel in Christianity with its cult of saints in the early church, not to mention its emphasis upon a hierarchy of priest: patriarchs, popes, archbishops, metropolitans. But again, the Shi'a cult of religious leadership finds a closer parallel with the Zoroastrian magi, and Iran is the only country in the Islamic world with a priestly hierarchy as we have observed. Finally, even the huge cult of mourning for the martyrdom of Imam Husain, marked throughout Iran every year in the month of Muharram with public processions, displays of flagellation and passion plays, has been suggested to be a survival of the pre-Islamic cult of mourning for the martyrdom of the Zoroastrian warrior-hero Siyavush, brutally cut down by Afrasiyab the tyrant king of Turan.[13]

Iran also transformed mainstream Islam—indeed, much of the history and practice of Islam is a result of this transformation. Islam was born, of course, in Arabia, and soon afterwards was nurtured in Damascus under the Umayyad Caliphate, the capital of the first Muslim dynasty for the first century of its existence. But Islam was transformed when the Caliphate moved to Baghdad after 750 with the so-called 'Abbasid Revolution'. To begin with, the 'Abbasid Revolution was brought about by many disaffected elements within Islam, not only Shi'a elements, but other Sunni elements as well, in particular those who were discontented with the way that Arab Muslims discriminated against non-Arab converts. These various discontented elements were almost entirely in the eastern Islamic world, chiefly Iran. Much of the disaffection was from older aristocratic Iranian families—recent converts to Islam, but heirs to a thousand years or more of ruling great empires—who resented being ruled by people whom they viewed as newcomers and upstarts.

All of these disaffected elements were united under the black banner of Abu'l-ᶜAbbas, and came to a head with the revolt under his leadership that led to the overthrow of the house of the Umayyads and the move of the capital to Baghdad. His own family, the ᶜAbbasids, were established as Caliphs from 750 until the dynasty was in turn overthrown by the Mongols in the thirteenth century.* Not only was the creation of the ᶜAbbasid Revolution largely brought about by Iranians, but the move of the capital to Baghdad brought it immediately under the influence of the older Iranian civilisation. Many of the early ᶜAbbasid dynasties of viziers and local rulers were Iranian, such as the Barmakids in the ninth century and the Buyids of northern Iran in the tenth. Indeed, the Buyids (or Buwayhids) consciously tried to bring about an ancient Persian renaissance: ᶜAdud ad-Daula, for example, tried to revive the Middle Persian language, encourage Zoroastrianism and even proclaimed himself 'Shahinshah' on one occasion. The ᶜAbbasids adopted older Iranian trappings of kingship, interest in pre-Islamic Persian literature and culture revived, and Iranian cultural forms dominated the caliphal court in Baghdad. Most importantly, Islam itself turned eastwards, not only as its natural heartland but also for its further expansion, and today Islam is regarded as an 'eastern' rather than a 'western' religion. This Iranian filter remains a part of Islam to this day.

This long excursus on Iranian religion is essential in order to understand its impact upon the west. This took two forms: first, its impact upon the development of Christianity in Anatolia, and second the spread of dualist ideas from Iran into Europe. It is to this that we turn in the next two chapters.

---

* In fact nominal ᶜAbbasid caliphs remained until the title was taken over by the Ottomans under Selim the Grim in the early sixteenth century.

Chapter 8

THE SHADOW OF ZOROASTER
Iranian Religion in Anatolia and Armenia

The nation of Magusaeans [Zoroastrians] ... is widely scattered amongst us throughout almost the whole country, colonists having long ago been introduced to our country from Babylon [i.e., Persia].

Bishop Basil of Caesarea in 377 [1]

Anatolia was the first major new area of outward expansion for the Achaemenid Empire during the time of Cyrus.* Sardis became one of the most important regional capitals of the empire, perhaps the most important city after the royal capitals themselves, and Asia Minor was colonised by Iranian settlers. At the same time it is important to stress that Asia Minor was a major centre for the development of Greek civilisation, as important for the Greeks as Athens and the cities of Greece itself were. We thus have in Anatolia direct and intimate contact between two of the more influential cultures of the ancient world: Persian and Greek. And this contact did not end with the fall of the Persian Empire. On the contrary, the contact not only remained but assumed political form with the rise of neo-Persian kingdoms in Anatolia that combined Persian and Hellenic elements: a Graeco-Persian civilisation. The contact, therefore, was direct, it was fundamental, and it was long term.

Anatolia, of course, was home to more peoples and cultures than just Greeks and Persians. Indeed, it is probably true to say that Anatolia has witnessed a greater and older variety of different cultures, civilisations and

---

* Babylonia was already a part of the Median Empire that Cyrus inherited, as opposed to newly incorporated for the first time.

peoples than any other single region in the world. It was the centre of civilisations older than either Persian or Greek: the Hittite of the Bronze Age, for example, was one of the more important civilisations—and empires—of early antiquity, and the region was also a centre for the Mitanni, the Urartian and the Phrygian civilisations, to name just some. Indeed, recent archaeological discoveries have revealed the existence of elaborate monumental building—at Göbekli Tepe near Urfa—some eleven and a half thousand years ago. That we are neglecting these cultures here does not mean that they are unimportant: to cover even a fraction of them would make this book impossibly long. But they do emphasise that any cultural fusion in the incredibly rich background of Anatolia is important.*

Into this cultural melting pot there entered yet another element in the first few centuries AD, this time from the Semitic world: Christianity. The resultant mixture was to change the world. To understand this it is necessary to return to some of the events covered in Chapters 2 and 5 to examine the religious elements that the Persians brought with them to Anatolia.

Persian Anahita meets Anatolian Artemis

Very little is known of the religion of the Achaemenids. No Achaemenid temple has been definitely identified: the so-called 'Ka'ba-yi Zardusht' at Naqsh-i Rustam near Persepolis and its near identical twin, the 'Zendan-i Sulaiman' at Pasargadae (Pls 5, 24), have defied efforts to identify them as temples or any other types of buildings. Indeed, Herodotus specifically notes that the Persians did not have temples but worshipped in the open air, preferably in high places, and there are references elsewhere to sacred fires. This, and the invariable invocation to Ahura Mazda in Achaemenid royal inscriptions, has led to the assumption that Zoroastrianism was the official state religions. However, Zoroaster himself is never actually mentioned in any of the surviving texts. This has been cited as evidence that the Achaemenids did not practice Zoroastrianism—but equally, there is no evidence to the contrary. All that we can be certain about is that the Achaemenid kings practised an official policy of toleration of religious beliefs and that a wide variety of beliefs—including Zoroastrianism—were practised. Cyrus certainly made a point of placating local religious sentiment amongst the Greeks of Asia Minor, for example at the sanctuaries of

---

* This will be further emphasised in Volume 3 of this series.

Didyma, Claros and Aulai (near Magnesia on the Maeander). This policy was largely followed by his successors: even Xerxes in his occupation of Greece was careful to protect places of worship (the Acropolis of Athens being a notable exception, although that was a political rather than religious issue), and many of the Greek sanctuaries remained largely pro-Persian as a result.

Probably the main cult that was brought into Anatolia by the Persians was that of Anahita. Anahita was the goddess of sweet waters, in Zoroastrianism an emanation of Ahura Mazda. She became one of the main cults of Iran throughout antiquity, becoming Anaïtis or the 'Persian Artemis' in Anatolia and an important vehicle for the transmission of Iranian religious ideas. The temple of Hiera Come, or 'Sacred Village', about thirty kilometres north-west of Sardis in Lydia was an Iranian sanctuary that was probably dedicated to Anahita. It was founded by Cyrus (presumably the younger, who was killed in 401 BC) and confirmed by Attalus III (138-133 BC), according to Tacitus, and so testifying both to the early arrival and the continuity of the cult. Archaeological remains indicate a temple of the Roman period, but they have not been investigated in detail. Another Anahita shrine was that at Hypaipa, 25 kilometres south-west of Sardis, where there are remains of a large colonnaded temple (attested by later inscriptions to be dedicated to Anaïtis) that would have been highly visible on the main road leading from Sardis to Ephesus. Several other smaller Anahita temples are known to have existed in Lydia which, like Hiera Come and Hypaipa, were located in the countryside rather than cities. This is consistent with Persian colonial settlement of landed aristocratic families occupying large country estates around a capital. In Sardis itself, the main city cult temple of Artemis was probably assimilated to Anahita (Pl. 27). Although its foundations probably date from the period of the Lydian kingdom, the main building phase was during the Persian period following its destruction by Athenians during the Ionian Revolt.

At Amyzos in Caria, hereditary priests bearing Iranian names are documented at the temple of Artemis from the time of Alexander's conquest to the time of Antiochus III in the first century BC. There is evidence of an Iranian religious presence in the early fourth century BC Temple of Artemis at Ephesus, with possible religious assimilation to Anahita, where the name of the high priest is recorded as Megabyzos, a Hellenised form of a Persian theophoric name. There is some suggestion in the layout of the temple of Didyma near Miletus of assimilation with Persian cult practices as well (Pl. 39). The Temple of Artemis at Ephesus was in fact largely built during the Persian period and was still being administered by the magi as late as the first century AD. There is considerable further evidence, both historical and epigraphic, for the cult of Anahita/Anaïtis—almost invariably described in ancient sources as 'the Persian Artemis'—elsewhere throughout Asia Minor and other former lands of the Persian Empire and beyond. Arrian, for example, notes a local goddess at the mouth of the Phasis in Colchis that might be a local variant of Anahita.[2]

The assimilation of Anahita with Artemis calls for comment. The mother-goddess fertility cult was one of the main cults of ancient Anatolia, embedded deep in Anatolian prehistory, with evidence found in excavations of Neolithic sites going back to the seventh millennium BC. In Archaic Ionia in the seventh century BC, the Greek cult of Artemis was grafted onto it, producing in architecture one of the Seven Wonders of the World at Ephesus (Pl. 40). But the cult of Ephesian Artemis had little, if any, resemblance to the goddess more familiar from Classical Greek mythology, and the Temple of Artemis at Ephesus was the embodiment in stone of the ancient Anatolian mother-goddess, the Classical style of its architecture notwithstanding, as well as elements of the Iranian Anahita cult.[3] In Ephesus, Christianity—in the person of St Paul—encountered some of its stiffest resistance with opposition from the 'Diana of the Ephesians'. However, over time the cult of the Virgin Mary was grafted on to the cult of Ephesian Artemis. For according to a Christian tradition, several years after the death of Jesus, the Virgin Mary was brought to Ephesus where she lived out her days in retirement—her purported house outside Ephesus is still a place of veneration today. It is notable that the cult of the *Theotokos*— of Mary the Mother of God*—was first articulated and legitimised at the Second Church Council at Ephesus in 431.

The regions of Asia Minor examined above were, it must be emphasised, major centres of Greek culture—Ephesus and Miletus in particular were two of the most important cities for the development of Greek civilisation in general (and the latter for Greek philosophy in particular). The Zoroastrian elements incorporated into religious worship there might have been nothing more than superficial, particularly against the established background of Greek philosophy reaching far back to Thales and the Milesian school. Equally, the philosophical environment of Greek Asia Minor would have been receptive to new religious ideas.

---

* In fact *Theotokos* translates literally as 'God bearer' rather than 'Mother of God', a subtle but important difference.

The contact that the Greeks had with Iranian religion was to have huge implications for subsequent Greek civilisation.

Not surprisingly, it was in the Neo-Persian kingdoms of Anatolia that deeper Iranian religious influence existed. The temple of Comana, near Cabeira (modern Niksar) in Pontus, became an important centre for the cult of Anaïtis.* The cult was administered by hereditary magi, presumably descendants of those who came from Iran during the Achaemenid period. All priests that are recorded bore Greek names, but the term for 'high priest' for this cult is derived from the Iranian title *mowbed*, meaning 'priest.' The Comana priestly caste also became priests for other cults, even, on occasion, of a Temple of Rome. These priests wore a diadem and ranked second behind the kings of Pontus themselves. Another major Anaïtis cult centre in Pontus was the temple of Zela (Pl. 56), probably founded during the Achaemenid period. No trace of it survives today apart from a fragmentary Corinthian capital of the Roman period, but contemporary descriptions (mainly by Strabo) attest to a fire cult as well as other large and elaborate ceremonials in an extensive temple complex.

MEETINGS WITH THE MAGI

Of all the neo-Persian kingdoms, it was the neighbouring kingdom Cappadocia where Iranian religion proved to be the most tenacious with the most far-reaching effects. Mt Argaeus (modern Ercyes Dağ), which dominates Cappadocia so dramatically (Pl. 88), would have provided an appropriate Iranian 'sacred landscape' for the Iranians, with its superficial resemblance to the Zoroastrian sacred mountain of Damavand in Iran, which figures so highly in their homeland myths (Pl. 83). Hence, it is suggested that the area would have attracted settlers and religious communities from Achaemenid times, and Iranian communities—mainly rural—continued to flourish throughout the Roman period. There is accordingly archaeological evidence for Iranian religious presence and colonisation in Cappadocia (see Chapter 5), and religion remained an important factor in Cappadocian society throughout its history. Strabo describes Zoroastrianism—fire worship and the magi, as well as the worship of Anaïtis and Omanus—as particularly strong in Cappadocia in his day,

---

* Usually designated Comana Pontica to distinguish it from Comana Cappadocia, where Anaïtis was also worshiped—see below.

having witnessed its practice himself.[4] A Persian relief stele depicting magi performing a Zoroastrian style sacred rite has been found near Kayseri. The volcano of Argaeus might well have attracted Iranian fire worship, and Strabo refers to 'many temples of the Persian gods' in Cappadocia where fire worship was practised. Interestingly, Strabo includes his description of Cappadocia in his section on Iran. Inscriptions and other sources suggest an important Iranian element in the population until well into Roman times—and the kings bore Iranian names.[5]

In the first century AD there emerged an important religious leader and cult in Cappadocia. This was the remarkable mystic Apollonius of Tyana, who was born in Tyana sometime in the early first century AD. Tyana, it will be recalled, was the satrapal capital of Cappadocia under the Achaemenids, and so was a particular focus for both influence and settlement from Iran. Apollonius espoused an extreme form of mysticism and asceticism, whose beliefs appear to combine elements of Pythagoreanism and even Brahmanism. He believed in reincarnation and claimed to speak all languages, including those of birds and animals. Apollonius supposedly undertook a journey to the east, travelling through Iran to India, where he held conversations with the magi and the Brahmans, as well as several secular rulers such as the Parthian King Vardanes in AD 43/44. On his return he attracted a wide following, and his cult was seen as a rival to that of Christ. Indeed, it is tempting to see the second century *Life of Apollonius* by the philosopher Philostratus as a pagan answer to the Gospels. As late as the beginning of the fourth century, Apollonius was being venerated by pagans as a viable alternative to Christ with his philosophy contrasted with Christianity.

Religion seems to have been the most important cultural import from Iran, both during the time of the Cappadocian kingdom and subsequently. The great temple of Comana in Cappadocia, dedicated to the Iranian goddess Anaïtis, had over six thousand temple servants and we read of many more such Iranian cults within Cappadocia. Iranian priests—the magi—were particularly prominent in Cappadocia and many ancient writers describe the rites of the magi and fire worship elsewhere in Anatolia. We also learn of magi practising in Syria, Mesopotamia, Arabia and Egypt, with instances as far as the western Mediterranean, as late as the fourth century. Apollonius of Tyana may well have been descended from the Cappadocian magi (spiritually if not genetically). The name 'Apollonius' in fact was often consciously chosen by the Hellenised Iranians of Anatolia because of the equation of Greek Apollo with Iranian Mithras or (occasionally) with Anahita (and inscriptional evidence of Mithraism has been recorded at Tyana).[6]

THE NATURE OF ZOROASTRIANISM IN ANATOLIA

The cult of Anaïtis developed into an independent cult divorced from its Zoroastrian roots (although not as much removed as Mithraism became), and the mere mention of magi in the sources does not necessarily mean anything more than their existence in the 1999 Stephen Sommers movie, *The Mummy*. Our two main authorities on the subject, historians Mary Boyce and Frantz Grenet in their monumental *Zoroastrianism under Macedonian and Roman Rule*, emphasise that such elements do nonetheless indicate the presence of Zoroastrianism, at least in the Achaemenid period. Was this anything more than superficial appearances, or did it take root and survive?

Pausanias' description of the temples at Hypaipa and Hierocaesarea in the second century AD are virtually 'classic' Zoroastrian: even as late as Roman times they were attended by 'magi' using 'foreign' (presumably Avestan?) liturgical language. The existence of magi and an archimagus (high priest, or Persian *mowbedan-mowbed*) is confirmed by inscriptions. At ancient Nacoleia, modern Seyitgazi in western Turkey, a Roman period inscription invoking 'Zeus of the Persians', i.e. Ahura Mazda, has been recorded. The Romans themselves related their ancient cult of Vesta to the Zoroastrian fire cult, in particular to the great Fire Temple of Adhur Gushnasp at Shiz in Azerbaijan. Kartir, the Zoroastrian high-priest under Shapur I, claimed to have encountered Zoroastrian communities, presumably descendants of the original Persian colonial families from the Achaemenid period, throughout central and eastern Anatolia—particularly in Cappadocia—and other parts of the occupied Roman East during the Persian campaigns of the third century. Kartir, together with his successors, was responsible for establishing Zoroastrian orthodoxy, so would have been well qualified to recognise its practice as something more than superficial observances (although this might have been mere propaganda). [7]

The Zoroastrian concept of the *saoshyant*, the saviour, arrived in the Hellenistic world through the Anatolian Iranian kingdoms in the second century BC in the tradition of the *Book of Hystaspes* or the *Oracle of Hystaspes*. This was a collection of prophecies, similar to the Sybilline Oracles, that had been revealed by a boy in a dream and recorded by 'Hystaspes, king of the Medes long ago' according to Lactantius that prophesied, among other events, the fall of both Macedon and Rome. Hystaspes is the Hellenised form of Vishtaspa, the name of a king of Bactria who may have ruled about 1000 BC that has been preserved in Zoroastrian sacred texts. Vishtaspa was also the name of the father of Darius the Great. According to the *Avesta* the *saoshyant*, or redeemer, is to be born of the house of Vishtaspa. Lactantius also cites Hystaspes/Vishtaspa when he writes of the end of the world when 'the pious and the faithful will separate themselves from the evil and ... Jupiter will look upon the earth, hear the voices of men and destroy the impious.' 'Jupiter' in this context is Ahura Mazda, and the text echoes very accurately Zoroastrian eschatological texts. By the Christian era the Oracle of Hystaspes had become equated with Christ. [8]

The tenacity of Zoroastrian communities in Cappadocia is demonstrated in a letter by Bishop Basil of Caesarea composed in 377 when he writes: 'the nation of Magusaeans [the regular term for Zoroastrians at this time] ... is widely scattered amongst us throughout almost the whole country, colonists having long ago been introduced to our country from Babylon [i.e., Persia]. And these have practised their own peculiar customs, not mingling with other peoples; and it is altogether impossible to employ reasoning with them, inasmuch as they have been preyed upon by the devil according to his wish. For there are neither books amongst them, nor teachers of doctrine, but they are brought up in an unreasoning manner, receiving their impiety by transmission from father to son. Now apart from these facts, which are observed by all, they reject the slaying of animals as a defilement, slaughtering through the hands of others the animals necessary for their needs; they rave after unlawful marriages; and they believe in fire as God; and other such things. But regarding their descent from Abraham, no one of the magi has up to the present told us any myths about that, but in fact they claim a certain Zarnuas as the founder of their race.'[9] 'Zarnuas' here refers either to Zurvanism, a later Zoroastrian heresy, or to Zuraon, the 'Father of Light' in Manichaeism.

The *Chronicle* of Pseudo-Dionysius of Tel-Mahre tells of the conversion of important Zoroastrian aristocratic families (whom he calls 'magian') in 509/10.[10] Zoroastrianism was still flourishing in Anatolia as late as AD 562 when its Zoroastrian communities (their fire-temples are specifically referred to) were recognised by Constantinople as lying to some extent within Sasanian jurisdiction. Official Byzantine recognition of extra-territorial status for a community in its heartland is astonishing, for this, remember, was at a time of major conflict between the two super-powers (Chapter 6). [11]

Just to the south of Cappadocia was the remote mountain kingdom of Commagene, and the extraordinary dynastic cult centre of the kings of Commagene on top of Mt Nemrut where Ahura Mazda, Mithras and Verethragna were overtly and publicly worshipped (see Chapter 5; Pls 63-66). Places of worship on top of high places was a feature of ancient Iranian religion; equally, it existed throughout the ancient Semitic Near East—Syria and northern Arabia, most famously at Petra—and the Hellenistic features of Mt Nemrut has already been remarked upon. In fact combining different religious elements into a dynastic cult centre was entirely consistent with ancient Iranian religious practice. Zoroastrians were still recorded in nearby Samosata as late as the end of the eleventh century.

The spread of Mithraism throughout the Roman Empire was promoted by Commagenians. The cult of Jupiter Dolichenus, which achieved considerable popularity throughout the Roman world spreading westwards as far as northern Britain, had its origins at Doliche in the Commagenian kingdom (modern Dülük). Its iconography probably derives from the Hittite god Teshup, but of more significance in the present context is that alone of Roman cults, that of Jupiter Dolichenus had a structured, hereditary clergy, surely deriving from the Iranian magi. Dolichenus altars also bore a superficial resemblance to Zoroastrian fire altars.[12]

On the fringes of ancient Commagene, there is evidence of Zoroastrianism in the Tur ᶜAbdin before Christianity, continuing until the Arab conquest. A monk of Tur ᶜAbdin extinguished a 'magian' fire shortly before the Arab conquest, and there was still a large Zoroastrian community in Nisibis in the mid-eighth century.[13] In this context, it is interesting to observe the striking Persian features in the architecture of the monastery-church at Hah in the Tur ᶜAbdin, despite the otherwise Byzantine nature of the architecture: it is in the form of a Persian *chahartaq* (a four-way arch, typically used in Zoroastrian fire-temples of the Sasanian period), it has Iranian style squinches rather than the more usual Roman-Byzantine style pendentives, and the exterior is adorned with rows of blind arches in the style of Ctesiphon (Pls 89-90). This becomes all the more curious in view of the origin of the Church of the Mother of God at Hah which, according to local legend, was founded by the Three Magi returning from Bethlehem, who rejoined there the nine others who originally set out from the east but remained in Hah.[14]

Synesius, the late fourth-early fifth century Bishop of Cyrene and man of letters—at once both Neo-Platonist and Christian—includes

Zoroaster in his list of the wise men of antiquity.[15] Of course, the late antique 'Hellenistic Zoroaster' doubtless bore little resemblance to the original Zoroaster of the *Avesta*. But Zoroaster had become an important metaphor for the Greeks for 'ancient wisdom' generally, and that aspect at least is in keeping with the *Avesta*, just as Cyrus had become for the Greeks a metaphor for the ideal king.

The figure of Zoroaster—or at least his shadow—was to have a curious footnote in the Byzantine world not long before the fall of Constantinople. In the early fifteenth century, the neo-Platonist philosopher George Gemistos Pleithon—who has been described as the last of the Greek philosophers—formulated a neo-pagan philosophy in his *Book of Laws*, whereby all wisdom and knowledge descended from Zoroaster, although there the resemblance to orthodox Zoroastrianism stops: Zoroaster was simply the first and most prominent of philosophers, followed by Minos, Lycurgus, the Brahmans, the magi and the Greek philosophers. Zeus was regarded as the supreme deity, but even there the resemblance to the pagan Greek god was superficial: the supreme being was a rigorously abstract concept. In fact such an abstract concept is closer to the Zoroastrian—not to mention the Muslim—idea of deity, and there is perhaps a Manichaean (or at least Gnostic) element in suggestions such as Poseidon being an emanation of Zeus (rather than his brother). To say that such ideas in the rigidly Orthodox world of Constantinople shortly before the conquest were regarded as heresy is, of course, an understatement, and Pleithon was hurriedly moved out of the way to remote Mistra in the Peloponnese for his own protection (and thereby contributed to the last upsurge of Byzantine cultural fluorescence before the empire disappeared forever). But however non-Zoroastrian Pleithon's philosophy was, it does represent the very last meeting of Greek philosopher and Persian magus.[16]

IRANIAN RELIGION IN ARMENIA

Chapter 5 has already explored the Iranian connections of Armenian dynasties since the Achaemenid period. With the dynasties came the deities, particularly under the Artaxiads of the second and third centuries BC. These deities consisted of Armazd or Armazi (Ahura Mazda), the chief deity associated with the worship of the sun and fire, Anahit (Anahita), Mithra, Ahriman, Vahagn (Verethragna) and Tir (Tishtriya). In addition, the Armenian pantheon included a number of Avestan spirits such as *divs* and *druj* (male and female demons), as well as *paris* and *kaj* (fairies and their male consorts). The Iranian religious element remained under the succeeding Arsacid dynasty of Armenia. Indeed, there are suggestions that the founder of the dynasty, Tiridates I, in accounts of his journey to Rome for his coronation by Nero in 66, was a Zoroastrian priest or magus. The fire altar is depicted on some of the Arsacid coins in Armenia, and the Arsacid period saw a re-assertion of Iranian influences, that included Zoroastrian elements.

Furthermore, a major cult in Armenia was that of the sun, worshipped as Ara or occasionally Armazi or Armazd, the latter two variations of Ahura Mazda. Thus, the Armenian worship of the sun in this instance can be viewed as a variation of the Zoroastrian veneration of the god of light, Ahura Mazda. It remained a potent symbol in Armenia, and can still be seen in Armenian architecture through the prevalence of sun discs and sundials on Armenian churches (Pl. 91).*

Dualism certainly formed a part of ancient Armenian religion, although dualism is by no means exclusive to orthodox Zoroastrianism. This came later in the Sasanian period, particularly under Yazdegird II (439-45), who attempted to enforce strict orthodox Zoroastrianism throughout Armenia as a part of the new state policy of making it a state religion. We read that fire temples were built in all villages in Armenia which, whilst no doubt exaggerated, does at least indicate that it became widespread. We have already observed that the earliest circular planned Armenian churches might have been based upon Zoroastrian fire temples (Pl. 49). Since Zoroastrianism had by then become an arm of the Sasanian state, resistance to it was seen as rebellion, and dissidents suffered persecution as a result. The importance of dualist and other Zoroastrian derived beliefs in Armenia was to have huge implications on subsequent European history with the rise of the Paulician movement in Armenia (see Chapter 9).

Iranian influence was only marginally less in neighbouring Georgia in antiquity, where we have already observed that the ancient capital itself of eastern Georgia, Armazi, was named after Ahura Mazda. Georgia too experienced the same late Sasanian enforced Zoroastrianism and subsequent persecutions as Armenia did, and a fire temple has been excavated in eastern Georgia (Pl. 48). However, it is unlikely that Iranian religious influences were as strong in Georgia, Yazdegird II's zeal notwithstanding, and it was not to have as widespread an influence as Armenia has.

---

* I am indebted to Julian Lush for this observation.

ANTICIPATING CHRISTIANITY

The implications of the Zoroastrian redeemer or *saoshyant* (born of a virgin, although this might be a later interpolation) for the development of Christianity are obvious, although the idea of a redeemer or saviour was common to a number of other ancient eastern religions, both pagan and monotheist.* 'Magian' beliefs offering future resurrection were recorded by Greek authors as early as the fourth century BC. Of far greater implications for Christianity was the position of a priestly hierarchy in the Zoroastrian religion. Whilst priesthoods are known from elsewhere, a structured, elaborate hierarchy had few counterparts. The Judaic institution of the Pharisees only occurred after Judaism came into contact with—and under the influence of—Zoroastrianism during the Babylonian exile. The contact transformed Judaism.[17] Pagan Rome had many priests, of course. But their function was limited to the temples to which they were attached; there was no structured hierarchy, no concept of administering to a flock or of overseeing the religion, in both spiritual and administrative terms, such as became familiar under the Christian Church. The magi of Zoroastrian Iran was practically the only institution that functioned in this way in the ancient world. The Christian idea of a priestly hierarchy and even the term 'priest' applied to Christian ministers does not emerge until the end of the second century.[18] The idea entered Christian mythology with the visit of the Three Magi to the infant Christ—symbolically, the older monotheistic religion giving its blessing to the new one being born in Bethlehem.

The Iranian institution of the magi was to have repercussions for the west politically as well as religiously. Under Shapur I in the third century,[19] the religious reforms of the Zoroastrian high-priest Kartir established for the first time a monotheistic religion as a structured, state religion and the Zoroastrian 'church' as an extension and instrument of Iranian state policy (Pl. 92). This was the culmination of a movement begun by Tansar, high-priest under Shapur's father, Ardeshir, who writes in his *Letter*: 'Know that royal authority and religion are two brothers in perfect agreement with each other.'† The position that Kartir created, of arch-priest with state

---

* Although Boyce and Grenet (1991: Ch. XI) stress the origin of the Judaeo-Christian belief in a day of judgement, a messiah and the physical resurrection in a hereafter in Zoroastrianism.

† The prevailing opinion now is that the text of the *Letter of Tansar* which has come down to us was re-written or perhaps just fabricated in the late Sasanian period (Frantz Grenet, pers. comm.). This translation in Gutas 1998: 80-1.

responsibilities to oversee both official religious formalities and religious orthodoxy, foreshadowed the papacy of Christianity. Such a revolutionary step might have found precedent in Buddhism, such as Kanishka's patronage of Buddhism in the second century AD or even Ashoka's in the third century BC. The precedent thus set was followed by the Romans: Constantine, a short time after Shapur, established his own state monotheistic and monolithic church, a structure that was to be an instrument of state policy and a means for centralising his own rule. The ensuing structure became the keystone of subsequent European history down to the Reformation. Constantine's letter to Shapur extolling the virtues of Christianity seems to have been an echo of King Abgar of Edessa's letters to fellow rulers following his conversion to Christianity over a century before, or even Ashoka's letters to the Hellenistic rulers of the west following his conversion to Buddhism in the third century BC.[20]

Some further Zoroastrian religious practices are relevant in this context. The Zoroastrian practice of praying five times daily, involving the ritual washing of face, hands and feet before prayer, has obvious implications for the emergence of the same practice in Islam. So too does the overseeing of charitable institutions and religious endowments demanded by Zoroastrianism. The ritual bathing for purification anticipates the Christian rite of baptism. The Christian regard for holy water might have derived from the cult of Anahita, where holy water is central to its ritual. The Zoroastrians also practised the confession of sins, although this might be a later tradition. Although Christianity rigidly rejected dualism (violently so as we shall see in the next chapter), the dualism that dominates Zoroastrian belief—the conflict between the forces of light and darkness—is echoed in Christianity with its emphasis on good versus evil, as well as heaven and hell, god and Satan. This dualistic belief has been suggested as an explanation for the eastern orientation of the early churches: east, being the source of light, symbolised good, as opposed to the west, the source of darkness symbolising evil. The idea of evil is quite different to the Christian tradition, being always distinct and uncreated, unlike Christianity where even evil ultimately stems from the original creation by God (and the Devil is a fallen angel).[21]

A single almighty god, a god furthermore of goodness, a creator, a creation story, heaven and hell, a first man and woman, a redeemer born of a virgin, the promise of redemption, resurrection and a hopeful hereafter, angels and other spirits, a hierarchical college of priests to administer the religion—it all sounds very familiar. All, some, or even none of this may have directly influenced Christianity. But what is important is that many of the elements were already in place in Anatolia by the time Christianity arrived: in the ideas sown by Zoroastrianism in Anatolia, Christianity found the way already prepared.

THE COMING OF CHRISTIANITY

It comes as no surprise to learn that these former Iranian kingdoms in Anatolia with their long religious traditions rooted in Zoroastrianism became important centres of early Christianity, both for its development and its spread. The historian Stephen Mitchell in his monumental *Land, Men and Gods in Asia Minor* contrasts the (sometimes contradictory) literary and epigraphic evidence for the spread of Christianity, and notes how it did not spread or even seem to relate to St Paul's activities, but how its spread must be related to other factors: 'There is virtually no evidence to show how the gospel had spread.' He concludes that Christianity found fruitful ground by existing religions paving the way, particularly in the emergence of the belief in the supreme abstract god in earlier religious belief. Although not specified, it is very easy to see the magi and Zoroastrianism behind Christianity in Pontus and Central Anatolia: 'the Christianization of much of central Anatolia from the mid-3rd century onwards was intense, but patchy. Areas where virtually the entire population had been converted contrasted, sometimes starkly, with others where pagans still prevailed.'[22]

The bishopric of Pontus, particularly under St Gregory in the third century, was one of the most important Christian centres in the east,[23] while the vast numbers of churches that still litter the landscapes of Cappadocia and Commagene today—the underground churches, for example, or the Binbir Kilise (the 'Thousand and One Churches') of the Black Mountain, or the monasteries of the Tur ʿAbdin—attest to its strength and tenacity in those regions (e.g., Pls 92, 93, 97). The Cappadocian brothers Basil ('the Great'), Bishop of Caesarea, and Gregory, Bishop of Nysa, were from a Christian priestly family from Cappadocia,[24] Gregory of Nazianzus was the son of a bishop of Nazianzus, and a large number of other early church figures also hailed from Cappadocia. In this context, it is worth recalling that Armenia, a similarly Iranised kingdom on the fringes of Anatolia, was the first kingdom in the world to proclaim Christianity as a state religion (with the possible exception of Edessa, also on the fringes of Anatolia), with Georgia following soon after. The evangeliser of Armenia, St Gregory the Illuminator, spent many years in Cappadocia where he became a Christian, while the evangeliser of Georgia, St Nino, was a Cappadocian. We thus see a strong continuity of priestly castes in Cappadocia from the magi of Anatolia to the priests of early Christianity.

We also see in Anatolia in late antiquity the final outcome of the contact between Persian and Greek in early antiquity. For it is important to emphasise how quickly Christianity, at first a religion born in the Semitic religious climate of Palestine, came to be dominated by Greeks. The Greeks were heirs to very different philosophical and religious traditions to Judaism, and sought to 'explain' perceived inherent contradictions in Christianity in their own terms: mainly the contradictory human and divine natures of Christ in terms of Greek logic. It is notable that the Christological debates were largely restricted to the Greek east but were of relatively little concern to the Latin west (indeed, much of the issues that obsessed the Greeks baffled western Europeans). It is tempting to see in the debates over the different natures of Christ the influence of Manichaeism in its recognition of the three natures of Jesus. This led to endless disputes and to the early oecumenical councils, which were held mainly in Anatolia (successively Nicaea in 325, Constantinople in 381, Ephesus in 431 and Chalcedon in 451, with two further councils held in Constantinople and another in Nicaea), ultimately leading to a split after Ephesus. All western churches to this day—Orthodox, Catholic, Protestant—follow the Council of Chalcedon of 451 that was dominated by the Greeks, while the eastern churches—Coptic, Ethiopian, Syrian, Armenian—reject the terms of Chalcedon. Thus, Christianity in the form that was eventually transmitted to the west was transformed in Anatolia by its contact with Hellenic and Iranian traditions.

Of course, the suggestion that Iranian magi quite literally became Christian priests cannot be documented, and whether or not Christianity incorporated Iranian elements is perhaps not the issue here. The real issue is that the spread of Iranian religions westwards *paved the way* in the very region where Christianity first took root, was transformed by the contact and in turn spread further west. The spread of other Iranian religious ideas into Europe is explored in the next chapter.

Chapter 9

THE DUALIST CHALLENGE
Manichaeans, Paulicians, Bogomils, Cathars and the Albigensian Crusade

When they [the barons] had stripped them [of their booty],
they gave a shout:
'Raze it to the ground!' those filthy, wretched rogues cried
out (...)
(...) who burned the town, the women, and their babes,
young men and old, and the priests who sang at mass
dressed in their vestments, within the monastery gates.
They took Béziers and razed it to the ground,
and for want of greater injury, they slaughtered all they found.
They killed all those who, gathered in the monastery,
no help could find in cross, or altar or crucifix.
That mad and low-born rabble killed the priests,
and women and children, and none, I think, escaped.

'Song of the Cathar Wars',
thirteenth-century Occitan troubadour's song[1]

The dualist concept (examined in Chapter 7) is central to Zoroaster's message. In its essence, it is the idea of two completely separate and uncreated concepts of good and evil, light and darkness, locked in perpetual struggle and expressed in Zoroastrianism as Ahura Mazda and Angra Mainyu. The concept was further refined and broadcast by the prophet Mani in the third century. Whilst the Zoroastrian religion did not spread much beyond people of Iranian descent, in its refined and derived form under Manichaeism it spread throughout the ancient world. In this way, the relationship between Zoroastrianism and Manichaeism is parallel to that between Judaism and Christianity.

Dualist ideas are not exclusive to Zoroastrianism and Manichaeism. There are aspects of dualism in ancient Egyptian, Judaic and Greek religious ideas. The idea also exists in Gnosticism, although unlike the Iranian religions, it is not central to it. Gnosticism, however, was never a structured, organised religion in the way that Zoroastrianism or Christianity is, and still less with a set of canonical beliefs: it was more a religious movement or even just a school of thought rather than a specific religion. The term derives from the Greek word *gnosis* meaning simply 'knowledge', applying specifically in this case to an inner, more mystical knowledge of God or the 'Divine Being'. Gnosticism was first articulated as a movement in the second century AD in Egypt and the Near East. It incorporated elements of Christianity, but some aspects of it also contain elements of Judaism, neo-Platonism, Pythagoreanism and other pagan beliefs, so its origins might be earlier.[2] Mani was certainly influenced by the Gnostic movement, but his dualist ideas derive from Zoroastrianism—as, indeed, dualist ideas in Gnosticism probably do. Given the former spread of the Persian Empire throughout western Asia—not to mention its resurgence under the Parthians—and the huge foment of religious and philosophical ideas that spread as a result of unifying this vast area, it seems unlikely that dualist ideas would emerge completely independently of each other. The dualist ideas thus spread was to have a huge impact worldwide, particularly in medieval Europe where it posed a major challenge to both of the established churches, Catholic and Orthodox—indeed, it was probably the greatest challenge that the Church has ever faced.

MANICHAEISM IN THE WEST

Dualist ideas spread into Europe soon after Christianity did. The Prophet Mani himself was a vigorous evangelist and actively proselytised in the Roman Empire, accompanying Shapur's armies in the mid-third century into Syria. Indeed, a historian of Manichaeism, Samuel Lieu emphasises that Mani was an 'indefatigable missionary' and further writes that: 'A remarkable feature of Mani's religion is its extraordinarily swift spread from Persian-held Mesopotamia, the land of its origins, westwards to the Roman Empire. This westward diffusion was achieved within a century of the founder's death in 276.'[3]

Between 224 and 226 Mani sent missions under his disciples Addai and Thomas to Alexandria and elsewhere in the Roman Empire. These missions supposedly converted, amongst others, Zenobia of Palmyra (according to Manichaean documents in the Sogdian language discovered in China) and 'the religion of the Apostle [Mani] flourished in the Roman Empire.'[4] Sogdian manuscripts also describe how another disciple, Gabryab, actively proselytised in Armenia in about 260, as well as a possible mission to Georgia. This was to assume significance in the light of the subsequent development of the Paulician movement in Armenia, described below. Manichaeism enjoyed particular success generally in the western border states of the Sasanian empire—precisely where Paulicianism was to later flourish.

The persecution of Manichaeism as a Zoroastrian heresy after Shapur's death further drove many Manichaeans into the Roman Empire. Alexandria was a particular focus of early proselytisation. The success of Manichaean missions in Egypt is supported in Roman sources as well as archaeological evidence, notably the discoveries of genuine Manichaean texts at Medinet Madi and Lycopolis. The latter is probably the find spot of the *Cologne Mani Codex*, the most complete ancient Manichaean text to survive. Both the literary evidence and the discovery of major original Manichaean texts 'have shown beyond doubt that the religion was well established in Egypt.'[5]

By the 290s Manichaeism had spread into North Africa and had reached Rome soon after, from where it spread through Italy and into Gaul and Spain. During the time of Diocletian (284-305) a Manichaean called Boundos who taught in Persian practised in Rome, and his schism was called the Daristhenians. The name might derive from *dryst-dyn*, a Manichaean Middle Persian word meaning 'right religion', and Boundos has been suggested as deriving from the Middle Persian *bundg* meaning 'perfect', the Manichaean elite. By this time, Manichaeism was so widespread in the Roman Empire that Diocletian felt it necessary to issue an edict specifically against this 'shameful and utterly disreputable creed, ... the teaching of the Persians.'[6]

Antioch also became an important early centre, possibly originating with Mani's own visit there under Shapur's army of occupation. Its importance is stressed by Lieu when he writes that 'Antioch-on-the-Orontes was the gateway to Asia and the Balkans. Once Manichaeism had secured a firm foothold in this great metropolis, its passages to the inland cities of Asia Minor and the Aegean seaboard would have been relatively straightforward.'[7] Thus, we read of its spread into Anatolia and the Balkans during subsequent centuries. An early fourth century Manichaean tomb has been found at Spoleto (Split on the Dalmatian coast), and sources report of Manichaeans in Constantinople in the fifth and sixth centuries, where they were being persecuted during the time of Justinian (although many of the Byzantine reports of Manichaeans might have been prompted by official Orthodox propaganda attempting to depict Monophysite Christians as Manichaeans).

Although Manichaeism was born some two centuries after Christianity—indeed, it incorporated elements of Christianity and regarded Jesus as a precursor of Mani—it is important to remember that much of Christian practise in its present form did not become doctrine until the fourth century and even later. Hence, influences went both ways. One of the earliest Christian apologists, Lactantius, appears to be expressing Manichaean ideas when he wrote: 'Man is therefore composed of elements which are contrary and hostile just as the world is composed of good and bad, light and dark and life and death; and god arranged for these two to fight it out in man so that if the spirit which springs from god is victorious man will be immortal and live in perpetual light, but if the body conquers the soul and brings it under his control, man will be in everlasting darkness and death.' A particular category of Monophysite monks in the Syrian desert in the sixth century were referred to as the 'Perfects', which might also suggest Manichaean influence. [8]

St Augustine, more than anybody else the father of western Christianity, practised for many years as a Manichee among flourishing communities in Carthage and Rome. Even after he renounced Manichaeism, elements of it remained with Augustine, including some aspects of dualism. Others have seen Christian dualism—the belief in the sharp division between good angels versus bad demons in the unseen world—as deriving from Zoroastrianism via Judaism. The doctrine of original sin is an essential element of Catholic Christianity and has virtually no place in the Orthodox Church. Although its foundation has been traced to the Gospels, its origins lie more in the teachings of the western church fathers, Tertullian, St Cyprian and St Ambrose. However, it received its final form from St Augustine who, in his recognition of humanity as a pre-existing *massa damnata*, moved the doctrine closer to the Manichaean recognition of the pre-existence of the forces or darkness within humanity, diminishing considerably the idea of free will. [9]

Manichaeism was to have an even greater history in the east, where it was adopted as the state religion of the Uighur Empire of Central Asia in the eighth and ninth centuries, remaining active in the region down until thirteenth century when it eventually died out. Nearer to its original homeland elements of Manichaeism still survive in the Mandaean religion of southern Iraq and the Yazidi religion of Kurdistan. (Indeed, it is notable that the Yazidis today occupy more or less the same region as the Paulicians discussed below: Armenia, eastern Anatolia and northern Mesopotamia.) This spread and survival of Manichaeism serves to illustrate just how much Mani's universal message spread. But eastern Manichaeism does not form so much a part of our present story, which is concerned more with its effect upon Europe.

THE PAULICIANS

Manichaeism as a practising religion appears to have disappeared in Europe in late antiquity: persecutions by the church during the fifth and sixth centuries appear to have successfully extinguished it (at least in the open) throughout the empire. Hence, it is not possible to trace direct continuity from Manichaeism to the dualist sects of the Middle Ages. But the dualist ideas espoused by the Manichaeans revived in Europe with a movement that has been traced back to the Paulician sect of Armenia.

The Paulicians were described by contemporaries as Manichaeans— although it is always difficult to disentangle the term from one of religious belief or one of religious abuse. They certainly owed some at least of their doctrines to Manichaeism, notably the dualist idea of the two principles. The Paulicians took their name from Paul of Samosata, a town in south-eastern Anatolia (modern Samsat). Although Paul was Patriarch of Antioch in the third century, he was said to be a practising Manichaean and a member of a prominent Manichaean priestly family (both his brother and father were active proselytisers). It is tempting to see in this family of priests a remnant of the Zoroastrian magi, active in this part of Anatolia as we have seen. It is also possible that Paul might have received his Manichaeism direct from the source: Mani, one recalls, accompanied the army of Shapur I in his capture of Antioch. However, there is some dispute whether Paul of Samosata was the founder of the movement: the name might originate from the Epistles of St Paul, which the Paulicians particularly revered.

The region of Samosata was in any case subject to considerable Zoroastrian influence in antiquity. Samosata was one of the cities of the neo-Persian kingdom of Commagene where Iranian religion is so visibly manifested at Mt Nemrut as we have seen (Chapters 5 and 8; Pls 63-68). It was also in Samosata and adjacent the regions of the Tur ͨAbdin and Nisibis where Zoroastrianism remained longest, as late as the eleventh century in the case of Samosata.[10] It is not difficult, therefore, to recognise where the Paulicians received their doctrines.

From Samosata an Armenian known as Constantine of Mananali took the religion into Armenia in the mid-seventh century, founding the Paulician church. The sect was condemned by the Byzantine authorities and Constantine was ordered to be stoned to death. This act was carried out by Constantine's adoptive son, Symeon, who later repented and became the new leader of the Paulicians. They were savagely persecuted by the Catholicos of Armenia, forcing the Paulician community to found their own semi-independent principality on the upper Euphrates just beyond the Armenian border, from where they were a constant thorn in the side of Constantinople, co-operating with the new Muslim powers to the south.

We have already emphasised the Zoroastrian background to this region, remaining a factor there even after the spread of Christianity. Hence, Paulicianism would have found fertile ground in Armenia and adjacent areas of eastern Anatolia. Equally important was the nature of Armenian Christianity in contrast to that in the Roman Empire. In the Roman Empire Christianity came from below: a religion of the lower classes that gradually filtered upwards. In Armenia it came from the top—the conversion of King Tigranes in the early third century—and filtered downwards. Such movements happened elsewhere—notably in Georgia and Ethiopia, where the royal houses were converted before spreading below to the populace. But both Georgia and Ethiopia experienced 'second waves' of evangelisation by Syrian and Cappadocian monks who worked among the ordinary people. This did not happen in Armenia, and Christianity (in the early years at least) remained a religion of the elite.* Hence, Christianity imposed by the court and the landowning wealthy families would have encountered considerable resistance amongst the ordinary people, finding a ready expression in the Paulician movement.

It has been suggested that the iconoclast movement initiated by Leo III of the Isaurian dynasty (717-741), was due to Paulician influence.[11] The Isaurian dynasty originated in the mountainous southern part of Anatolia

---

* It is notable, for example, that most early churches in Armenia are tiny—far too small to hold a congregation—and could only hold a small number of clergy and nobles. It was only in the twelfth century that churches were enlarged by the addition of the *gavit*, a peculiarly Armenian architectural feature comprising a large hall or vestibule that was added onto the original church, often larger than the church itself.

bordering Syria, hence coming under Muslim influence. Leo III spoke Arabic as his first language, and the dynasty's fanatic iconoclasm has been seen by some as derived from Islam.

In the ninth century the Empress Theodora attempted to stamp out the Paulician movement and instigated a general persecution. Church accounts gloatingly record a hundred thousand Paulicians killed, many by impalement and other forms of torture. The remaining Paulicians in the empire fled to their strongholds in the eastern fringes of Anatolia (such as Amara and Tephrike—modern Divriği, Pl 98) from where they openly sided with the Muslims and raided deep into the Byzantine heartland, often with spectacular success. Finally, following the capture and execution of the charismatic Paulician leader Chrysocheir in 870 by Emperor Basil I, effective Paulician resistance collapsed. This brief history very closely anticipates that of the Cathars in medieval France.

Armenians had been deported to Thrace as early as the reign of Emperor Maurice (582-602). The Emperor Constantine V had deported a community of Paulicians to the Thracian frontier in the seventh century. He might have hoped that they would gradually be wiped out in border warfare, but they survived and spread. These colonies were increased by Emperor John Tzimisces in 975 who, anxious to move the Paulicians away from the sensitive Muslim frontier where their loyalty was doubtful, transplanted large numbers to Thrace (some sources speak of up to 200,000), settling them around Philippopolis. There they flourished—indeed, often at the encouragement of Constantinople, grateful for their help in defending the vulnerable Balkan borders. These colonies formed the core of the later Bogomil movement.

THE BOGOMILS

Bogomilism—*Bogomilistvo*—was supposedly named after the shadowy Bulgarian priest Bogomil (although its exact meaning is disputed) who preached in the middle part of the tenth century during the time of Tsar Peter of Bulgaria. Very little is known about him, although both his teaching and his following appear to have drawn heavily upon the older Paulician communities of Bulgaria, as well as of Thrace and Macedonia. There were doctrinal differences between Paulicianism and Bogomilism and even doctrinal differences between early and late Bogomilism. But the dualist

64. Nemrut Dağ

65. King Mithradates I of Commagene and Heracles/Verethragna at Arsameia

66. *Commagene royal burial ground at Karakuş*

67. *Relief of Parthian warriors at Hatra in Iraq*

68. *Ardashir's investiture relief at Naqsh-i Rustam. Ardashir on the left is trampling the last Parthian king, Artabanus V, underneath; opposite is Ahuramazda trampling Ahriman.*

69. *Shapur's victory relief at Naqsh-i Rustam. The captive Emperor Valerian is standing behind Shapur, and Emperor Philip the Arab is kneeling in supplication. The high-priest Kartir (upper right) looks on.*

70. *Shapur's great victory relief at Bishapur depicting Roman prisoners of war*

71. *Shapur's victory relief at Bishapur depicting the captured Emperor Valerian standing, Emperor Philip kneeling and Emperor Gordian III being trampled underfoot.*

72. *The palace of Ardashir at Firuzabad*

73. *The palace of Shapur at Bishapur*

74. *A Sasanian jousting relief at Naqsh-i Rustam.*

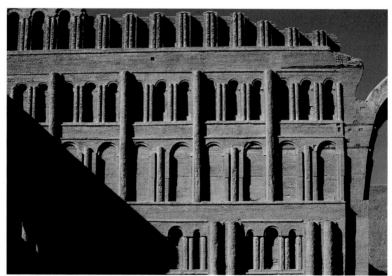

75. *The late Sasanian palace at Ctesiphon in Iraq, the capital for much of the Parthian and Sasanian periods.*

XXXVIII

76. Dariel Gorge in the Caucasus Mountains in Georgia

77. Remains of the city gateway in the fortress city of Dara

78. *The Roman stronghold of Petra overlooking the Black Sea, modern Tsikhisdziri in Georgia.*

79. *The immense Roman legionary fortress of Gonio in Georgia*

80. Relief of Khusrau Parviz at Taq-i Bustan outside Kermanshah

81. Narikala Fortress overlooking Tbilisi

82. The fire temple at Absheron in Azerbaijan

83. Mt Damavand in the Alburz Mountains north-east of Tehran

84. Interior of the Median fire temple of Nushijan in western Iran

85. Exposure towers or 'towers of silence' outside Yazd

86. Modern Zoroastrian fire temple in Yazd

87. The Mithraeum at Hadrian's Wall in Northumberland

88. Mt Argaeus—modern Erciyes—in Cappadocia

89. The Church of the Mother of God at Hah in the Tur ʿAbdin, founded in the 6th century.

90. Interior of the Church of the Mother of God at Hah

91. Sun disc sundial on the church of Noravank in Armenia

92. Relief of the Sasanian high-priest Kartir at Naqsh-i Rajab

93. One of the rock-cut churches at Gülşehir in Cappadocia

94. The fortress of Tephrike, modern Divriği, in eastern Anatolia, one of the Paulician strongholds.

95. The Cathar castle of Peyreperteuse, Aude, France (photo: Julian Lush).

message remained its central belief throughout. It is also suggested that Bogomil dualism drew upon Iranian elements that arrived with the migrating Bulgar tribes from Central Asia, where they would have come into contact with Manichaeism, which formed the state religion of the Uighur Empire in the ninth century. In this context it must be noted that the Volga Bulgars used the Manichaean Sogdian script, borrowed from the Uighurs, prior to their conversion to Islam in the tenth century.* There has been further speculation on possible direct Manichaean influence upon Bogomilism following the last diaspora of Manichaeans from Iraq in the tenth century. However, this and the possible Central Asian influences are speculative, but the chain of transmission from the Paulicians to the Bogomils is not seriously in doubt.[12]

Ironically, it was the establishment of the Orthodox Church as the official state religion of the new Bulgarian Empire after the ninth century that contributed to the spread of the Bogomils. For Bogomilism stood as a real alternative to the pomp, wealth and oppression of the state church associated with the ruling classes, prompting many ordinary people to go over to the Bogomils as a protest (thus echoing the Paulician spread in Armenia). Manichaean dualism appealed to the peasants and lower classes, having far more experience of the wickedness and suffering in the world than of the wealth and corruption of the high clergy and state which appeared remote and alien to them. The high church contrasted with the asceticism and simple devotion of the Elect, or Perfect, of the Bogomils. There may also have still been residual elements of the older Bulgar heaven worship religion of the steppes among ordinary Bulgarians, leading to further resentment of the newer Christianity of the ruling classes.

The Bogomils also actively proselytised, and thus soon spread their faith throughout the Balkans—particularly into the Slavic areas (missions were recorded as far away as Kiev)—as well as eastwards to Constantinople. In the religious foment—and dissent—of the imperial capital Bogomilism found fertile ground and its numbers grew quickly, to the alarm of the church and court. The leader of the Constantinople Bogomils, Basil, was arrested by the Emperor Alexius I and he, along with many of his followers, were burnt at the stake. This setback was only a temporary one for the Bogomils and they soon revived, and proselytising missions were recorded as far as southern France by 1167. This was to have huge repercussions for the rise of Catharism, discussed below.

---

* The Bulgar migrations are discussed further in Volume 4 of this series.

After the Fourth Crusade of 1204 we hear little more of the Bogomils in Constantinople, but they continued to flourish elsewhere in the Balkans, particularly in Bulgaria, throughout the thirteenth and fourteenth centuries. Bogomism is even recorded to have penetrated the Orthodox stronghold of Mt Athos in the early fourteenth century. From Bulgaria it spread into Serbia and Bosnia where Bogomilism was to enjoy its greatest success. Under the name of Patarenes, Bogomilism was adopted by members of the Bosnian aristocracy and for the first time large scale religious establishments were built; for a while in the fourteenth century the Patarene church even enjoyed equal status in Bosnia with the Orthodox and Latin churches.

In the late fourteenth century a new religion entered the Balkans with the arrival of Islam under the Ottomans. There is no record of any persecution of the Bogomils by the Ottomans, who exercised an official policy of religious tolerance for all faiths under their rule. At the same time the Ottomans would not have tolerated any repression by the Bulgarian Church either, so that the Bogomils in theory would have enjoyed more freedom than at any time in their history. All the same, Bogomilism seems to have declined after the Ottoman conquest and virtually disappears; perhaps, like many movements, it flourished best in adversity.

THE CATHARS

The most spectacular advance of a dualist movement was in western, rather than eastern Europe. In the south of France its growth provoked a major backlash by the Roman church, involving what was probably the greatest efforts in its history to eradicate another belief. It is uncertain when or how it arrived in France, whether from Constantinople or from the Balkans, although it was probably in Italy that the first Cathars appeared. Certainly by 1022 the Church was already burning 'Manichaeans' at the stake in France.

The name used by the Cathars to describe their religion was simply 'the Church of God' (anticipating later Protestant movements). Many of them were known under the name 'Publicani', thought to derive from the original Paulicians of Armenia. They were described as 'Manichees' by the Church, although this probably meant little more than a reference to St Augustine. The name 'Cathar' was first applied in 1030 in Italy, probably deriving from the Greek word for 'pure' (although this is disputed), a reference to the belief in the community of the Elect or Perfect (which is a Manichaean element). A Greek term might imply a Byzantine origin, but Bogomils from the Balkans were in any case actively proselytising in the west as well—in France the Cathars were occasionally known as 'Bosnians'. In the thirteenth century the Cathars in France were also referred to as 'Bougres', deriving from Bulgars—a clear indication of its origins in Bogomilism.* The centres of Catharism in France were inland rather than on the Mediterranean coast, suggesting that it came overland rather than by sea. The period of the Crusades in any case was a period of increased communication between western Europe and the lands of the Byzantine east. It is also not certain how much residual Manichaeism—or at least dualist beliefs—would have survived underground in the west from late antiquity, when it had been widespread under the late Roman Empire, paving the way for the arrival of new dualist ideas. Certainly by 1125 some Cathars at least in France were identified specifically with those Manichees described by St Augustine. Although there is scant evidence for the distribution of Manichaeism in the Roman Empire, it is nonetheless significant that the main centres of Catharism in the Middle Ages where in those parts of western Europe most Romanised: northern Italy and southern France.

As in Bulgaria, the growing luxury and hypocrisy of the church, associated by much of the peasantry with the landowning aristocracy, contrasted with the ethical appeal of the Cathar Perfects: their simplicity, abstemiousness, poverty and asceticism. The Perfects also included women as well men in their number, and were furthermore required to work for a living within the community, in contrast to the church clergy. There is much evidence too for the simple hospitality of the Perfects, extended to both Christians and Cathars alike: meals (bread and nuts—the Perfects were vegetarian) were always shared. Election to the Perfects, according to one version that has been recorded, involved being asked 'first if they wished to give themselves to God and the Gospel; secondly, if they would promise not to eat meat, eggs or cheese or any fat except vegetable oil or fish; not to take any oath, not to lie, not to satisfy any bodily desire—all this for the rest of their lives.'[13] The Cathar 'baptismal' rite is expressed in similar vein: 'This holy baptism, by which the Holy Spirit is given, in the Church of God has preserved from the apostles until this time and it has passed from Good Men to Good Men until the present moment, and it will continue

---

* Later on the term—in Christian eyes—assumed a pejorative meaning implying sodomite, a part of the anti-Cathar propaganda war, from where we get our word 'bugger'.

to do so until the end of the world.' The initiate was then enjoined not to commit adultery, kill, lie, swear an oath or steal, and should 'hate the world and its works and the things of this world.'[14] The Perfects—both male and female—also made home visits, paying particular care to the well-being of children, the comfort of the sick and the care of the poor. All of this made fertile ground for a protest movement in western Europe.

From Italy and France the religion spread to Flanders, Germany—there was a wholesale burning of Cathars in Cologne in 1163—and England, where it was publicly denounced in Oxford in the 1160s. A Cathar was burnt at the stake in London as late as 1210 and there were still numerous communities in Bavaria as late as the 1230s. But France remained the main centre. In Languedoc, the Cathars' greatest stronghold, Catharism and Catholicism were not the only faiths recorded. There were also Arians and Waldensians, both of them Christian heresies, as well as a large community of Jews. The latter arrived from Andalusia following the rise of the Almohads there in the 1140s, who were less tolerant of non-Muslims. Indeed, it has been suggested that Jewish Cabbalistic ideas might have partially paved the way for Catharism.[15] In the countryside of southern France Catharism, when not greeted with outright sympathy and conversions, was at least tolerated by the minor gentry, who allowed it to grow and multiply. In the towns, where the Church and orthodoxy had a greater hold, it was less successful. This was in contrast to Italy, where Catharism tended to be more urban, gaining converts among the tradesmen and craftsmen.

The most powerful Cathar see was Albi in Provence, which soon became the effective centre of the religion. Indeed, Albi eventually gave its name to the movement itself: Albigensian. By 1167 there were Cathar bishoprics at Toulouse, Albi, Carcasonne, Agen, Razès and Montségur, and they were even powerful enough to hold a great public church council in Félix-de-Caraman near Toulouse in 1176. Cathar bishops from all over Europe as far as Constantinople attended, and they obviously enjoyed the patronage of a number of noble families. Cathar doctrine, structure and hierarchy was formalised, and the Council was presided over by Bishop Nicetas from Constantinople, who was entitled *Papa,* i.e., Pope. Clearly, the Cathar church was becoming a force to be reckoned with. By the early thirteenth century it was beginning to attract minor nobility—the house of Foix, for example—and even Raymond VI of Toulouse was sympathetic (albeit not a practising Cathar).[16]

THE ALBIGENSIAN CRUSADE

In 1199 a young Italian nobleman, Lotario di Segni, assumed the papal throne under the name of Pope Innocent III, and the church began to fight back in earnest. Pope Innocent was one of the more vigorous popes of the medieval church. He enforced papal ascendancy and openly interfered with secular states and rulers in Europe (King John in England, for example). He would not tolerate any deviation from Rome's view of Christianity—it was during Pope Innocent's time that the notorious Fourth Crusade was launched against Christian Constantinople—and he viewed the struggle against the Cathars as even more important than that against Islam. Hence, a crusade against the Cathars in 1209 was launched: the Albigensian Crusade. Innocent promised his warriors not only the full indulgences that were standard in the Crusades against Muslims but also—a greater incentive—land that was to be confiscated from the Cathars. The first blow was struck in July at the town of Béziers, where the order was supposedly given by the papal legate and leader of the Crusade, Arnau Amalric, to 'kill them all for the Lord knows his own.' The words are probably apocryphal, but they do nonetheless accurately express the fanatic hatred of the Cathars by the Church and the brutal efforts to suppress them at any cost. A general massacre of both guilty and innocent followed—many were burnt to death in the cathedral where they sought sanctuary—even though the Cathar population of Béziers was probably less then ten percent. The indiscriminate slaughter and utter horror felt at the time by both Cathars and non-Cathars is appropriately expressed in the contemporary troubadour's song quoted at the beginning of this chapter.

Narbonne and Carcasonne then meekly submitted to the crusading army, but campaigning continued for some years as many Cathars were in well defended strongholds, such as the great fortresses of Peyreperteuse and Montségur. Punishment for captured Cathars—or even suspected Cathars—was horrific: stonings, beatings, blindings, rapings were routine, usually culminating in mass burnings. The war was fought with equal viciousness on the propaganda front. The Church accused the Cathars of practising mass night-time orgies where sex was completely indiscriminate and without distinction, between same sexes, between brothers and sisters and between parents and children. Babies born of such unions claimed by the Church to be burnt and their ashes ritually eaten in a mockery of the Catholic eucharist.[17]

11. Languedoc (after Barber 2000)

After the initial blood-letting there was an easing of tensions in the 1220s and 1230s, when many Cathars in the south of France came back out into open. After 1240, however, the crusade was revived with renewed vigour under Pope Gregory IX and King Louis IX of France. Following the assassination of some inquisitors at the village of Avignonet in 1242 by Cathar sympathisers, it was decided to destroy the Cathar stronghold of Montségur once and for all. Knowing their fate, the Cathar Perfects defended their fortress to the bitter end with no surrender countenanced.

When the end seemed inevitable they divided all their possessions and gave them away to the survivors. Many of the non-Cathar garrison were inspired to convert in the final hours by the faith and devoutness of the Cathar Perfects. After a long siege, Montségur fell in March 1244. The lay defenders of Montségur were allowed to go free, but for the Perfects—including those who converted during the siege and others who insisted on following them who otherwise might be allowed to go free—an inevitable fate awaited. Some two hundred of the leading Cathars were put onto a massive pyre and burnt to death. 'The great days of Catharism in its heartland thus ended in both tragedy and glory, in an episode that demonstrated yet again the remarkable power of Catharism in the gravest adversity.'[18]

Montségur was thought to have been impregnable. With its fall, surviving Cathars were forced underground. There followed what was probably the largest police style investigation until the advent of the institutionalised secret police services of the twentieth century. The need for the Church to recognise Catharism as a heresy, and then to punish its adherents, gave rise to a specialist group within the Church whose decisions would be final and who had absolute powers of life and death over the people whom they were trying. This group would be formalised as the Inquisition, perhaps the most notorious body in the history of Christendom. The Inquisition—or *Inquisitio heretice pravitatis*, the 'Inquiry concerning heretical depravity' to give it its full title—was created by Innocent III specifically to root out Catharism. Its officers were answerable solely to the pope, and it was to be above any other existing laws. Over a period of nine and a half months every male over fourteen and every female over twelve in the region were routinely interrogated, often re-interrogated and cross-questioned, all statements painstakingly recorded and cross-referenced.

The Inquisition did not always proceed smoothly. Of particular repugnance was the exhumation by the inquisitors of 'suspected heretics' and the burning of their bones. This attracted widespread opposition—amongst Cathars and non-Cathars alike—resulting in inquisitors being mobbed and beaten on several occasions and some on one occasion even being hacked to death. In the end, the Church had to halt exhumations.

There was some revival at the end of the thirteenth century and in the early years of the fourteenth. The last important Cathar leader, Pierre Autier, was betrayed and captured and, after a long period of interrogation, was burnt in front of a great assembly in 1310, defiant to the last. But despite Autier's revival and defiance, the heart had gone out of the Cathar movement in the ashes of Montségur, and the subsequent thoroughness and ruthlessness of the inquisitorial techniques ensured that it disappeared into oblivion.

WERE THE CATHARS MANICHEES?

Throughout history—from the Middle Ages, if not antiquity, down to the modern era—Manichaeism and Catharism are almost invariably referred to as 'heresies'. This is not only a pejorative term, but it is a moot point whether Catharism was technically a heresy, just as Christianity is not generally regarded as a heresy of Judaism or Islam as a heresy of Christianity.* The dualist movements, particularly Manichaeism but also Bogomilism and Catharism, were not breakaway movements from the established Church such as the later Protestant movements were, but were separate movements altogether. The differences of Catharism from Christianity were so fundamental that it must surely be described as a separate religion, not a heresy. Just how 'Iranian' was this religion that posed as a viable alternative to—and came so close to seriously challenging—the power of the Catholic church in western Europe?

Unfortunately, there is so little known. On the one hand, the Cathars were never secretive about their beliefs but actively proselytised; their religion was—at the time—a matter for open record. On the other hand it is important to remember that the sole records we have of Cathar beliefs are from their Church detractors, who viewed them with abhorrence: the Church not only went out of its way to present Cathar beliefs as negatively as possible, but to eradicate all traces of them. To be fair to the Church, there were genuine efforts by the inquisitors to understand their beliefs if only to understand what they were up against. Nonetheless, the ultimate goal of the Church was complete extinction, to root out all traces not only of the movement but of the beliefs as well. We have, therefore, very little to go upon, and the little amount that we do must be viewed with the above caveats in mind—it is as if one had to reconstruct Marxism based solely upon the records of the inquiries of Senator McCarthy and the Committee for Un-American Activities.

---

* Although C S Lewis notably—and erroneously—wrote that 'Islam is only the greatest of the Christian heresies', in *Christian Apologetics*, p. 158.

The basic belief is unambiguously dualist: that there existed uncreated and entirely separate concepts of good and evil. The belief that evil/Lucifer then attacked Good/God and captured part of his essence, that mankind is then the result of this combination thus containing both good (the soul) and evil (the body) appear to be pure Manichaean. However, there appears on the surface to be elements in Cathar belief that were not Manichaean but which seem to have been adopted from Christianity. Baptism, for example, was incorporated into Cathar practice, and this has no counterpart in eastern Manichaeism. But it was performed by the laying on of hands rather than by water, which might be viewed as polluting the sacred element of water and so in keeping with Zoroastrian sentiment. Similarly, the Cathar abhorrence of the sacrament which, being of material substance, had to be by definition the work of the devil, so that associating it with the worship of god was seen to be blasphemous. One must remember, too, that Mani himself incorporated elements of Christianity into his beliefs, as well as Buddhism and—of course—Zoroastrianism. This has led to Manichaeism being labelled a 'parasitic' religion by its detractors, but it did at least mean that it could be 'grafted on' to other existing religions: similar difficulties, for example, have been encountered in disentangling Manichaeism from Buddhism in Central Asia.

A core Cathar belief was that, given the existence of evil (which even the Christians admitted), it was inconceivable that it could have been created by God. Hence, good and evil had existed as entirely separate, uncreated concepts since the beginning of time. Then, in a time before the creation, the kingdom of heaven was invaded by Satan, or evil, and did battle against God and heaven. Satan was evicted, but had managed to capture and come away with some of the powers of heaven—sometimes expressed as captive angels. These captive life-giving powers from heaven enabled Satan to then create the material world from which to make war against heaven. He then created mankind through procreation, thus to use them to wage war against God. There are thus two worlds: the visible material world that was corrupt, and the invisible incorrupt world that was eternal. Because Satan had used elements captured from heaven with which to create mankind, there was an essence of heaven—of goodness—within each person: the soul, which was a part of heaven, captive within the material body which was created by Satan. Hence, it was the belief of the Cathars to make known the inner goodness within everybody, and for the soul to eventually return to its origin. Jesus was one of the beings who had been sent by heaven to make mankind aware of the captive soul (although it is unclear exactly what the Cathar concept of Jesus implied; he could not have been born of a woman, as this implied procreation, which was the work of Satan). The material world would continue only so long as souls remained captive: once all souls had returned from the evil world back to heaven, the material world would come to an end. This would happen when another redeemer would be sent from heaven. There are seven ascending levels of heaven, each more pure than the last, so as to maintain absolute purity uncontaminated by the battle against evil.

The Cathar movement had obviously lost some of the original Manichaeism in its journey to the west and absorbed many non-Manichaean elements on its way. But these beliefs appear consistent with Manichaeism. There is no evidence that Mani himself was cited, except perhaps indirectly (for example, 'preserved by the apostles … and passed on by Good Men to Good Men … and will continue to do so until the end of the world').[19] There is little evidence, too, for some of the more cerebral aspects of Manichaeism, and no writings of Mani nor any of Manichaean sacred writings seemed to have been used in Europe; the Cathars only used the New Testament. This in fact is consistent with Manichaeism, for Mani admitted underlying truth in all religions (although the Cathars abhorred the Old Testament, regarding it as sacrilegious). In any case it must be remembered that Manichaeism was so ruthlessly exterminated that many of its more cerebral—and more Manichaean—elements might no longer be visible.

Contemporaries, such as the Catholic inquisitors in Western Europe and Princess Anna Comnena in Constantinople, equated Catharism and Bogomilism unambiguously with Manichaeism, although the term probably was little more than a term of abuse in such cases. There is little doubt that Catharism owed much to Bogomilism and modern studies almost invariably confirm this link.[20] That Bogomilsm in turn came from Paulicianism also seems beyond doubt. With Paulicianism we are back to where Manichaeism itself flourished, and the Paulician movement in Armenia has been specifically linked to Manichaeism.[21] There was, therefore, a continuous 'chain of transmission' leading Catharism back to Manichaeism, and many modern scholars of Manichaeism affirm such a connection.[22]

Some trace Catharism and Bogomilism directly back to Zoroastrianism, by-passing both the Paulicians and the Manichaeans. Equally, others assert that the European dualist movements were entirely independent with no connections to the Manichaeans. Some authorities see the origin of the

Cathar movement in the Carolingian debates of the ninth century on the nature of good and evil, not necessarily derived from the Bogomils (although both were aware of each other): that Catharism was completely independent, in other words, of either Bogomilism or Manichaeism.[23] Both extreme views, however, simply reflect how *little* we know of the Cathars, and the real answer to the question posed at the beginning of this section of 'were the Cathars Manichees?' can only be 'we do not know.' They were almost certainly not Manichaeans in the original ancient sense of the term: there was no direct link to the Manichees who practised in the Roman Empire. However, the Cathar-Bogomil-Paulician links were real. In this way the dualist ideas of the Cathars led back to the source. What cannot be in serious doubt is that the concepts of dualism as first articulated by Zoroaster and later refined by Mani had a major effect on the world's religious beliefs, and this was adopted and carried forward with such enthusiasm in the west that its adherents would rather face hideous torture and death than renounce this fundamental belief.

THE IMPACT UPON THE WEST

What effect did it ultimately have upon the west? The main legacy of Catharism is probably seen in the development of the late medieval Church of Rome and the position of the papacy. The crisis of Catharism forced the Church to examine itself and the nature of its beliefs, its practice and its position. In deciding matters of doctrine and consequently condemning and exterminating heterodoxy—real or perceived—the Church assumed ultimate authority on all religious and moral issues, allowing no rival. All decisions came to be centred ultimately on the authority of the pope and papal infallibility. It is notable that none of the eastern churches have this element. This was the culmination of the emergence of the papacy as an independent force and supreme bishopric that had been under way since about 800. In the early church, the papacy was but one of the four ancient apostolic patriarchates—Jerusalem, Antioch, Alexandria and Rome—and were in any case theoretically subject to the Great Church in Constantinople. Before about 750 the pope was not necessarily recognised as supreme bishop in Spain, France or even northern Italy. It is notable that the title of 'pope' only became exclusive to the bishop of Rome after the eighth century (and even after that date was still used to describe the head of the Cathar Church in the twelfth century as we have noted).[24] Then, by investing itself with the power to create emperors with Pope Leo's coronation of Charlemagne in 800, the papacy began to claim supremacy over all Christendom. The ruthless answer to the challenge posed by Catharism was a culmination of this process. It was, after all, during this period that the Papacy launched its greatest claim to supreme Christian leadership, the Crusades—and it was no accident that one of those Crusades (the Fourth) was launched against Rome's only serious rival: Constantinople. It was also this period that saw the struggle between the papacy and the Emperor Frederick II for moral and political leadership of Western Europe, culminating in the triumph of the papacy in 1250 with the death of Frederick II and the collapse of the Hohenstaufen supremacy.

As a protest movement, Manichaeism in Europe anticipated many aspects of Protestantism, as did its emphasis on more ascetic values: its belief in the absolute depravity of Man, for example, and its emphasis on the body of men known as the Perfect or Elect as the only ones for redemption. In much the same way, Manichaeism had earlier been a protest movement against orthodox Zoroastrian Iran. The Hohenstaufen and the Cathar movements both, in their very different ways, anticipated Protestantism in its resistance to the power of the established church. It is notable that the French Protestant strongholds and the Wars of Religion of the sixteenth and seventeenth century were in the same region of France as Catharism.

The emergence of the Dominicans and Franciscans in the late twelfth/ early thirteenth century was in part a response to the Cathars. The vows taken on election to the Perfects anticipated many of the medieval Christian mendicant teaching orders, especially the Franciscans—indeed, it is notable that many Cathars who escaped martyrdom later entered monasteries and convents. Some elements of Catharism, such as the evil of matter and the importance of an ascetic life, were adopted—presumably unconsciously— by St Francis, who would have encountered (and tolerated) them amongst the Cathars of Italy.

The Zoroastrian concept of evil influenced Christianity in one important respect. Up until the Middle Ages, the Christian 'Devil' was not the embodiment of evil he has become now, but was more a tempter, a fallen angel. The more evil and 'demonic' attributes of the Devil probably came after the contact with the Cathars, which derived its idea of evil from Zoroastrianism. Indeed, the Catholic Church's view of—and concern with—the concept of evil owes more to the Manichaean concept of evil than to early Christianity: it is notable, for example, that the eastern Churches do not have the same emphasis on evil.

Up until the time of the Albigensian Crusade, the area loosely known as the ill-defined region of Occitania—largely southern France and adjacent regions in Italy and Spain—was only nominally under the Kingdom of France. The conquest of this region—particularly of the powerful County of Toulouse—of which the Albigensian Crusade provided an excuse was one of the more important developments in the emergence of the Kingdom of France roughly in its modern form. Hence, by 1240 King Louis IX was able for the first time to provide visible form to the extension of his kingdom to the Mediterranean by the construction of the new fortress city of Aigues-Mortes at the mouth of the Rhône.

Ironically it was perhaps Catharism's very tolerance that contributed to its ultimate failure in Europe. For its incorporation of some elements of Christianity led the Church to regard it merely as a 'heresy'—and hence as a divergence from orthodox Catholicism to be suppressed—and not the separate religion that it was (Islam, for example, was rarely if ever described as a 'heresy'). This meant that recognition of its very existence was denied. Even today Manichaeism can still arouse strong passions. In the introduction to the Penguin Classics edition of St Augustine's *Confessions*, for example, Mani is referred to as a 'fanatic' and the religion written off simply as 'fantastic theories'. Elsewhere we read that 'for us, looking at it so many centuries later, the doctrine of Manes or Mani, "the many-headed monster," seems a misleading jumble, in which someone of considerable intelligence, but lacking any cohesive thought, has tossed together a thousand badly assimilated ingredients, Buddhism, Gnosticism, and Judaic-Christian traditions, the whole thing relying on the substratum of old Persian dualism. The collection of myths—some pretty, others silly—gives the crazy impression of a spiritual universe in utter chaos.'[25] One is left almost admiring the power that a long dead religion can still exert.

The twentieth century has seen a revival of interest in the Cathars and a recognition of their suppression as one of the more shameful aspects of European history. To be sure, some of this revived interest has been on the extremer fringes of fantasy, associating the Cathars with everything from the Templars, the Holy Grail and mysterious 'lost treasures of Montségur' to the Turin Shroud, the Freemasons, the Rosicrucians and mysterious codes. It makes excellent fiction, but is hardly history. Although not fantasy, the creation in 1989 of a 'Pays Cathare' brand in Languedoc geared mainly to tourism and applied as a stamp of approval to everything from standards of accommodation to organic goat's cheese, is hardly more relevant to the Cathars than Dan Brown's *Da Vinci Code*. More serious was the establishment of the Centre National d'Études Cathares in Carcasonne in 1982, with the aim of promoting their study and uncovering more of its past. More recently, 'the terrible tragedy of the Cathars or "Good Men" and their witness to their faith' has been recognised by the Catalonian musician, Jordi Savall, with the monumental production in 2009 of *The Forgotten Kingdom. The Albigensian Crusade.* This is a compilation on three compact discs of music from the time, together with accompanying 560 pages of notes in Occitan, Catalan, German, Italian, French, English and Castellan, as a tribute that 'deserve[s] our unreserved respect and determined effort to preserve their historical memory.'[26]

Ironically, it was in its very persecution that we ultimately see how powerful an effect the dualist ideas had on Europe. For its suppression was so fanatical and so ruthless that it demonstrated just how much the challenge posed by the dualists was as a very persuasive threat to the established church: it so nearly won.

Chapter 10

AN IRANIAN WORLD
Conclusion

The dynasties of ancient Iran were not only those well-known great opponents of Greeks and Romans on the battlefield, but also their cherished trading partners. Under the Achaemenids, Greek philosophy flourished in Ionia, Greek mercenaries fought for Persian interests, and Greek statesmen served as counsellors to the great kings. The Parthians counted Greek citizens and settlers among their subjects and were impressed by Greek culture and learning. The Sasanians, though deporting Greeks and Romans from Syria, at the same time offered protection and refuge to the persecuted minorities of the Roman empire, guaranteeing religious freedom and the chance of economic and social promotion to all those who prove loyal.

Josef Wiesehöfer[1]

In examining how cultures from beyond Europe contributed to what we consider to be 'the west', I have strictly limited myself to those cultures (civilisations, empires or other forms—the exact definitions need not concern us here) that actually extended geographically into Europe, whether by colonisation, conquest or other ways of direct interaction. Hence—regretfully—I have set aside the effects that other non-European cultures have had upon the west: the enormous impact of Jewish culture or Chinese civilisation, for example. Volume 1 of this series conformed to my self-imposed limits: the Phoenicians by colonisation and the Arabs by conquest, both extending over significant parts of Europe for a very long time. In devoting an entire volume to a power that extended only to a tiny part of south-eastern Europe for a very brief period it might at first appear that I am stretching my own constraints, but I hope in this book to have demonstrated that Persia's foothold of a mere sixty years on the fringes of Europe has had as profound effect as the Phoenicians' six hundred, or the Arabs' or Turks' far longer periods. In summing up, therefore, we may examine Iran's legacy not only in the making of the west, but towards the making of a single world.

Towards One World

In writing a single world history, the historian J M Roberts emphasises that 'Persian culture ... was one always open to influence from abroad and would continue to be. ... The base of a future world civilisation was in the making.'[2] The area of Western Asia—roughly the area covered by the Persian Empire—has a longer history of unity than, say, the Indian subcontinent or Europe have had. In uniting this vast area, the Persian Empire encouraged the transmission of ideas across it long after its collapse. Never mind the largely mythical Silk Route, it was the Persian Empire that first created an international world that allowed peoples, goods, ideas and artistic creativity to move on a vast scale. The area remained a natural unit: the Parthian and Sasanian Empires soon assumed much the same shape, and with the advent of Islam the Arab Islamic Empire very rapidly assumed similar borders to that of the former Persian Empire, borders that were established again by the Seljuks in the eleventh century. The Persians imposed a unity on the region that long outlasted its collapse.[3] It also meant that Iran has been continuously open to outside influences: it is a civilisation that both gives and receives.

For the civilisation of Iran has never been isolationist or looked inwards: it has always looked outwards to other cultures, adopting, embracing and adapting them. A subject of the Persian Empire once remarked that 'no race is so ready to adopt foreign ways as the Persian.'[4] This is as true now as when Herodotus made this observation. In the sixties modern Persian was using the term *gharbzadeh*, which can be roughly translated as 'west-struck', a term used to describe those who were captivated by western (and particularly American) culture. We have already observed how in Herodotus' day Persian culture borrowed extensively from Egypt, Greece, Anatolia, Central Asia and Mesopotamia (occasionally reflected in the architecture of just a single column: see Pl. 15). Often such borrowings would be almost unquestioning, such as with the *gharbzadeh* youth of Tehran in the seventies.

But ultimately such borrowings transcended the mere imitative: out of all the styles imported into Susa and Persepolis emerged a style that was at the same time both international and uniquely Persian, a style that underpinned the arts of the Near East and beyond for centuries to come.

The pattern of borrowing, imitating and then transforming became a permanent characteristic of Persian civilisation. A further example from the days of Herodotus concerns one of history's more important revolutions: the establishment of a monetary economy and an international currency. Lydia in Anatolia was the first country to invent coinage. The idea was soon adopted by both the Greeks and the Persians, but it was the latter with the introduction of the 'Daric' that set up the first international currency based upon a single standard. Modern economy still revolves around this. But perhaps the greatest example of Iran's transformation of a foreign import lies in religion.

The Idea of a Universal Religion

For the civilisation of Islamic Iran proved no less adaptive than that of ancient Iran. Once again Iran absorbed an entirely foreign culture along with much of what it entailed: the religion of Islam along with its legal system, and the script—and much of the vocabulary—of Arabic. Iran then proceeded to transform Islam. For after the Caliphate moved east to Baghdad in 750, Islam became increasingly Iranised. This was explored more in Volume 1 of this series,* but for the moment it is worth emphasising some of the more salient points and results of this first 'Islamic revolution' which, like its modern equivalent, was essentially Iranian in character. The 'Abbasid Revolution' which moved the Caliphate to Baghdad was largely a revolt by non-Arab Muslims, particularly by Iranians. Hence, although the Caliphate in Baghdad remained Arab it soon came to be dominated more by powerful Iranian families of viziers, such as the Barmakids, who came from Balkh, and later the Buyid dynasty, governors from northern Iran. Although writing in Arabic (new Persian did not become established as a literary language until after the tenth century), many of Islam's earliest intellectuals who established Islamic ideas, practice and jurisprudence were Iranian. Iran then became the leading centre of Islamic learning between about 850 and 1130: al-Razi, al-Majusi and Ibn Sina (Avicenna) in the medical sciences, for

---

* *Out of Arabia,* Chapter 7.

example, and al-Khwarazmi and al-Biruni in mathematics and astronomy. Al-Razi was still consulted well into the nineteenth century as an authority on smallpox and measles, and Avicenna underpinned medicine in Europe until well after the Renaissance. It was Iranians who did much to transform the religion from one of Arabia to that of a truly universal one.

The idea of a universal religion was embedded in Iran's earliest history even before the Iranians migrated from Central Asia to the land they gave their name to. The religion of Zoroaster hardly spread beyond the Iranian peoples themselves, but the figure of Zoroaster became a powerful metaphor in subsequent philosophies. Greek philosophers were fascinated by him, from Plato in fifth century BC to Synesius in the fifth century AD to Pleithon in the fifteenth. Both the fascination and the metaphor were taken up by modern philosophers from Nietzsche to Bertrand Russell. Nietzche's 'Zarathustra' has probably reached more audiences through Richard Strauss' tone poem, *Also Sprach Zarathustra*, if only through the masterly use of its opening by Stanley Kubrick in his classic 1969 science fiction movie, *2001: A Space Odyssey*. Richard Strauss was not the first composer to fall under his spell: in 1749 Jean-Philippe Rameau's five-act opera *Zoroastre* was a remarkable attempt to explore the actual message. Set in ancient Bactria, the opera's theme was the struggle between good represented by Orosmade and evil represented by Arimane. A Zoroastrian musical theme can perhaps also be perceived in another work by a contemporary of Rameau's, *Les Elemens* by Jean-Féry Rebel, a court musician of Louis XIV, which explores musically the four sacred elements of Zoroastrianism.

Of course, the works of Rebel, Rameau or Strauss can no more be described as 'Zoroastrian' than those of Russell, Nietzsche or Pleithon, but they nonetheless bear witness to the power of universal themes first articulated by Zoroaster. A more direct influence of the universal message of Zoroaster was through Manichaeism, one of the earliest to become a world religion. This had a profound effect upon the dualist religious movements of medieval Europe as we have seen, although the Bogomil and Cathar Churches cannot be described as a part of a universal Manichaean religion. But Manichaeism was to spread more in the east than in the west. It found great favour after the third century amongst the Soghdians of Central Asia (who were an Iranian people). Through them the religion was passed on to the Turks, first under the Turk Empire in the seventh century and then the Uighur Empire in the tenth, both of which adopted Manichaeism at state level. The Soghdian-Manichaean lobby in the Turk and Uighur empires was able to exert a disproportionate influence, not only in these empires but beyond in China. Indeed, in the early eighth century China came very near to being ruled by an Iranian dynasty when a major rebellion was led by the Sogdian An Lushan, which almost toppled the infant T'ang dynasty. Although Manichaeism never became a major religion in China, it did continue to spread, particularly after the Mongol conquest allowed religious freedom. The Manichaeans were noted in Fukien by Marco Polo in 1292, which remained a pocket of Manichaeism throughout the Ming period. Indeed, an active Manichaean temple still remained in use at Huabiao near Quanzhou in Fukien as late as the early twentieth century when the Manichaean religion finally became extinct. The temple still survives, becoming the only Manichaean monument on the UNESCO World Heritage list in 1991.[5] Today, elements of Manichaeism remain with the Yazidis of Kurdistan and the Mandaeans of southern Mesopotamia.

IRAN AND THE FIRST WORLD CHURCH

It may come as a surprise—or, in view of the above, no surprise—to learn that of all religions, it was Christianity that first became a world religion through ancient Iran. The combination of Christian missionary activity and the Sasanian deportations from Syria had already made Christianity an important minority religion in Iran by the third century, with missionaries reaching Merv in Central Asia by AD 200 or earlier. However, it was the Nestorian Christians who assumed particular prominence in Sasanian Iran. The Nestorian Church (the 'official' and more appropriate name is the Church of the East or the Assyrian Church) came into being following the condemnation of Bishop Nestorius at the Council of Ephesus in 431 as a heresiarch over a dispute concerning the nature of Christ. Its followers were consequently persecuted by the orthodox court in Constantinople, being forced to flee progressively further eastwards. Nestorian Christians were not only welcomed as refugees from the rival Roman Empire, but encouraged to establish their own church. It even became an autocephalous church, the first in Christendom, established under Sasanian protection, when it was encouraged as an official Iranian church in opposition to the Orthodox Church of Constantinople with its patriarchate at the Sasanian capital of Ctesiphon. The Roman world's loss not only reinvigorated intellectual life in Iran but also stimulated much of the trade of Asia, both overland and maritime. In the Persian Gulf and

Indian Ocean regions the Nestorians established a number of communities, with bishoprics throughout southern Iran, southern Mesopotamia, northern Arabia and western and southern India. Metropolitanates were established in Charax, Rev Ardeshir (Bushehr) and Qatar. They were similarly active inland. In 410-415 Syrian sources describe the establishment of a Metropolitan See in Samarkand. In 635 Chinese sources mention a Nestorian missionary from Syria establishing a church in Xinjiang, with further missions taking Nestorian Christianity to China after the early eighth century. It took root in Central Asia as early as the fifth century, becoming (along with Manichaeism) one of the main religions of the Soghdians after the sixth century and of the Uighur Empire of Xinjiang after the eighth century.

The Islamic conquest saw the high point of the Church of the East. With the foundation of Baghdad and establishment of the ᶜAbbasid Caliphate after 750 the Patriarchate moved to Baghdad and was able to benefit from the huge world-wide reach as well as the religious tolerance of the ᶜAbbasid Empire. By the tenth century the Patriarch in Baghdad was consecrating metropolitans as far away as Central Asia, China and southern India. The power of the church further increased with the Mongol conquest, as Nestorianism had spread amongst the Mongols from Soghdian and Uighur influence, forming an important element—not to mention a strong Christian lobby—in the Mongol aristocracy. By the beginning of the fourteenth century there were 27 archdioceses under Baghdad stretching from the Mediterranean to the China Sea. The Church of the East in Central Asia was the main origin of the medieval European legends of Prester John, the 'oriental Christian Empire' which would supposedly join forces with western Christendom to drive the Muslims from the Holy Land. One Nestorian priest from Peking even performed mass for Edward I of England at his court in 1297.[6]

Today, the Church of the East is only a shadow of its former self with about forty thousand adherents in north-western Iran and neighbouring parts of Turkey and Iraq (although the Keralan Christians of southern India are descendants of the Church). But it was the Church of the East that became a world church long before the rise of the medieval papacy of Rome with its claim to supremacy and Christian universality—a salutary corrective, if nothing else, to the common preconception of Christianity and the Christian Church as wholly 'western'.

There was another Iranian religious element that had a profound, albeit indirect, effect on the growth of Christianity in the Greek mind. This came via Alexander. One of the most controversial acts (to his contemporaries) of Alexander's career was his insistence upon *proskynesis*, the Persian ritual obeisance, during and after his Central Asian campaign. Failure to observe it meant death to Greeks and Macedonians on several occasions (most notoriously to Alexander's 'friend' Cleitus in Samarkand, whom Alexander impaled). The increasing numbers of Iranians in Alexander's court and army saw nothing wrong with *proskynesis*, being standard practice before a Persian monarch. But to the Greeks and Macedonians it was abhorrent to the point of blasphemous. For *proskynesis* was reserved solely for a god, and Alexander's insistence on it implied divine status. In the end, Alexander had his way and it became standard, if reluctant, practice at his court in recognition of Alexander's spurious claim to be the son of god (of Zeus Ammon). The cult of the living god in a king was then renewed under the Seleucids, especially Antiochus Epiphanes, when it was imposed as an official cult to unify disparate peoples.[7] Alexander thus paved the way for the idea of Christ in the Greek mind, that a man could be at once human and divine, a god and the son of a god, a concept that continued to plague the Greek mind for another thousand years with their concerns over the human and divine natures of Christ.

FROM PLATO'S ACADEMY TO THE ITALIAN RENAISSANCE

Following the Battle of Edessa in AD 260, sixty-thousand Roman prisoners-of-war were captured with Emperor Valerian and settled in Assyria, Susiana, Persia and elsewhere. Shapur founded several cities peopled by these prisoners, including Gundishapur in Susiana, built along the lines of a Roman military camp, which became the main centre for Roman deportees.[8] Gundishapur (or Jundeshapur) was to have a long and illustrious history. When Justinian closed down Plato's ancient Academy at Athens, it was, significantly, to Gundishapur that the heirs to the Greek philosophers moved.[9] It evolved into a major religious and intellectual centre, attracting some of the greatest minds of both the Roman and Iranian worlds with a famous observatory and medical school that lasted well into the Islamic period. It also became a centre for the translation of Greek texts into Syriac—mainly scientific and philosophic works. This was regarded as a priority for the Sasanian kings, for in Iranian historical tradition Greek learning was viewed as Persian that was stolen by Alexander and the originals destroyed, until recovered and re-translated by the Sasanians and ᶜAbbasids in the Middle Ages.[10] Hence, Ibn Khaldun in the fourteenth century wrote in his *Introduction to History*:

> Among the Persians, the intellectual sciences played a large and important role, since the Persian dynasties were powerful and ruled without interruption. The intellectual sciences are said to have come to the Greeks from the Persians, when Alexander killed Darius and gained control of the Achaemenid empire. At that time, he appropriated the books and sciences of the Persians.[11]

Ibn Khaldun then describes how in becoming heirs to Greek learning, the Muslims through them were ultimately able to recover the 'stolen' world of Persian learning. Whether or not this tradition is true (and it probably has little real foundation) is not the issue. What made this of huge importance for the development of later European history was that the translations of the Greek classics at Gundishapur (as well as at other translation centres in the Sasanian and ᶜAbbasid empires) preserved much of Greek learning that was otherwise lost in the west, only to be transmitted to Europe subsequently by the Arabs.* By the sixth century Gundishapur had become a centre of learning where Roman, Greek and Syrian scholars were able to meet their Iranian counterparts in an atmosphere of religious and intellectual toleration not known in the Roman world at the time. The glory that was Gundishapur is a tribute to both of the civilisations that produced it.

Religion and learning was a major legacy of ancient Persia, but it is not often appreciated just how much impact it had in politics as well. For all the west's trumpeting of democratic ideals based on the Greek model, it is significant just how much Iranian monarchism proved ultimately the ideal that was more imitated. For the Greeks there is, of course, Xenophon's unabashed panegyric of Persian monarchism in the *Cyropaedia*, as a challenge to Plato's *Republic*. But more importantly, whenever ancient republicanism came into contact with Iran, it was the west that changed, not the east. Hence, soon after Greece's victory against Persia in the fifth century BC, Athens adopted imperial trappings. And soon after Republican Rome entered the east, it created its own 'Shahinshah' and became an empire.

---

* See Volume 1 in this series, *Out of Arabia*.

TOWARDS A UNIVERSAL LANGUAGE

The huge range of nationalities that came under the Persian Empire created the need for the first time of a single international language to administer the empire and hold its disparate parts together from Egypt to the Indian borderlands. The Old Persian language, written in a script adapted from the cuneiform of Mesopotamia, was the official language of the royal inscriptions, together with Elamite and Babylonian. But for everyday administrative purposes and communications throughout its vast empire, the Persians adopted the Aramaic language and—more importantly—the Aramaic script of Syria, which had evolved from the first alphabetic systems of the ancient Phoenicians in the second millennium. Known as Official or Imperial Aramaic, this was the first time that an international language had been used to any significant extent in history, stimulated by similar Persian needs for an international coinage noted above.

The use of Aramaic as an international language declined after the collapse of the Persian Empire, at least in the Persian heartland, although it remained in use throughout much of the Near East for many centuries and today is still spoken in some pockets of Syria and Turkey. However, the Aramaic script has a longer history, particularly on the eastern borderlands of the Persian Empire. It remained as the script for the Middle Persian language of the Parthian and Sasanian Empires, and the script, and developments of it, continued to be used to write the Iranian related languages of Central Asia long into the early first millennium AD: Bactrian, Kharoshti (the language of the Kushan Empire) and Soghdian. In the ninth century the Uighurs adopted the Soghdian-Aramaic script for writing Turkish. With the establishment of the Mongol Empire, Genghis Khan required the Mongolian language—hitherto an entirely unwritten language—to be written for administering his empire, so engaged Uighur scholars to adapt the Aramaic script for Mongolian. This script was still used to write the Mongolian language in the Republic of Mongolia until it changed to the Cyrillic in the 1920s, and is still used in the Mongolian Autonomous Region (Inner Mongolia) of China to this day. As one of China's five official languages, the Aramaic script thus appears on modern Chinese banknotes.

The Persian language itself was also one of the first international languages of the modern era. It became the language of Iran again after it re-emerged following the Muslim conquest, stimulated by its adoption as the court language of Samanid Bukhara in the tenth century and its revival as a literary language by Firdausi and his contemporaries. With the establishment of the Mongol Empire in the thirteenth century, large numbers of Iranians were incorporated into the Mongol administration, so that Persian became probably the main language of administration throughout the empire. Iranian officials and the Persian language remained a major administrative component of the successor Mongol Yuan dynasty in China down to the fifteenth century, when the Ming eventually replaced it with Chinese.

The Persian language also spread into India, at first with the conquests of Mahmud of Ghazna from eastern Afghanistan in the eleventh century. Although the Ghaznavids themselves were Turks, they were major patrons of the Persian language and Persian poets (such as Firdausi himself), and the spread of Persian into India stimulated the development of the Urdu language. But Persian came to be used as an administrative and literary language in India after the sixteenth century with the conquest of Babur and the establishment of the Mughal dynasty. Although the Mughals were again Turkish, Persian was widely used as a court language and, faced with the large numbers of different native languages of the peoples they ruled, Persian was used as the *lingua franca* of India until it was in turn replaced by English (indeed, many of the early East India Company employees had to learn Persian).

Another Turkish dynasty also took the Persian language westwards. This was the Ottoman, particularly after the fourteenth century. Persian already had a history as a literary language in Anatolia by the Seljuks through their patronage of Persian writers, such as Jalal al-Din Rumi (who also wrote in Turkish and Greek). Although Ottoman Turkish remained the main administrative language throughout the Ottoman Empire, Persian was also largely used—indeed, many educated Ottomans (such as Mehmet the Conqueror himself), spoke, read and wrote literary Persian. In addition to Iran itself, Persian remained the main language of communication and trade throughout Central Asia and western China right down until the beginning of the twentieth century.

*   *   *

More than anything else, what Iran contributed to posterity was an idea. In articulating the concept of a single universal creator, ancient Persian civilisation was the first to grope towards the idea of a single universal world, an all embracing world where 'distinct units of history in the Near East [were] over' in the words of one historian, with 'the base of a future world civilisation … in the making'.[12] The idea of one world was to remain. The ancient Iranian idea of a single world transcending political and ethnic boundaries makes it appropriate that today, the inscription over the entrance of the United Nations building in New York, is that of a Persian poet:

> *The sons of Adam are limbs of each other,*
> *Having been created of one essence.*
> *When the calamity of time affects one limb*
> *The other limbs cannot remain at rest.*
> *If thou hast no sympathy for the troubles of others*
> *Thou art unworthy to be called by the name of a human*

Saᶜdi, Gulistan, Book 1, x

NOTES

INTRODUCTION

1 Pagden 2008: xiv & xix.
2 Pagden 2008: 3, 56, 62, 66 & 76.
3 Holland 2005: xx,145, 146; Pagden 2008: 67-8.
4 Le Goff 2005: 53-4.
5 Le Goff 2005; Bartlett 1993.
6 Davies 2006: 39.
7 Council of Europe 1998.
8 T S Elliot, '... the whole of the literature of Europe from Homer', *Critical Essays* (London 1932): 14-15; Edward W Said, '... one belongs to a part of the earth [Europe] with a definite history of involvement in the Orient almost since the time of Homer' (in the context of 'European or American' writers of the Orient); '... every [European] writer on the Orient (and this is true even of Homer)', *Orientalism* (London 1978): 11, 20; 'European literature ... from Homer to Virginia Woolf', *Culture and Imperialism* (London 1993): 54; Norman Davies, 'Homer's *Iliad* and *Odyssey* were traditionally regarded in Europe ... as the oldest examples of European literature', *Europe. A History* (Oxford 1996): 114; J M Roberts, 'together with the Bible, they [the *Iliad* and *Odyssey*] are the source of western literature', *The Pelican History of the World* (London 1980): 181.
9 Davies 2006: 114.
10 Mehmet Güldiz, *Mythology* (Istanbul 1997).
11 Erskine 2001: 27.
12 Carr 1987:30.
13 Braudel 1972-3: 764.

1—THE LEGACY OF CYRUS

1 Potts 2006 argues a very convincing case.
2 Roberts 1980: 172.
3 Grainger 2007: 21.

4 Boardman 2000: 225.
5 As Boardman 2000: 220.
6 Frye 1984: 119; Dandamaev 1989: 130 & 132; Miller 1997: 106; Briant 2002: 602.
7 Found at Neirab south-east of Aleppo; see Akkermans & Schwartz 2003: 389.

2—Persians and Greeks

1 From 'Returning from Greece' by Cavafy C P Cavafy, *Collected Poems.* Translated by Edmund Keeley and Philip Sherrard (London 1998)145.
2 Davies 1996: 139.
3 Carr 1987: 13.
4 The historian Wilfried Nippel (in Harrison 2002), in a thought provoking paper argues that the Greek view of and relationship with the 'barbarian' has coloured all later European views of the 'other': Muslims, Turks, slavery in the New World, etc.
5 Drews 1988.
6 See, for example, the arguments in Burkert 1992 and 2004 and Mitchell 2007: 116-8.
7 Burn 1962: 1-2; Dandamaev 1989: 153.
8 Frye 1984: ix.
9 Strabo XIII.4.13; Briant 2002: 556, 723-4, 794.
10 Summers 1993; Boardman 2000: 204-6, n. 159, 160.
11 Miller 1997: 91-7; Keen 1998; Boardman 2000: 204-6, n. 159, 160; Cahill 1988; Cormack 1989. Bayburtluoğlu 2004: 222 and 2005: 63-4.
12 Boardman 2000: 222.
13 McNicoll 1997; Ruzicka 2001: 46-50.
14 The 'precise nature of his [Mausolus'] involvement in the [Satrap's] revolt is unknown. Most likely Maussollus' role was not great.' Ruzicka 1992: 79-80.
15 The Phoenician's role in the development and transmission of the planned city has already been discussed in Vol 1.
16 Miller 1997: 94.
17 See Ball 2000: Chapter 8.
18 Cook 1962: 122.

3—The Ionians beyond the Sea

1 E.g., Burn 1962: 226, 258.
2 Green 1970, all on the very first page.
3 Green 1970: 5.
4 Pagden 2008: 30; Holland 2005: xvii.

5   Green 1970: 8, 14-15; Holland 2005: 145 & 146.
6   Green 1970: 5.
7   Green 1970: 34-40.
8   When the Melians refused to submit to Athens: Thucydides Book XVII (p. 331 of the Modern Library edition).
9   Burn 1962: 242; Green 1970: 101.
10 Burn 1962: 318; Frye 1984: 118. Opinion, however, is divided as to whether these 'wages' were ample or starvation.
11 Cawkwell 2005.
12 Erskine 2001: 27; Mitchell 2007: 13-19, 78-80.
13 E.g., Wiesehöfer 1996, Briant 2002, Cawkwell 2005.
14 Wiesehöfer 1996: 86.
15 Hammond 1991: 14-19; Miller 1997: 129; Briant 2002: 201-2; Grainger 2007: 3.
16 Herodotus 358.
17 Herodotus 337-8. See also Burn 1962: 187; Green 1970: 19; Dandamaev 1989: 158-9.
18 Herodotus: 350.
19 Holland 2005: 203.
20 Briant 2002: 160-1.
21 See Green 1970: 28-30.
22 Briant 2002: 567.
23 Burn 1962: 313-4.
24 Herodotus 421-1, 457-9.
25 Cawkwell 2005.
26 Cawkwell.
27 Green 1970: 120; Pagden 2008: 5.
28 Burn 1962: 471.
29 Mitchell 2007: 77, 78 & 10.
30 Herodotus 515.
31 E.g., Burn 1962: 226, 258.
32 Herodotus 520 & 533.
33 Dandamaev 1989: 291-2.
34 Starr 1989: 46.
35 Miller 1997: 241.

4—THE DEMON KING

1   Aubrey de Sélincourt, 'Introduction' to the Penguin Classic edition (1958) of *Arrian's Life of Alexander the Great*: xv-xvi; Roberts 1980: 172.
2   Boyce and Grenet 1991: 361.
3   Lane Fox 1973: 11.
4   Bosworth in Bosworth and Baynham 2000.
5   Green 1996: 163.

6 Spencer 2002: 37.
7 Bosworth in Bosworth and Baynham 2000: 4.
8 Billows in Bosworth and Baynham 2000: 288.
9 Trogus 12.5.7, following the execution of Parmenio and Philotas; Green 1990: 311; Briant 2002: 839-40.
10 Bosworth and Baynham 2000: 25.
11 Briant 2002: 862-4.
12 Briant 2002: 862-4; 1 *Maccabees* 1. 2-3, 9; Trogus 11.6.4; Heckel in Roisman 2003: 225. See also the *Ardashir Romance*. See Wiesehöfer 1996: 168, Gutas 1998: 34-40. Alexander from the Zoroastrian viewpoint Boyce and Grenet: 3-17. Contemporary Babylonian references to Alexander: Sachs and Hunger 1988. The transformation of Alexander into the quasi-Persian hero he becomes in the *Shahnameh* belongs to a much later, mainly Qur'anic, tradition.
13 Spencer 2002: 212.
14 Davies 348.
15 Green 1996: 6, 13and 40.
16 Quoted in Mitchell 2007: 12-13.
17 See Billows in Bosworth and Baynham 2000: 290.
18 Green 1991: 157-8. See also Heckel in Rosiman 2003: 112-3.
19 Grainger 2007: 79.
20 Frye 1984: 144-8; Fraser 1996.
21 Green 1990: 309, 431.
22 Ammianus Marcellinus 18: 3-4.
23 Trogus 11.2.7-8 and 11.4.9-12.
24 Ball 2008: 59-71.
25 Mitchell 2007: 173 and 176.
26 See the Preface in Pandermalis 2004.
27 Potts 2006.
28 Livy 9.18.3, quoted in Spencer 2002: 42.
29 Gutas 1998: 40-4.
30 Ibn Khaldun: 373.
31 Wiesehöfer 1996: 168.Gutas 1998: 34-40. Alexander from the Zoroastrian viewpoint: Boyce and Grenet: 3-17, Yarshater: 472-3.
32 Al-Biruni *Chronology*: 48-9. See also Yarshater: 472-3, Stoneman 2008: Chapter 2; Ball 2000: 97.
33 Kiani 1982: 12-13.
34 Trogus 11.5.4.
35 Briant 1979: 1414, and 2002: 876; Frye 1984: 135. See also Wiesehöfer 1996: Chapter 5. This is strongly refuted by Lane Fox in Tuplin 2007.
36 Billows in Bosworth and Baynham 2000: 294-6.
37 Briant 2002: 696, 812-13.
38 Spencer 2002: 218.
39 Grainger 2007: xviii.
40 Quoted and discussed in Spencer 2001: 69-79.

.5—AN 'IRANISTIC' AGE

1 Erciyas 2006: 1.
2 Boardman 1994: 108; Ball 2000: Chapter 7. See also the remarks on the essential unity of this region by John Curtis (1998-99) Keynote Speech. British Near Eastern Archaeology and Museology on the Eve of the Millennium. *BANEA Newsletter* 11 and 12: 9-10.
3 Ball 2000: Chapter 7.
4 Strzygowski 1923.
5 Lang 1983: 533.
6 Matyszak 2008: 101.
7 Mayor 2010: 157-8.
8 Mayor 2010: 359.
9 Summerer in Højte 2009.
10 Green 1990: 557 and Chapter 31.
11 For recent biographies see Matyszak 2008 and Mayor 2010.
12 Erciyas 2006: 17-18 and 121.
13 See Yarshater in Sarkhosh and Stewart 2008: 410.
14 Mayor 2010: 34 and 46.
15 Quoted in Boyce and Gretet 1991: 293.
16 See Mitchell I, 1993: 86; Erciyas 2006: 124-34.
17 Erciyas 2006: 67-115.
18 Erciyas 2006: 134-43.
19 Fleischer in Højte 2009: 115.
20 Butcher 2004: 91-2.

6—TWO SUPER-POWERS

1 Witakowski 1996: 83.
2 By Howard-Johnston (2006), although he was mainly referring to the latter part.
3 I am grateful to Eberhad Sauer for discussions on his excavations at the Gurgan Wall. See Omrani *et.al.* 2007.
4 Sebeos 9-10 and 69-70, although this was just wishful thinking on Sebeos' part according to Howard-Johnston p. 165.
5 Dignas and Winter 2007: 106 (quoting Procopius).
6 Quoted in Greatrex and Lieu 2002: 136-7.
7 Whitehouse and Williamson 1973: 38-9; Greatrex and Lieu 2002: 136-7; Kleppe 2007: 91-2. See also Chapter 4.
8 Whitby 1989: 614-628; Thomson *et.al.* 1999; Palmer 1993.
9 This reconstruction is put forward by James Howard-Johnston (1999) in his Commentary on Sebeos: 103-4 and 183-7.
10 Witakowski 1996: 135-7.

11 Witakowski 1996: 135-7.
12 E.g., Dignas and Winter 2007.

7—Light And Darkness

1 Boyce 1997: 1.
2 For Zoroastrianism generally, see Boyce 1979, 1992, 1996, 1997, Boyce
   and Grenet 1991. See also Curtis 1993, Sarianidi 1998, Grenet 2006.
3 Sarianidi 1998; Stronach and Roaf 2007.
4 Boyce 1996: 116; Boyce 1997: 27.
5 Boyce 1979: 42-3; Boyce and Grenet 1991: 451. See also Corbin 1976.
6 Razmjou 2004.
7 Daryaee 2003: 199-200.
8 Turcan 1996: 209-15.
9 Ball 2000: 431-3.
10 Hopkins 1979; Colpe 1983: 853-6; Boyce and Grenet 1991: 468-90; Curtis 1993; Turcan 1996: Ch. 4.
11 Widengran 1983, Klimkeit 1993, Lieu 1994, Boyce and Grenet 1991:
   460-5.
12 Stoyanov (2000) in his seminal history of dualism also traces it in ancient
   Egyptian and Judaic doctrine.
13 Curtis 1993: 74.

8—The Shadow of Zoroaster

1 Boyce and Grenet 1991: 277.
2 Raditsa 1983: 105-6; Boyce and Grenet 1991: 235-8; Braund 1994: 190;
   Miller 1997: 94; Boardman 2000: 207-8; Briant 2002: 37-8, 702-5; Burkett
   2005: 105-7. See also Mitchell I, 1993: 188-9, and II, 1993: 43-51.
3 Boyce and Grenet 1991: Ch. VIII; Turcan 1996: Ch. 1 and 254-8; Elsner
   1997: 180-91. See also Frazer 1911-36: I, I: 37-8.
4 Strabo 15.3.15. See also Mitchell II, 1993: 73.
5 Duchesne-Guillemin 1983: 872.
6 Colpe 1983: 826-31; Boyce and Grenet 1991: Chs X and XI; Kingsley
   1995; Turcan 1996: Ch. 4.
7 Procopius II. xxiv. 1-3. For Vesta see Frazer 1911-36: I, II: Ch. XIV.
   Boyce and Grenet 1991: 70-9, 254-8, 261; Dodgeon and Lieu 1991: 65.
8 Lactantius, tr. Bowen and Garnsey 2003: 423, 427; Colpe 1983: 831-4;
   Boyce and Grenet 1991: 376-87.
9 Boyce and Grenet 1991: 277.
10 Witakowski 1996: 11.
11 Boyce and Grenet 1991: 239 and 256-7.
12 Boyce and Grenet 1991: 352; Turcan 1996: 159-69.
13 Colpe 1983: 840-3; Boyce and Grenet 1991: 309-51 and 352; Turcan

1996: 159-69; Palmer 1993 *et.al.* 16; Palmer in Holleweger 1990: 30, 78

14 See Hollerweger 1999: 169.

15 Dzielska 1995: 77-8.

16 Runciman 2009: Ch. 10; Woodhouse 1986: Ch. 17.

17 See Boyce and Grenet 1991: Ch XI with refs. On pp. 409-10 they discuss the possible derivation of the word Pharisee from 'Persians'. See also Stoyanov 2000: 54-6.

18 Boyce 1996: 236; Cross and Livingstone 1997: 'priest'.

19 Or probably under Hormizd I in 272, rather than Shapur, according to Colpe 1983: 877-84.

20 Frye 1963: 247-9; Boyce 1979: Chapters 6 and 7; Blockley 1992: 10-11; Wiesehöfer (1996: 199-200, 210-11) however, discards this view. See also Fowden 1993: 80-85. For Constantine's letter, see Lane Fox 1986: 636-7.

21 Colpe 1983: 831-4; Boyce and Grenet 1991: 376-87 and 481; Peña 1996: 80; Boyce 1996: Chapter 12; Daryaee 2003: 200; Le Goff 2005: 61-2, 91-2.

22 Mitchell II, 1993: 43-51, 62.

23 Lane-Fox 1986: 532-8.

24 See Mitchell II, 1993: 68.

9—THE DUALIST CHALLENGE

1   Savall 2009: 475.

2   Stoyanov 2000.

3   Lieu 1994: 22.

4   Klimkeit 1993: 202-3, 208-9; Lieu 1994.

5   Lieu 1994: 61.

6   Lieu 1994: 130-1; Lee 2000: 66-7; Lancel 2002: 32.

7   Lieu 1994: 105.

8   Lieu 1994: Ch. II; According to John of Ephesus. See Pseudo-Dionysius of Tel-Mahre: 115; Lactantius 2.12.7; John Malalas 12. 42; Lieu 1994: 130-1; Klimkeit 1993: 202-3, 208-9; Dodgeon and Lieu 1991: 65; Pseudo-Dionysius of Tel-Mahre: 70.

9   Cross and Livingstone 1997: 'Original Sin'; Lancel 2002: 52; Wickham 2009: 56.

10 Colpe 1983: 840-3; Boyce and Grenet 1991: 309-51 and 352; Palmer 1993 *et.al.* 16; Palmer in Holleweger 1990: 30, 78.

11 Lang 1978: 185.

12 Stoyanov 2000: Chapter 3.

13 Quoted by Lambert 1998: 75.

14 Barber 2000: 78.

15 Forcano in Savall 2009: 82-6.

16 Barber 2000; Stoyanov 2000.

17 Barber 2000: 109.

18 Lambert 1998: 169.

19 Quoted by Lambert 1998: 76.
20 Stoyanov 2000: 184.
21 Lang 1978: 178-83.
22 Stoyanov 2000: xi.
23 Sanchez in Saval 2009: 80-1.
24 Wickham 2009: 58, 171-2; Ball 2009: Ch 6.
25 R.S. Pine-Coffin, 'Introduction', *The Confessions of St Augustine*, Daniel-Rops: 27.
26 Montserrat Figuearas and Jordi Savall in the preface to Savall 2009.

10—An Iranian World. Conclusion

1 Wiesehöfer 196: 243.
2 Roberts 1980: 172.
3 See also the remarks on the essential unity of this region by John Curtis (1998-99) Keynote Speech. British Near Eastern Archaeology and Museology on the Eve of the Millennium. *BANEA Newsletter* 11 and 12: 9-10.
4 Herodotus: 70.
5 Lieu 'Manichaeism in China' in the *Encyclopaedia Iranica*.
6 Baum and Winkler 2000; O'Mahony (ed) 2004; Baumer 2006.
7 Boyce and Grenet 1991: 30-3; Bosworth 1996: Ch. 4. See also Frazer 1911-36: I, II: 50-1.
8 It was built on the 'Hippodamian' grid plan. See Adams and Hansen 1968.
9 Wiesehöfer 1996: 218-9; Ball 2000: 115 and refs.
10 Gutas 1998: 40-4.
11 Ibn Khaldun: 373.
12 Roberts 1980: 172.

BIBLIOGRAPHY

Note: references to Herodotus, Arrian and Livy are to page numbers in the Penguin Classic editions.

Akkermans, Peter and Schwartz, Glenn, *The Archaeology of Syria. From Complex Hunter-Gatherers to Early Urban Societies* (ca., *16,000-300 BC)*. Cambridge, 2003.
Arrian, *Life of Alexander the Great*. A new translation by Aubrey de Sélincourt. Harmondsworth, 1958.
Ascherson, Neal, *Black Sea. The Birthplace of Civilisation and Barbarism*. London, 1995.
Athanassiadi, Polymnia, and Frede, Michael (eds), *Pagan Monotheism in Late Antiquity*. Oxford, 1999.
Augustine, *City of God* (transl. Henry Bettinson), London, 1984.
Austin, M M, *The Hellenistic world from Alexander to the Roman conquest. A selection of ancient sources in translation*. Cambridge, 1981.
Bakir, T., Samcisi-Weerdenburg, F. et al. (eds) *Achaemenid Anatolia: Proceedings of the, 1st international Symposium on Anatolia in the Achaemenid Period*. Leiden, 2001.
Ball, Warwick, *Rome in the East. The Transformation of an Empire*. London, 2000.
—*The Monuments of Afghanistan. History, Archaeology and Architecture*. London, 2008.
Barber, Malcolm, *The Cathars. Dualist Heresies in the Languedoc in the High Middle Ages*. Harlow, 2000.
Bartlett, Robert, *The Making of Europe. Conquest, Colonization and Cultural Change 950-1350*. London, 1993.
Baum, Wilhelm and Winkler, Dietmar W, *The Church of the East. A Concise History*. London, 2003.
Baumer, Christoph, *The Church of the East. An Illustrated History of Assyrian Christianity*. London 2006.
Bayburtluoğlu, Cevdet, *Arykanda. An archaeological guide*. Istanbul, 2005.
—*Lycia*. Antalya, 2004.
Boardman, John, *Persia and the West. An Archaeological Investigation of the Genesis of Achaemenid Art*. London, 2000.
—*The Diffusion of Classical Art in Antiquity*. London, 1994.
—*The Greeks Overseas. Their Early Colonies and Trade*. London, 1980.
Bosworth, A B, 'The Heritage of Rulership in Early Islamic Iran,' *Iran, 1* 1: 51-62, 1973.
—*Commentary on Arrian's History of Alexander*. Oxford, 1995.
—*From Arrian to Alexander. Studies in Historical Interpretation*. Oxford, 1988.
—*Alexander and the East. The Tragedy of Triumph*. Oxford, 1996.
Bosworth, A B and Baynham (eds), E J, *Alexander the Great in Fact and Fiction*. Oxford, 2000.
Boyce, Mary *A History of Zoroastrianism. Volume One. The Early Period*. Leiden, 1996.
—*Zoroastrianism. Its Antiquity and Constant Vigour*. Costa Mesa, California, 1992.

—*Zoroastrians: Their Religious Beliefs and Practices.* London, 1997.

Boyce, Mary and Grenet, Frantz, *A History of Zoroastrianism. Volume Three. Zoroastrianism under Macedonian and Roman Rule.* Leiden, 1991. Braudel, Fernand , *The Mediterranean in the Ancient World.* London, 2001.

Braudel, Fernand, *The Mediterranean and the Mediterranean World in the Age of Philip II.*, 2 vols, London, 1972-73.

Braund, David, *Georgia in Antiquity.* Oxford, 1994.

Bregel, Yuri, *An Historical Atlas of Central Asia.* Leiden, 2003.

Briant, Pierre, *From Cyrus to Alexander: A History of the Persian Empire.* Winona Lake, Indiana, 2002.

Brosius, Maria, *The Persians. An introduction.* London, 2006.

Browning, Robert, *Justinian and Theodora.* London, 1971.

Burkert, Walter, *Babylon, Memphis, Persepolis. Eastern Contexts of Greek Culture.* Cambridge, Massachusetts, 2004.

—*The Orientalizing Revolution. Near Eastern Influence on Greek Culture in the Early Archaic Age.* Cambridge, Massachusetts, 1992.

Burn, A R, *Persia and the Greeks; the Defence of the West, c. 546-478 B.C.* London, 1962.

Burstein, Stanley M (ed), *The Hellenistic Age from the battle of Ipsos to the death of Kleopatra VII.* Cambridge, 1985.

Butcher, Kevin, *Roman Syria and the Near East.* London, 2003.

Cahill, N, 'Taş Kule: A Persian Period Tomb near Phokaia', *American Journal of Archaeology* 92 (1988): 481-501.

Cardini, Franco, *Europe and Islam.* Oxford, 2001.

Carr, E H, *What is History?* London, 1967.

Cawkwell, George, *The Greek Wars. The Failure of Persia.* Oxford, 2005.

Chadwick, Henry, *The Early Church.* London, 1990.

Colledge, Malcolm A R, *The Parthians.* London, 1967.

Colpe, C, 'The development of religious thought,' in *Cambridge History of Iran* 3 (2): 819-65. Cambridge, 1983.

Cook, J. M., *The Greeks in Ionia and the East.* London, 1962.

Corbin, H, *Spiritual Body and Celestial Earth. From Mazdean Iran to Shi'ite Iran.* Princeton, 1976.

Cormack, Sarah, 'A Mausoleum at Ariassos', *Anatolian Studies* 39 (1989): 31-40.

Council of Europe, *Gods and Heroes of the Bronze Age. Europe at the Time of Ulysses.* Copenhagen, 1998.

Cribb, Joe and Herrmann, Georgina (eds), *After Alexander. Central Asia Before Islam.* London, 2007.

Cross, F L and Livingstone, E A (eds), *The Oxford Dictionary of the Christian Church.* Oxford, 1997.

Curtis, John and Tallis, Nigel (eds), *Forgotten Empire. The world of Ancient Persia.* London, 2007.

Curtis, Vesta Sarkhosh, *Persian Myths.* London, 1993.

Curtis, Vesta Sarkhosh and Stewart, Sarah (eds), *The Birth of the Persian Empire. The Idea of Iran Vol., 1.* London, 2005.

—*The Age of the Parthians. The Idea of Iran Vol., 2.* London, 2007.

—*The Sasanian Era. The Idea of Iran Vol. 3.* London, 2008.

Curtis, Vesta Sarkhosh, Hillenbrand, Robert and Rogers, J M (eds), *The Art and Archaeology of Ancient Persia. New Light on the Parthian and Sasanian Empires.* London, 1998.

Dandamaev, M. A., *A Political History of the Achaemenid Empire.* Leiden, 1989.

Daniel-Rops, H, *The Church in the Dark Ages*. London, 1959.

Darmesteter, James (transl.), *The Zend-Avesta*. 3 vols. Oxford, 1880.

Daryaee, Fouraj 'The Effect of the Arab Muslim Conquest on the Administrative Division of Sasanian Persia/Fars', *Iran* 41 (2003):, 193-204.

Davies, Norman, *Europe East and West*. London, 2006.

—*Europe. A History*. London, 1996.

Dawson, Christopher, *The Making of Europe. An Introduction to the History of European Unity*. London, 1934.

Dignas, Beate and Winter, Englebert, *Rome and Persia in Late Antiquity. Neighbours and Rivals*. Cambridge, 2007.

Dodgeon, M H and and Lieu, S N C, *The Roman Eastern Frontier and the Persian Wars (AD, 226-363). A Documentary History*. London, 1991.

Drews, Robert, *The Coming of the Greeks. Indo-European Conquests in the Aegean and the Near East*. Princeton, 1998.

Duchesne-Guillemin, J, 'Zoroastrian religion,' in *Cambridge History of Iran* 3 (2): 866-908. Cambridge, 1983.

Eckstein, Arthur M, *Rome Enters the Greek East. From Anarchy to Hierarchy in the Hellenistic Mediterranean, 230-170 BC*. Oxford, 2008.

Eder, Walter and Renger, Johannes, *Chronologies of the Ancient World. Names, Dates and Dynasties. Brill's New Pauly*. Leiden, 2007.

Elsner, Jas', 'The Origins of the Icon: Pilgrimage, Religion and Visual Culture in the Roman East as Resistance to the Centre,' in Alcock, Susan E (ed), *The Early Roman Empire in the East*. Oxford, 1997, 178-199.

Elton, G R, *The Practice of History*. Sydney, 1967.

Erciyas, Deniz Burcu, *Wealth, Aristocracy and Royal Propaganda under the Hellenistic Kingdom of the Mithradatids*. Leiden, 2006.

Erskine, Andrew, *Troy Between Greece and Rome. Local Tradition and Imperial Power*. Oxford, 2001.

Ferdowsi, Abolqasem, *Shanameh. The Persian Book of Kings*. A New Translation by Dick Davies. New York and London 2006.

Finley, M I, *Ancient History. Evidence and Methods*. London, 1985.

Fowden, Garth, *Empire to Commonwealth. Consequences of monotheism in late antiquity*. Princeton, 1993.

Fraser, P M, *Cities of Alexander the Great*. Oxford, 1996.

Frazer, James, *The Golden Bough*, 13 vols. London, 1911-1936.

Frye, Richard N, *The Heritage of Persia*. London1963.

—*The History of Ancient Iran*. Munich1984.

Gershevitch, Ilya (ed.), *The Cambridge History of Iran. Volume, 2. The Median and Achaemenian Periods*. Cambridge, 1985.

Gibbon, Edward, *The History of the Decline and Fall of the Roman Empire*. 7 vols, ed. J. B. Bury. London, 1900.

Gnoli, Gherado, *Zoroaster's Time and Homeland. A Study on the Origins of Mazdeism and Related Problems*. Naples, 1980.

Golden, M. and Toohey, P. (Eds,) *Inventing Ancient Culture*. London, 1997.

Goody, Jack, *The East in the West*. Cambridge, 1996.

Grainger, John D, *Alexander the Great Failure*. London, 2007.

Greatrex, Geoffrey and Lieu, Samuel N. C., *The Roman Eastern Frontier and the Persian Wars. Part II. AD 363-630. A Narrative sourcebook*. London, 2002.

Green, Peter, *Alexander of Macedon, 356-323 B.C. A Historical Biography*. Berkeley, 1991.

—*Alexander to Actium. The Hellenistic Age*. London, 1990.

—*The Greco-Persian Wars*. Berkeley, 1996.

Grenet, Frantz, *La Geste d'Ardashir fils de Pâbag. Kārnāmag ī Ardaxšēr ī Pābagān*. Die (France), 2003.

Gutas, Dimitri, *Greek Thought, Arabic Culture. The Graeco-Arabic Translation Movement in Baghdad and Early 'Abbāsid Society (2nd-4th/8th-10th centuries)*. London, 1998.

Hammond, Nicholas G L, *The Miracle that was Macedonia*. London, 1991.

Hammond, N G L and Scullard, H H (eds), *The Oxford Classical Dictionary*. Oxford, 1970.

Harrison, Thomas (ed.), *Greeks and Barbarians*. Edinburgh, 2002.

Herrmann, Georgina, *The Iranian Revival*. London, 1977.

Hobsbawm, Eric, *On History*. London, 1997.

Hobsbawm, Eric and Ranger, Terrence (eds), *the Invention of Tradition*. Cambridge, 1983.

Hobson, John M, *The Eastern Origins of Western Civilisation*. Cambridge, 2004.

Højte, Jakob Munk (ed), *Mithridates VI and the Pontic Kingdom*. Aarhus, 2009.

Holland, Tom, *Persian Fire. The First World Empire and the Battle for the West*. London, 2005.

Hollerweger, Hans, *Living Cultural Heritage. Turabdin*. Linz, 1999.

Howard-Johnston, James, *East Rome, Sasanian Persia and the End of Antiquity*. Aldershot, Hampshire, 2006.

—'The Destruction of the Late Antique World Order' in Kennet and Luft (eds), 2008: 79-86.

Jeppesen, Kristian *Maussolleion at Halikarnassos 5: The Superstructure*. Jutland, 2002.

Justin, *Epitome of the Philippic History of Pompeius Trogus. Volume I. Books, 11-12: Alexander the Great*. Translation and Appendices by J C Yardley. Commentary by Waldemar Heckel. Oxford, 1997.

Karageorghis, Vassos (ed), *The Greeks Beyond the Aegean: From Marseilles to Bactria*. New York, 2003.

Keen, Antony G, *Dynastic Lycia. A Political History of the Lycians and Their Relations with Foreign Powers, c.545-362 BC*. Leiden, 1998.

Kennet, Derek and Luft, Paul (eds), *Current Research in Sasanian Archaeology, Art and History*. Oxford, 2008.

Kiani, M Y, *Parthian Sites in Hyrcania, the Gurgan Plain*. Archaeologische Mitteilungen aus Iran, Ergänzungsband 9. Berlin, 1982.

Kingsley, P, 'Meetings with the Magi: Iranian themes among the Greeks, from Xanthus of Lydia to Plato's Academy.' *Journal of the Royal Asiatic Society* 5, 2 (1995).

Klimkeit, Hans-Joachim, *Gnosis on the Silk Road. Gnostic Parables, Hymns and Prayers from Central Asia*. New York, 1993.

Kohl, Philip L. and Fawcett, Clare (eds,) *Nationalism, Politics and the Practice of Archaeology*. Cambridge, 1995.

Kriwaczek, Paul, *In Search of Zarathustra. The First Prophet and the Ideas that Changed the World*. London, 2002.

Kuhrt, Amélie, *'Greeks' and 'Greece' in Mesopotamian and Persian Perspectives*. The Twenty-first J. L. Myers Memorial Lecture. Oxford, 2002.

Lactantius, *Divine Institutes*. Translated with an introduction and notes by Anthony Bowen and Peter Garnsey. Liverpool, 2003.

Lambert, Malcolm, *The Cathars*. Oxford, 1998.

Lancel, Serge, *St Augustine*. London, 2002.

Lane Fox, Robin, *Alexander the Great*. London, 1973.

—*Pagans and Christians in the Mediterranean world from the second century AD to the conversion of Constantine.* London, 1986.

Lang, David Marshall, *The Georgians.* London, 1966.

—*Armenia. Cradle of Civilization.* London, 1978.

Le Goff, Jacques, *The Birth of Europe.* Oxford, 2005.

Lee, A D, *Pagans and Christians in Late Antiquity. A Sourcebook.* London, 2000.

Lieu, Samuel N C, *Manichaeism in Mesopotamia and the Roman East.* Leiden, 1994.

Livy, *The Early History of Rome,* trans. Aubrey de Sélincourt. Harmondsworth, 1960.

Lowenthal, David, *The Past is a Foreign Country.* Cambridge, 1985.

Lytton, Edward Bulwer, *Athens: Its Rise and Fall.* Ed Oswyn Murray. London, 2004.

Macmullen, Ramsay, *Christianity and Paganism in the Fourth to Eighth Centuries.* New Haven, 1997.

Mango, Cyril and Dagron, Gilbert (eds), *Constantinople and its Hinterland.* Aldershot, 1995.

Matheson, Sylvia, *Persia: An Archaeological Guide.* London, 1976.

Matyszak, Philip, *Mithridates the Great. Rome's Indomitable Enemy.* Barnsley, 2008.

Mayor, Adrienne, *The Poison King. The Life and Legend of Mithradates Rome's Deadliest Enemy.* Princeton, 2010.

McNicoll, A. W., *Hellenistic Fortifications. From the Aegean to the Euphrates.* With revisions and an additional chapter by N. P. Milner. Oxford, 1997.

Miller, Margaret *Athens and Persia in the Fifth Century BC: A Study in Cultural Receptivity.* Cambridge, 1997.

Mitchell, Lynette, *Panhellenism and the Barbarian in Archaic and Classical Greece.* Swansea, 2007.

Mitchell, Stephen, *Anatolia. Land, Men, and Gods in Asia Minor,* 2 vols. Oxford, 1993.

Momigliano, Arnaldo, *Alien Wisdom. The Limits of Hellenization.* Cambridge, 1971.

Nizam al-Mulk, *The Book of Government or Rules for Kings.* Translated by Hubert Darke. London, 1960.

Olmstead, A T, *A History of the Persian Empire.* Chicago, 1948.

O'Mahony, Anthony (ed), *Eastern Christianity. Studies in Modern History, Religion and Politics.* London 2004.

Omrani, Hamid *et.al.,* 'An Imperial Frontier of the Sasanian Empire: Further Fieldwork at the Great Wall of Gurgan' *Iran* 45, 2007: 95-136.

Owens, E J *The City in the Greek and Roman World.* London, 1991.

Pagden, Anthony, *Worlds at War. The, 2,500-Year Struggle Between East and West.* Oxford, 2009.

Palmer, Andrew, *Monk and mason on the Tigris frontier. The Early history of Tur 'Abdin.* Cambridge, 1990.

Palmer, Andrew, Brock, Sebastian and Hoyland, Robert , *The Seventh Century in the West-Syrian Chronicles.* Liverpool, 1993.

Pandermalis, Dimitrios, *Alexander the Great. Treasures from an epic era of Hellenism.* New York, 2004.

Potts, D T, *The Archaeology of Elam. Formation and Transformation of an Ancient Iranian State.* Cambridge, 1999.

—'Cyrus the Great and the Kingdom of Anshan' in Curtis and Stewart (eds), 2005: 7-28.

Procopius, *History of the Wars, Books I and II.* London, 1914.

Pseudo-Dionysius of Tel-Mahre, *Chronicle. Part III.* Translated with notes and introduction by Witold Witakowski. Liverpool, 1996.

Pseudo-Joshua the Stylite, *Chronicle.* Translated with notes and introduction by Frank

R Trombley and John W. Watt. Liverpool, 2000.

Quintus Curtius Rufus, *The History of Alexander*. Translated by John Yardley with an introduction and notes by Waldemar Heckel. London, 1984.

Raditsa, L, 'Iranians in Asia Minor,' in *Cambridge History of Iran* 3 (1), 100-115. Cambridge, 1993.

Razmjou, Shahrokh, 'The *Lan* Ceremony and Other Ritual Ceremonies in the Achaemenid Period: The Persepolis Fortification Tablets', *Iran* 42 (2004), 119-130.

Redgate, A E, *The Armenians*. Oxford, 1998.

Regan, Geoffrey, *First Crusader. Byzantium's Holy Wars*. Stroud, 2001.

Rietbergen, Peter, *Europe. A Cultural History*. Oxford, 1998.

Roaf, Michael, *Sculptures and Sculptors at Persepolis (Iran, 21)*. London, 1983.

—*Cultural Atlas of Mesopotamia and the Ancient Near East*. Oxford, 1990.

—'Persepolitan Echoes in Sasanian Architecture: Did the Sasanians attempt to re-create the Achaemenid empire?' in Curtis, Hillenbrand and Rogers (eds) *The Art and Archaeology of Ancient Persia. New Light on the Parthian and Sasanian Empires*. London, 1998:, 1-7.

Roberts, J M, *The Pelican History of the World*. London, 1980.

—*The Triumph of the West*. London, 1985.

Roisman, Joseph (ed), *Brill's Companion to Alexander the Great*. Leiden, 2003.

Rudolf, Kurt, *Gnosis. The Nature and History of Gnosticism*. Edinburgh, 1983.

Runciman, Steven, *The Medieval Manichee. A Study of the Christian Dualist Heresy*. Cambridge, 1947.

—*Lost Capital of Byzantium. The History of Mistra and the Peloponnese*. London, 2009.

Russell, Bertrand, *History of Western Philosophy*. London, 1946.

Ruzicka, Stephen, *Politics of a Persian Dynasty. The Hecatomnids in the Fourth Century B.C.* Norman, Oklahoma, 1992.

Sachau, C Edward, *The Chronology of Ancient Nations. An English Version of the Arabic text of the Āthār-ul-Bākiya of Albīrūni*. London, 1879.

Sancisi-Weerdenburg, H and Drijvers, J W (eds) *The roots of European tradition: Proceedings of the, 1987 Groningen Achaemenid History Workshop*. Netherlands Institute for the Near East, Leiden, 1990.

Sarianidi, Victor, *Margiana and Protozoroastrianism*. Athens, 1998.

Savall, Jordi, *et.al.*, *The Forgotten Kingdom. The Albigensian Crusade*. (3 CDs and notes). Bellaterra, Spain,, 2009.

Sebeos, *Armenian History*. Translated, with notes, by R W Thomson. Historical commentary by James Howard-Johnston. Assistance from Tim Greenwood. Liverpool, 1999.

Sekunda, Nicholas, *The Persian Army 560-330 BC*. Oxford, 1992.

Sherwin-White, Susan and Kuhrt, Amélie, *From Samarkhand to Sardis. A new approach to the Seleucid empire*. London, 1993.

Shipley, Graham, *The Greek World after Alexander. 323-30 BC*. London, 2000.

Spencer, Diana, *The Roman Alexander*. Exeter, 2002.

Starr, Chester G, *The Influence of Sea Power on Ancient History*. New York and Oxford, 1989.

Stevenson, R B, *Persica. Greek Writing About Persian in the Fourth Century BC*. Edinburgh, 1997.

Stoneman, Richard (translation, introduction and notes), *The Greek Alexander Romance*. London, 1991.

—*Alexander the Great*. London, 1997.

—Alexander the Great. A Life in Legend. New Haven, 2008.

Stoyanov, Yuri, *The Other God: Dualist Religions from Antiquity to the Cathar Heresy.* New Haven, 2000.

Stronach, D and Roaf, M, *Nush-i Jan, 1. The Major Buildings of the Median Settlement.* Leuven, 2007.

Strzygowski, Joseph, *Origin of Christian church art: new facts and principles of research.* Oxford, 1923.

Summers, G, 'Archaeological Evidence for the Achaemenid period in Eastern Turkey', *Anatolian Studies* 43 (1993): 85-108.

Tatum, J, *Xenophon's Imperial Fiction.* Princeton, 1989.

Teissier, Beatrice, 'Texts from the Persian in Late Eighteenth-century India and Britain: Culture of Construct?', *Iran* 47:, 133-148 (2009).

Theophylact Simocatta, *History.* Translated with Introduction and Notes by Michael and Mary Whitby. Oxford, 1986.

Thomson, R W, Howard-Johnston, James and Greenwood, Tim, *The Armenian History attributed to Sebeos.* Translated with notes and historical commentary. Liverpool, 1999.

Trombley, Frank R and Watt, John W, *The Chronicle of Pseudo-Joshua the Stylite.* Liverpool, 2000.

Trümpler, Charlotte (ed) and Gerster, Georg (photographs), *The Past from Above.* London, 2003.

Tuplin, Christopher (ed), *Persian Responses. Political and Cultural Interaction with(in) the Achaemenid Empire.* Swansea, 2007.

Turcan, Robert, *The Cults of the Roman Empire.* Oxford, 1996.

Ure, Percy Neville, *Justinian and his Age.* Harmondsworth, 1951.

Valantasis, Richard (ed), *Religions of Late Antiquity in Practice.* Princeton, 2000.

Vogelsang, W J , *The Rise and Organisation of the Achaemenid Empire. The Eastern Iranian Evidence.* Leiden, 1992.

Wheeler, Mortimer, *Flames Over Persepolis.* London, 1968.

Whitby, Michael and Mary, *Chronicon Paschale, 284-628.* Translated with notes and introduction. Liverpool, 1989.

Whitehouse, David and Williamson, Andrew 'Sasanian Maritime Trade', *Iran XI,* 1971, pp. 29-49.

Wickham, Chris, *The Inheritance of Rome. A History of Europe from 400 to 800.* London, 2009.

Widengren, G, 'Manichaeism and its Iranian Background,' in *Cambridge History of Iran* 3 (2): 965-90. Cambridge, 1983.

Wiesehöfer, Josef, *Ancient Persia. From 550 BC to 650 AD.* London, 1996.

Witakowski, Witold, *Pseudo-Dionysius of Tel-Mahre.* Chronicle. Part III. Translation with notes and introduction. Liverpool, 1996.

Woodford, Susan, *The Trojan War in Ancient Art.* London, 1993.

Woodhouse, C M, *Gemistos Plethon. The Last of the Hellenes.* Oxford, 1986.

Worthington, Ian (ed), *Alexander the Great. A Reader.* London, 2003.

Yarshater, Ehsan (ed.), *The Cambridge History of Iran. Volume 3(1). The Seleucid, Parthian and Sasanian Periods.* Cambridge, 1983.

Yule, Henry and Cordier, Henri, *The Book of Ser Marco Polo.*, 2 vols. London, 1903.

INDEX